CultureShock!

A Survival Guide to Customs and Etiquette

Thailand

Robert Cooper

Marshall Cavendish
Editions

This edition published in 2008 by:
Marshall Cavendish Corporation
99 White Plains Road
Tarrytown, NY 10591-9001
www.marshallcavendish.us

Other Marshall Cavendish Offices:
Marshall Cavendish International (Asia) Private Limited. 1 New Industrial Road,
Singapore 536196 ■ Marshall Cavendish Ltd. 5th Floor, 32–38 Saffron Hill,
London EC1N 8FH, UK ■ Marshall Cavendish International (Thailand) Co Ltd.
253 Asoke, 12th Flr, Sukhumvit 21 Road, Klongtoey Nua, Wattana, Bangkok
10110, Thailand ■ Marshall Cavendish (Malaysia) Sdn Bhd, Times Subang,
Lot 46, Subang Hi-Tech Industrial Park, Batu Tiga, 40000 Shah Alam, Selangor
Darul Ehsan, Malaysia

Marshall Cavendish is a trademark of Times Publishing Limited

ISBN 10: 0-7614-5498-5
ISBN 13: 978-0-7614-5498-4

Please contact the publisher for the Library of Congress catalog number

Printed in China by Everbest Printing Co Ltd

Photo Credits:
All black and white photos from the author.
All colour photos from Photolibrary ■ Cover photo: Getty Images

All illustrations by TRIGG

ABOUT THE SERIES

Culture shock is a state of disorientation that can come over anyone who has been thrust into unknown surroundings, away from one's comfort zone. *CultureShock!* is a series of trusted and reputed guides which has, for decades, been helping expatriates and long-term visitors to cushion the impact of culture shock whenever they move to a new country.

Written by people who have lived in the country and experienced culture shock themselves, the authors share all the information necessary for anyone to cope with these feelings of disorientation more effectively. The guides are written in a style that is easy to read and covers a range of topics that will arm readers with enough advice, hints and tips to make their lives as normal as possible again.

Each book is structured in the same manner. It begins with the first impressions that visitors will have of that city or country. To understand a culture, one must first understand the people—where they came from, who they are, the values and traditions they live by, as well as their customs and etiquette. This is covered in the first half of the book.

Then on with the practical aspects—how to settle in with the greatest of ease. Authors walk readers through how to find accommodation, get the utilities and telecommunications up and running, enrol the children in school and keep in the pink of health. But that's not all. Once the essentials are out of the way, venture out and try the food, enjoy more of the culture and travel to other areas. Then be immersed in the language of the country before discovering more about the business side of things.

To round off, snippets of basic information are offered before readers are 'tested' on customs and etiquette of the country. Useful words and phrases, a comprehensive resource guide and list of books for further research are also included for easy reference.

CONTENTS

FOREWORD

Since the first edition of *CultureShock! Thailand* was published in 1982, Thailand has leapt forward economically. Change is evident everywhere: the excellent communication network throughout the country, the rapid construction of shopping centres, offices and condominiums in Bangkok, the introduction of the latest technologies and the industrialisation of the eastern seaboard. *CultureShock! Thailand* went through six editions during this period, each requiring substantive revision, as, to an extent that had never happened before, East met West in modernising Thailand.

During the quarter-century in which *CultureShock! Thailand* has become a standard text for foreigners coming to live and work in Thailand, rapid growth was becoming an accepted and expected part of Thai life. A whole generation of Thais grew up thinking that every day in every way, things would get better and better. But in 1997, the bubble burst. The economy almost fell apart, but Thai society did not totter with it. In some ways, traditional life was reinforced by the Thai response to an economic miracle that had seemed to promise them everything, before kicking them in the teeth, and in some cases, back where they came from. Those in need looked to relatives and friends for help, found solace in Buddhism and appealed to the spirits to intervene in their destiny.

Economic woes called a halt to the headlong rush into a brave new world, but did not reverse gains made in such things as education and democracy. Highways had been constructed, ports modernised, telecommunications revolutionised. Such benefits of social change or modernisation have been retained and strengthened through the leaner years, bringing us today to a time when Thailand is once more taking a leading economic and social role in the region—but a more reflective role than that of the 1980s and 1990s, a role built on a more solid base.

In revising this book substantively for this 2005 edition, I have given much thought to the double-edged sword of modernisation and change, and have decided that the Thai personality, which is really what this book is about, has learnt a few hard lessons related to the ups and downs of modern life, but that, not so deep down inside, the average Thai has not changed that much. Thus, the book has been revised much in the way that Thais have accepted change in their own culture—by a process of addition. This is not to belittle the changes that have taken place. Life expectancy is way up along with education, medical services rank among the best in the region if not the world and almost every home has electricity, a fridge, TV, water and sanitation. The achievements over the past couple of decades are enormous. That the Thais retain their traditional charms and smiles is perhaps the most amazing of these many achievements.

This is a book about Thailand and the Thais. It is written in English for a mostly non-Thai audience. The revision has been substantive. The non-Thai arriving in Thailand today is in a very different situation to his counterpart a quarter of a century ago. He is far more likely to find much that can help him through those early, difficult but exciting times. The last thing I want is to guide a 'reluctant expat' into a culture bubble, so along with the very significant new information on settling in, I include the many innovations that can help the newcomer come to terms quickly with Thai friends and colleagues. Most visitors to Thailand staying any length of time will read more than one book on the country and the people, but this book should be a good start, setting them on the way to a degree of integration without unnecessary shock from a culture which is different to their own but a culture which, if they give it a chance, will welcome them in, as far as they want to come in and have the required attributes for entry, one of which is a smile. I wish the reader success in Thailand and peace of mind.

Robert Cooper
July 2005

Note: This book is bang up to date in every way except for pronoun politics. The author uses 'he' throughout rather than varying gender and confusing the reader. He justifies this by reference to Thai language, which has a single word meaning 'he' or 'she'!

ACKNOWLEDGEMENTS

It is horribly unfair to single out a few individuals from the multitude of Thais and non-Thais who helped me produce this book, but not to do so would be even more unfair.

I thank my anthropology student at the University of Singapore, JoAnn Craig, who cleared the path ahead and guided me gently onto it. Denis Segaller, a dear friend who, but for a turn in the wheel of fate, would be the author of this book. Kieran Cooke who found the antidote to culture shock (a bottle of Mekhong, two bottles of soda and a *manao* cut in four). Webb and Renée who saw humour in madness and made me believe, or want to believe, that there is some kind of place, somewhere, wherever, for *farang* in Thailand.

I thank the Abbot of Wat Kingkeo, the *phu yai ban* and people of Bang Pli, the staff at the Social Research Institute and Department of Anthropology, Chulalongkorn University, and colleagues, Thai and non-Thai, in the United Nations family in Bangkok and Chiang Kham. I thank my friends Sirinthorn, who checked many of the facts for me, and Ayo, Sassi, Lung Jo and Souk Jumpathong, for being themselves. And Khun Orachart who helped more than she will ever know. In Chiang Mai, special homage to Pra Santi, Uncle Gerry and Phi Tiu, Ajarn Nok, Phong and Patcharin, Garnet and Tantawan.

I offer my thanks to the many readers who have written to me; many of the revisions and updates contained in this 2005 edition are a direct result of their suggestions. I will always be happy to hear from new and old readers and to reply to letters received through the publishers.

DEDICATION

To the girls
Tintin & Tessy
from
Daddy
xxx

The path towards understanding is a million lives long and
so narrow in places that each must pass alone.

MAP OF THAILAND

VIETNAM

LAOS

MYANMAR

THAILAND

BANGKOK

ANDAMAN SEA

CAMBODIA

GULF OF
THAILAND

VIETNAM

SOUTH CHINA SEA

INDIAN OCEAN

MALAYSIA

FIRST IMPRESSIONS

CHAPTER 1

'All generalisations are dangerous—even this one.'
—Kukrit Promoj,
ex-prime minister of Thailand and leading Thai author.

NON-THAIS ARE AN ODD LOT. Ask those who have been here what they think of Thailand and you will find that this amazing country is both ugly and beautiful, calming and infuriating, noisy and quiet, cheap and expensive, violent and passive, funny and sad. As to the Thais as individuals, visitors' first impressions are a mass of contradictions. Thais are friendly, everybody agrees with that. But some see this friendliness as covering a xenophobia—according to this view, the Thai smile simply hides the hate and fear the Thai feels towards you, the visitor. To some, the Thais are generous and hospitable; to others, Thais are the ultimate in avaricious scheming, their motive in every action being to empty the wallets of any foreign visitor. To some, the Thais are honest and ultimately tolerant; to others the Thais lie all the time and resort quickly to violence when attacked by jealousy. Will the real Thai please stand up? If you have never suffered from culture shock, Thailand is a great place to start.

Any human being, plucked from the world in which he functions and feels secure and plopped down into a culture as different as the Thai, is certain to have a few strange first impressions. Some people cry, others walk around with a broad grin on their dazed faces. Some love Thailand, some hate it and many both love it and hate it. Few remain indifferent. These feelings are the essence of culture shock. I would like to say that these are only first impressions: give things time and your second and third impressions will make sense of it all. I would like to say that. But one thing I can say with confidence is that Thailand is not a boring country. Don't rush into the Thais or Thailand, take things easy at first, play it cool. Do not trust your first impressions. Try to enjoy them. They are by nature spontaneous. They are also, to a large extent, superficial. They are, in some way, uniquely yours. You will, of course, never have them again.

Culture is a particular way of doing things. All people everywhere eat, talk, play, work and think; but not all people eat the same thing the same way, talk the same language, play the same games, do the same work or think the same thoughts. All people have families, places to live, tools, weapons and clothing; but not all people recognise the same boundaries to the family, live in the same type of place, use the same tools and weapons and wear the same clothes.

During your first-impression period, your senses are trying to adapt to new stimuli. You may think that everybody loves you, everybody finds you beautiful and interesting. Or you might become aware that your behaviour, which for years you had thought of as correct, polite and friendly, can be interpreted or misinterpreted as odd, rude and even hostile. Or you might feel both of these states. Those important first impressions will be gathered during a period in which your experience of life so far does not fully relate to life around you. Thailand will, if you allow it to do so, make your life more complete. First impressions, like love and hate, can be likened to temporary madness. You might well veer between the wonder of it all and the most depressing feelings you've ever had in your life. You will not be left indifferent. Enjoy your trip.

DISGUST AND RAPTURE

The initial impact of Thailand and Thai culture is likely to make the transplanted visitor very conscious of himself and the world he left behind. He will try to translate what he sees, hears, smells and feels into concepts with which he is familiar. When he is unable to make an adequate translation, he becomes confused, cannot function properly, and might veer wildly between love and hate for his new surroundings. It is at this point that the transplant is most at risk. This is the period when the transplant experiences CULTURE SHOCK. At the risk of simplicity, I feel all transplants experience something of two contradictory feelings: disgust and rapture.

The Disgusted

Some people feel culture shock in the popular, literal sense of the term. They are shocked and disgusted by the world in which they find themselves. Having made it through the glass doors at the modern airport and been ushered into an air-con limo that carried them in comfort along a fast and safe super highway to their bargain of a lovely hotel room, they are eager to experience their new world and they take a step outside the familiar and comfortable.

The chances are they step onto a pavement a bit different from the one back home. Here, pavements are for selling things on, riding motor-bikes on and placing deadly holes to keep your eyes glued to where your feet are going. If, as is likely, your hotel is in a tourist area, you might get the treatment most likely to turn any new arrival off of Thailand. "Hey you, where you go, you wan *tuk-tuk*/boom-boom?" The *tuk-tuk* has no meter, the taxi driver doesn't want to go where you want him to go, the buses are impossibly overcrowded and their routes inscrutable.

If you have the luck to be on a skytrain route, have a strong heart and no disability, you will find reasonable familiarity at the summit of a long climb in the heat. All you have to do is buy your ticket from a machine that is familiar enough, find out which way to go and note where to get off. But while such innovations as skytrains have done a lot to transform travel in Bangkok in recent years, there still comes a point where you are on that crowded pavement, looking for a street name which is probably there, written in large letters in Thai. Take out your telescope and you will make out a tiny English transliteration or translation, or an English name like 'New Road', which in Thai is Charoen Krung, the oldest road in Bangkok.

'As fungus sprouts chaotic from its bed;
So it spread;
Chance directed,
Chance erected, so they built;
On the silt.'
—Rudyard Kipling's first impression of Calcutta. He never came to Bangkok.

After your first venture with colourful Thai cooking that will be much more fiercely hot and spicy than that you sampled in the Thai restaurant back home, you rush to a toilet which is little more than a hole in the floor; while squatting, the used toilet paper stares at you from a basket; your clothes are soaked in sweat and, if you are lucky, there is a bucket of water or a shower-type hose to clean your backside. You want desperately to see something like the Thai temples and buildings that you have seen on TV and in the brochures back home. You approach a smiling face and ask the way, then you discover the Thais have a remarkable inability to read a map of Bangkok or anywhere else and directions, whether to the king's palace or the toilet in the restaurant, and whether given in Thai or English, are rarely more specific than 'over there'.

The senses begin to reel a little. The outside world is just not like the edited video you saw and loved before you came. The video carried no sound and sight of nostrils cleared without a handkerchief; it did not mention the non-drinkable water; it edited out the heat, the noise, the dirt, the flies, the mosquitoes, ants, spiders, lizards, dogs and snakes. Even real chicken soup has a chicken's foot floating in it. "Oh, what am I doing here? Why did I ever come to this country?"

All these first impressions have a lot to do with life in a recently-developed country and very little to do with Thai culture. The pavement salesmen are there to make a profit, which they do by serving mainly foreigners who want their pirated and porno VCDs, 'Louis Vuiton' bags, crocodile skin wallets and 'Guchi' watches at a tiny fraction of what they would pay back home. Apart from the chicken's foot soup, Thais dislike most of what might annoy you almost as much as you do. Most Thais would be happy enough if the seemingly never-ending strings of market stalls, all selling more or less the same things, disappeared overnight. But, being Thais, they don't complain. They just avoid it or ignore it. Thais have a gift for being able to ignore anything they don't try too hard to notice.

Once out of the tourist/girly-bar environment, most of the hassle disappears. Some things which don't disappear

Bangkok's Thai name runs to several lines. It is shortened in everyday language to the first two syllables: Krung Thep. This literally means 'city of angels'.

just have to be lived with. You will soon learn to squat on the toilet and to pack an emergency supply of toilet paper along with your toothbrush when you are going 'upcountry', or when you are discovering the inner reaches of Bangkok cuisine in an atmosphere that can only be described as genuine. Most people find they eventually adapt to most things—with a little help from mosquito repellents, imodium and air-conditioners!

The Enrapt

Other visitors react in a very different way. They fall madly in love with the cultural differences around them. Usually, the enrapt focus on a completely different part of life in Thailand to that experienced by the disgusted. The peaceful monks, passive faces on the crowded buses that are a lesson to the world, the fantastic serenity of the temples, the fun of the festivals and the mystique of the ceremonies. Thai dancing and handicrafts; the smiling, good-natured people. "Oh, how beautiful everything and everybody is."

The enrapt view of Thailand is infinitely more acceptable to the Thais than the opinion of the disgusted, but it is equally false and ethnocentric. Thailand, and the Thais, could never be as nice as the enrapt would like to think they are. Some of the enrapt manage to stay in Thailand for many years without adjusting their romantic image of the Thais, but many others fall victim to depression and disillusionment as soon as they realise that these 'wonderful, beautiful people' are really quite human after all. Beautiful, charming and tolerant, yes they are; saints they are not (and never pretend to be).

There is nothing wrong with telling Thais how beautiful everything and everybody is, since that is what they want to hear, but don't believe it too much, at least not 100 per cent. You might get hurt.

The Puzzled

Most visitors to Thailand, especially those with the prospect of spending some time here, feel very much like fish out of water when they first arrive. In a strange world, never quite sure what is going on, never sure what is the right thing to do, never sure if people approve or disapprove, surrounded by signs that can't be read, a language that doesn't make sense to them, strange food, strangers with strange customs, unsure if somebody really wants to help and befriend them or rip them off. One moment enrapt with the beauty of it all, the next moment disgusted with it all. And much of the time, puzzled.

One of the paradoxes of the modern world is that a man, or woman, can be uprooted, flown halfway around the globe, dropped down in another time, climate, culture, and expect to get up the following day and function as usual. Like a rice seedling torn from its protected nursery and transplanted in a big, strange field. Like the fragile seedling, the human transplant must either adapt and flourish or wither and perish. But unlike the pampered seedling, the man must survive without the loving care of the farmer and probably without the company of other seedlings of the same stock. It is a great tribute to the human race that most people in this position do manage to carry on somehow. Indeed, many of them revel in the novelty of their situation. But all feel at least something of the disorientation of culture shock.

A CHILD AGAIN

The newcomer finds himself suddenly unsure of when and how to go about the basic and 'natural' actions of daily life. He doesn't even know when to say 'good morning'. He may react by saying a hundred 'good mornings' to any Thai around him, when he made do with two or three back home. He doesn't know when it is appropriate to shake hands, make a *wai*, give tips, talk to strangers, make invitations, refuse invitations, arrive on time or arrive late. He has very little idea of what to say when he meets people, even if they speak his language, doesn't know when Thais are joking, and has no idea what people are thinking. Nothing seems to have a pattern and he finds it almost impossible to predict what will be happening next and how he will be feeling from one hour to the next. He is a child again.

Grown responsible adults suddenly find themselves back in infancy. Like children, they must rely on others, Thais who speak a few words of their language, for the simplest of things. Making phone calls, catching a bus, buying a packet of condoms and posting a letter become adventures; finding a place to live and hiring a maid become major preoccupations, and doing the shopping becomes an expedition. Like the world of children, the new world of Thailand is unknown, exciting, full of mistaken understandings and, potentially dangerous.

The Vet and the Mechanic

Roger had bought himself a beautiful little Golden Retriever. The time came to vaccinate the puppy and Roger asked his Thai neighbour if he knew a vet. He did. Then Roger bought himself a beautiful little red jeep with a reconditioned engine that was totally overhauled and as good as new. Roger was pleased with his bargain and showed it off to the neighbours. The next day, it refused to start. Roger angrily phoned the garage. They assured him they would send a mechanic to the house immediately. Ten minutes later, a man in greasy overalls turned up on a motor bike, carrying a small tool bag. Roger's Thai was good enough for him to lash into the man. "I bought this only yesterday." Roger pushed the man into the driver's seat, "Start the bloody thing," he shouted.

"I would if I could," replied the man in greasy overalls timidly. "But I can't."

"Ah, you see! Even you can't start it. Give me my money back."

The man looked blankly at Roger. "Money?" he said, as if he had never heard of the word.

"*Ngern, baht, tang*–money, I want it back." Roger was quite angry by this time and getting angrier.

The man in overalls shrank into the seat. "I'm sorry I can't start your car," he said apologetically.

"Sorry, my arse," said Roger. "Why the hell can't you start it? Call yourself a mechanic?"

"No," said the man. "I call myself a vet."

With no trouble the dog was vaccinated and the vet pleasantly took leave as two mechanics arrived, got into the car and started it immediately. Roger was surprised. "But I've been trying to start it for hours."

The mechanics looked at the poor foreigner. "This is a second hand car. It's how you turn the key that counts."

They showed Roger how to turn the key and Roger started the car. He felt foolish and reached into his pocket for a good tip. "No, no," said both mechanics, gave Roger a *wai* and wished him good luck.

Unfortunately for the foreign visitor, the Thais, tolerant as they are, do not extend childhood status to visiting adults. Young children, Thai or foreign, can do more or less as they like for several years and get away with almost anything; the adult visitor cannot. So get on those slippery slopes of the learning curve as soon as you have read this book. But, and I will emphasise this many times, take it easy, take it slowly, and if you don't like it, just don't take it at all (but don't throw whatever it is back in the faces of the Thais).

During a very short period of time, you must make essential adjustments to your behaviour and learn to reinterpret the world around you in a somewhat different way. The psychological pressure involved in attempting to adapt to two interpretations of the world can result in a feeling of euphoria in the morning and depression in the afternoon. The Thais are basically nice people (I think) and they (almost) certainly won't mind you smiling, giggling and laughing when euphoria strikes; but cry and you cry alone.

REACTION

The state of disequilibrium and confusion which characterises first impressions does not last long. Human beings hate being strangers, being 'left out', being helpless. Thus, very soon, the visitor strikes back. Seeking to defend his senses against the shock-waves of an alien world, he searches for, or tries to construct, a culture shock absorber.

In order to retain some sanity, the visitor responds to culture shock in one or all of the following four ways: escape, confrontation, encapsulation and integration.

Escape

Escape is the easiest way out. Short-term visitors who know they can 'escape' in a few days or weeks are free to enjoy their new experiences to the full. Good luck to them.

Other foreigners, working in Thailand for a year or more, may also respond by escape. They escape from the Thai world in which they feel uncomfortable, into their own homes, eat familiar imported food, watch satellite television of their favourite television programmes and mix socially with expats or foreign-educated Thais. Full-blown escapees are mentally always in the transit lounge.

Confrontation

Some visitors are always complaining—mostly to other visitors who feel the same way, but sometimes to Thais. Stated or implied in their criticisms of Thai values, competencies and behaviour is an assumption that things are better where they come from. Not-too-deep-down inside they enjoy feeling superior to the world around them. They make sense; the Thai world 'doesn't make sense'. For these visitors, Thai culture is there to fight against and to succeed in spite of.

Encapsulation

All foreigners, to a varying extent, retreat into a 'culture bubble' made up of people facing the same problems in an alien culture. They become part of the 'community of travellers' or of the 'expat community'. The culture to which they adjust is the lowest common denominator of many different parts: a culture of transplants. There are expat clubs, shops and mini-supermarkets catering essentially for non-Thais. Expats, whether from America, Japan, Africa or neighbouring Asia, meet on cocktail circuits and invite each other to their houses. A community of strangers in paradise, where the like-situated rub shoulders and where most of the Thais in the room are there to serve drinks, clear away the food and sweep the floor.

Belonging to a club because it shows movies and serves the kind of food you like and sending your children to an English-medium school, etc. is only normal, logical behaviour. Thais in America or Europe behave in much the same way. This very human grouping together to pursue a common goal need not exclude all the benefits of the Thai world. Comparatively, few foreigners in Thailand are completely encapsulated. Many find they grow out of (or bored with) the expat situation as soon as they have found their feet in the new environment. Others use such facilities sparingly, whenever they feel the need.

Integration

The non-Thai visitor has a good chance of integrating with Thais, if this is what he wants. In doing so, he will retain his original cultural identity and the Thais will maintain theirs. Integration is not assimilation; the visitor has practically no chance of really 'becoming Thai', however much he loves Thailand and however long he lives here.

> The meaning of integration is to fit together; to abolish segregation through the removal of social barriers that divide members of different cultures.

For integration to take place, the visitor consciously or unconsciously removes the social barriers that cut him off from Thais. This is usually a slow process. The foreigner finds himself decreasingly relying on the foreign community in Bangkok for friendship and entertainment, and feels increasingly at ease with Thais.

Integration takes place to a varying degree with most visitors who stay some time. It gives the best of both worlds. When the barriers are down, one's own culture can be enjoyed every bit as much as the new host culture. The individual has everything to gain and little to lose but intolerance (and, of course, culture shock).

REMOVING THE BARRIERS

Removing social barriers is a lot more difficult than it sounds. If you are working in Thailand, you are likely to be constantly expected and even required (by fellow expats and by Thais) to live up to the role demanded by 'expat culture'.

"Life is tiring enough, who has time and energy to reach out to the Thai community more than is absolutely necessary or immediately enjoyable?" The only answer to this question—repeated in one form or another by most expats I interviewed before beginning this book—is that I know coming to live and work in Thailand is tiring, at least initially, but getting to understand something about the Thais is likely to make it less tiring. By all means begin your personal study of the Thais with whatever you find immediately enjoyable, be it the massage parlour or Thai classical dancing; as you learn more about the Thais, many other aspects of their culture might attract you.

Culture Shock Relapse

Coming out of your early-days culture shock is not a simple lineal process. Within a few days, weeks or months, depending on your personality and past experiences of other cultures, you will get to find your way around and cope with

Minimising Culture Shock

- If possible, take a cultural orientation course before leaving home, although very few foreign companies offer such courses to their employees before sending them to Thailand. If there is no chance of a course, try at least to read some books before you leave (at the very least, this one!)
- Learn quickly the Do's and Don'ts set out in this book. For the really busy and tired, these are listed in easy reference form at the back.
- Learn the language. This will remove some of the communication barrier and teach you a lot about Thai culture. There are many private tutors in Bangkok who will fit their hours to your convenience. Better, if you have the time, is to attend the intensive courses at the American University Alumni Association Language Centre (AUA) on 179 Ratchadamri Road. There, apart from language laboratories and an experienced teaching staff, you will have the psychological prop of learning a difficult language in a small group of foreigners, all of whom find things just as difficult. Since the Thai course is an appendage to what is essentially an English language school for Thais, the minute you leave the classroom you are in a Thai-speaking environment, with lots of pleasant young people who have nothing much to do and will talk to you, preferably in Thai, for as long as you can stand it.
- Read about Thailand and the Thais, bearing in mind that a great deal of it has been written by a *farang* (foreigner) obviously enrapt by it all. An annotated

the obvious differences. The agony and ecstasy of culture shock is felt less intensely. You come to terms with being a foreigner. All around you, Thai is spoken and written; it perhaps remains unintelligible, but you have gotten used to it and it doesn't bother you anymore.

bibliography is to be found at the back of this book which should get you started on the mass of English language literature on Thailand. If in Bangkok for a time, request permission to use the AUA library on Ratchadamri. When you find yourself developing an interest in Thailand, you might decide to graduate to the Siam Society and its wide ranging library on Soi Asoke (you have to be a member). For the really hooked, or for those looking for specific information, the Thailand Information Centre in Chulalongkorn University has most things written on the country and an excellent subject index to help you find what you are looking for. (If you don't find what you want there, bear in mind that it takes a year or two for new stuff to get indexed so ask the staff.)

■ Take any of the English-language evening lecture courses on various aspects of Thailand (usually art or history), advertised periodically in the *Bangkok Post*. The Siam Society and the AUA also have interesting one-off lectures from time to time. This will help you respect the country and people.

■ Whenever you are tempted to criticise the Thais, remember that you are a transplanted foreign part in a culture that is very different from the one you are used to. Full acceptance by the host culture will take some time and involve some changes in you rather than it. Being a transplant is physically and mentally tiring, so take it easy, don't try to become Thai overnight (After 20 years in the country, maybe…).

After several months or years more, just as you think you are beginning to understand what being Thai is all about... culture shock relapse. A person to whom you have never spoken will send the servant with a basket of mangoes as a present for you; your trusted maid will go away for two days to visit her mother and never return; your friendly neighbour will ask you outright for US$ 10,000 to mend his beaten-up old car that is not worth US$ 500. Once again, it doesn't make sense.

LEARNING CULTURE

In many ways, as you get to know more about the Thais, the stranger they seem and the stranger you seem. When you have come to think of somewhere as 'home', it is very disturbing to be suddenly reminded that you are a foreigner. But try not to get too depressed about culture shock relapses, they are all part of the learning process.

Whenever culture shock strikes, in whatever form, and however euphoric or depressed it makes you feel, try to remember that the basic ingredient of culture shock is ignorance; a situation arises and you don't know how to act, once you have learnt to understand the situation from a Thai point of view, culture shock just fades away... almost.

COUNTING THE COSTS
First Meeting
Bangkok is by no means all there is to Thailand, but for most foreign visitors it is their first impression of the Thai world, and whether they like it or not, their first meeting with Thai culture.

Urbanisation and westernisation are now as much a part of Bangkok-Thai culture as the *wai* and the wat. Certainly, the culture of modern Bangkok is likely to relate much more to a visitor's initial culture shock than anything included in the tourist guides. To ignore Bangkok would be to ignore that part of Thailand's culture in which most visitors spend a large amount of their time.

Every Taboo Broken
In Bangkok, the visitor will see every taboo broken. Young girls swing braless along the street, hand in hand with a (usually foreign) boyfriend. Small men pretending to be big men talk loudly and rudely in restaurants. The waitress in Patpong Road looks askance at your *wai*-deserving tip and flips over the tray to throw your tip under the table and to show you the words CHEAPSKATE CHARLIE.

The fact that deviancy is evident publicly does not mean that Thai society does not value correct (i.e. Thai) behaviour. The great (silent) majority of the Thai population dislike bad behaviour and avoid the company of those who go for it. Nobody would deny that westernisation and urbanisation are rapidly taking place but, even in Bangkok, Thai ways of doing things are still very relevant.

The visitor should model his behaviour on the generally acceptable rather than the exceptional. One good reason for doing so is that the Thai population, used to hearing how decadent foreigners have corrupted Thai youth, love a foreigner who knows how to behave.

First Impressions
The first reaction of the visitor to this new world is likely to be bewilderment. Foreign tourists, long-term expats and Thais agree completely that Bangkok is hot, humid, dirty, noisy

and congested. The strange thing is very few Thais living here can ever be persuaded to live anywhere else and many visitors seem very reluctant to leave.

Second Impressions

Second impressions are not much better. New arrivals inevitably find that their centrally located hotel seems to be near nowhere they want to go. Everybody complains that there is no 'downtown', no city centre—'things are spread all over the place'.

Third Impressions

First and second impressions are none too kind. But, before you snap shut this book and, in true Bangkok style, flee the scene, let me assure you that many people who at first hate Bangkok grow to love it. Because of the people, the most positive factor in what may, at least at first, seem to be a largely negative world. In Thailand, third impressions are often the best.

So, if you are hesitant about the Thailand experience when you first arrive, and if your first impressions of Bangkok are the kind you would rather forget, you will (hopefully and before too long) come to realise that Thailand (even Bangkok) does have a heart. A cool heart, not worn on the sleeve. A Thai heart that, in spite of the smiles and the orchids, may not be immediately evident as you step out of the aircraft, but one which might well go on beating when Paris, New York, Moscow, Beijing and Timbuktoo are all dust in a Martian's museum. If you weep on arrival, you are likely to weep even more on departure, and for quite different reasons.

LAND, HISTORY & RELIGION

CHAPTER 2

'This country, free and fine.
There are fish in the rivers.
There is rice in the fields.'
—Oft-quoted line from a Thai folk song

GEOGRAPHY

Thailand covers 517,000 sq km (199,614.8 sq miles), making it about the size of France. With only a little imagination, its shape resembles the head of an elephant—and the Thais would have it no other way. Bangkok is the ever-hungry mouth and the trunk extends down between the slender leg of Myanmar (formerly known as Burma) and the Gulf of Thailand, all the way to the northern border with Malaysia, a distance from north to south of 1,860 km (1,155.8miles). It is bordered in the north and east by Laos and Cambodia, in the west by Myanmar, and in the south by Malaysia. The main rivers, which still serve as transportation routes for heavy products, tend to drain from the mountainous north into the fertile and flat areas around Bangkok, known as Central Thailand, which share a latitude and climate with Manila in the Philippines, Madras in India, Kartoum in Sudan, and Honduras in Central America.

Apart from the centre, Thailand is divided geographically into three other zones: the north-east, still perhaps the poorest area and one with predominantly rain-fed rice fields which suffer from periodic floods and droughts; the north, with the prosperous and historic centre of Chiang Mai, Thailand's second biggest city, surrounded by high mountains; and the south, an area of dwindling rain forests, with the longest coastline, a prospering if patchy tourist trade and a large fishing industry.

CLIMATE

Thailand has two seasons, dry and wet. The dry runs from November to June, the wet from June to October. The centre and the south are hot and sticky all year. The north and north-east enjoy a variable cool season from December to February and the hottest time of year all over is the months preceding the onset of the rains.

Monsoons get mixed up in the south of the country, where heavy rainfall is possible even in the dry season. And the monsoon sometimes comes late, or almost not at all in the north-east, creating significant economic problems for an agricultural area based on comparatively poor soil conditions (this is why so many people in Bangkok originate from the north-east). In the not too distant past, some areas, particularly Bangkok, experienced annual flooding in October when the flow of the rivers from the north was at its maximum and the sea tides were at their highest. Greatly improved sewage and water systems have almost eliminated this problem, but somewhere each year there is a flood to remind everybody of their traditions.

ECOLOGY

Just 50 years ago, most of Thailand was covered in forest and the people practised shifting ('slash and burn') agriculture on the assumption that resources would regenerate themselves. Part of Thailand's early attempts to leave the developing world took a significant toll on the forests, and the plants and animals living in them. Logging, and the unrestricted gathering of rattan, serviced a furniture industry which grew famous but is now in decline because raw materials are simply not available unless imported from poorer northern and western neighbours.

In 1988, a significant disaster occurred in Surat Thani province in the south. Hundreds of tons of cut timber was washed away, burying villages and people in its path. This disaster lent force to a growing environmentalist lobby and all logging was banned in Thailand in 1989. It is illegal to sell timber felled after that date; this accounts for the prosperous trade in old village houses. The government has introduced a number of measures to try to redress an environmental situation that approached the point of no return. These include the creation of 34 national parks and wildlife sanctuaries and seven national marine parks. It has also introduced specific legislation to protect endangered plants and animals, and hopes to raise the level of forest cover throughout the kingdom to 40 per cent by 2050.

Over recent years, there has been a raised awareness among Thais and visitors that Thailand must protect its environment, for economic reasons if for no other. Tourism, a significant contributor to the national product, has been responsible both for degradation, especially coastal-zone illegal tourism, and for assisting conservation through a growing eco-tourism. Thailand has signed the UN Convention on International Trade in Endangered Species, and has begun to tackle the problem of sewage in rivers and coastal areas and introduced a crackdown of sorts on restaurants with forest animals on the menu. As in many other countries, this has increased opportunities for corruption at all levels and the authorities, particularly the Royal Forest Department [#61 Phahonyothin, Bangkhen, Bangkok 10900;

tel: (02) 579-5266], are engaged in a continuous fight against those who destroy Thailand's beauty for short-term gains.

Environmental Organisations
- **Asian Society for Environmental Protection**
  CDG-SEAPO, Asian Institute of Technology Bangkok 10501;
  Tel: (02) 579-5266
- **Project for Ecological Recovery**
  77/3 soi Nomjit, Naret Road, Bangkok 10500
- **Wildlife Fund Thailand**
  Tel: (02) 521-3435; email: pisitnp@mozart.inet.co.th

Of course, the follies of man almost appear insignificant compared with the havoc wrought by the tsunami disaster of December 2004, which devastated some of Thailand's most beautiful regions in Phuket and the neighbouring Indian Ocean coast. However, there remains a role for the individual—Thai and visitor—in preserving and rebuilding the environment. Essentially, prevent further destruction by not buying coral or coral products (often acquired by 'dynamiting' reefs), by taking special care against fire when staying in forest areas (a discarded but unburied 'harmless' food can reflects powerful sun rays and can start a fire), and by avoiding and publicising negatively those restaurants that continue to offer forest food products. Contact any of the boxed organisations or write to the Tourism Authority of Thailand (TAT), 202 Ratchadaphisek Road, Huay Khwang, Bangkok 10310. The TAT should constantly be reminded that tourists do not flock to Thailand to see degrading environments and be offered items and services which further degrade nature. Tourists, for their part, must comply with occasional measures to promote regrowth, even if this means being refused admission at certain times in certain places.

HISTORY
Archaeology, or pre-history, is very clear in placing north-eastern Thailand as one of the first places in the world to

produce pottery, cultivate rice and enjoy a bronze age. It is quite probably the first place in the world to enter all three activities and a consensus of academic attention places the centre of such activities at what is now known as Ban Prasat and Ban Chiang, both easily visited by modern tourist buses. Should you visit, you will be offered 'genuine' Ban Chiang artefacts. For once, there is no problem in accepting. All are fakes. Prove it yourself—when asked US$ 500 for a genuine artefact, offer 50 baht; it will probably be accepted.

'Cheating' can have its charming side. At the Ban Chiang archaeological site, a beautiful old lady offered the author a 'genuine Buddhist monk's bowl guaranteed over 6,000 years old'. However, the Buddhist Era—and presumably Buddhist monks' bowls—began 543 years before the birth of Christ ushered in the modern Western calendar.

The Bronze Age arrived in north-east Thailand over 3,000 years BC, hundreds of years before Mesopotamia and China gave up their stone implements. At the time when the ancestors of the Thais (who probably spoke a Thai language, although certainly not Central Thai) were enjoying rice—possibly 4,000 years ago—the Chinese were existing on millet.

While the Thais take pride in the fact that they have never been colonised, the country had at certain times been under the control of one or more of its neighbours (it had equally controlled those neighbours for periods of time). Thus, from the 8th to the 13th centuries, much of what is now Southern Thailand was within the Malay-Indonesian Srivijaya Kingdom. Khmer kingdoms and cultures dominated much of Thailand, except for the far north and the south, between the 7th and 11th centuries; and the far northern Thai kingdom of Lan Na, which at its height controlled parts of Burma and Laos, fell to the Burmese in 1558. The first real Thai kingdom was Sukhothai, which declared its independence in 1238. It controlled much of contemporary Thailand, northern Laos and Malaysia. It is seen historically by many Thais as a golden age of peace and prosperity, and it was during this period that an early form of the Thai script came into limited use. However, conflict with the Burmese and Cambodians continued for two centuries. During this time, Thailand incorporated much of Cambodian Buddhism and royal ceremony, and Ayudhya, the capital of Thailand, was twice razed to the ground.

Ayudhya was one of the greatest and wealthiest cities in Asia for some 400 years. Many times the size of London at the time, it was a centre of east-west trade and much of the time used Malay as a lingua-franca between traders. The term *farang* might have originated in Ayudhya at this time, when *faringi* (Persians) were powerful in trade. It was during this period that the Thai monarchy became absolute and sanctified.

During the 400 years of what is usually referred to as the Ayudhya Period, 34 reigns maintained an unbroken succession, establishing the monarchy as a vital part of Thai structure and personality. A vital part of the Thai system, and one that continues in more democratic form today, was the establishment of the *Sakti Na* system, where every single Thai was graded within a complex hierarchy structure that related to wealth and social prestige and which controlled an individual's behaviour to others.

Sakti Na Gradings

One of the most significant of the Ayudhya kings was King Paramatrailokanatha, whose name, for obvious reasons, is usually shortened by Thais to Trailok. Lacking computers and any technological paraphernalia of a modern totalitarian state, he controlled feuding feudal lords by setting each against the other in a peaceful competition for the king's favours. Recognising that the amount of land a man controlled was the key to wealth and status, and often the cause of conflict, King Trailok rationalised the system of individual landholding (*sakti na* meaning the power of the fields) and made it possible for each man to increase his holdings and power through royal patronage.

Each landowner was accorded a number which corresponded to the amount of land held. Top officials, the *Chao Phya*, held a grading of 10,000 and were each allowed to own up to 1,618.7 hectares (4,000 acres) of land. Commoners, on the other hand, unless they had some special merit, held a *sakti na* grade of 20 and could own up to 4 hectares (10 acres) of land (8 are sufficient to support a family of 4–6 in comfort). Women were not excluded from the system. A man's *mia luang* (major wife) held half the *sakti na* grade of her husband. The *mia noy* (minor wife) held one quarter of her husband's grade. A slave wife held no grading but became a *mia noy* on bearing her husband's child. Some might argue that in the days of King Trailok, at least women knew where they stood—today the numbers have gone.

Disputes were settled with reference to *sakti na*. If a man was fined, the amount would relate to his grading. If a man was compensated, the compensation related to his *sakti na* grade. *Sakti na* permeated everything. A *sakti na* of 1,000 meeting a *sakti na* of 1,500 would *wai* first.

Brilliant in its simplicity, the system lasted a long time but was not really adaptable to bank managers, noodle sellers and long-nosed, red-headed merchants from strange lands. It was officially abolished, along with slavery, in 1905 by the great moderniser, King Chulalongkorn. The ghosts of *sakti na* live on and, if you care to look, are evident in much everyday behaviour of most Thais.

The Burmese continued to be a nuisance, threatening the peace and stability of Ayudhya. They were finally driven out by King Taksin in 1769. Taksin established a new Thai capital in Thonburi, just across the river from Bangkok. The current Chakri dynasty dates from 1782, when Chao Phraya Chakri became Rama I, the first king in a line that continues until today. One of his earliest actions was to move the capital across the river to the present location of Bangkok.

King Chulalongkorn

Perhaps the most revolutionary Thai who ever lived, King Chulalongkorn began his amazing rule by abolishing the obeisance laws which kept commoner heads below royal feet. By that time he had already introduced Thailand's first western-style school, with an English headmaster, in the Grand Palace. He went on to promote the spread of secular schooling throughout the kingdom and is today known as the 'father of modern education' and the founder of modern

Thailand. The king who did most to desanctify the kingship is today, one of the most revered of all Thai kings. The anniversary of his death is a national holiday and, on that day, the visitor will see students and civil servants stretching out in obeisance to his statue on Rajdamnoen Nok Avenue. This statue has become the centre of weekly urban cult gatherings, at which thousands of Thais of all classes pay homage and make vows to the father of the nation.

King Chulalongkorn is usually accredited with having kept Thailand free when every other South-east Asian state was collapsing to the forces of colonialism. The threat from outside required rapid modernisation of the armed forces, and the bureaucracy and King Chulalongkorn had the foresight and abilities to instigate and carry this through.

He also had some personal reasons for modernising the kingship. One of the most tragic ironies of Thai history is the death of Chulalongkorn's Queen Consort and daughter, which resulted directly from regulations which were designed to segregate and protect royalty. The Queen Consort Sunanda-Kumariratn died on a quiet waterway just a few metres from many devoted subjects. To explain why, I reproduce from H G Quaritch-Wales' great work on Thai royalty, *Siamese State Ceremonies*, a translation of the regulations existing at the time of the tragedy. More than anything else, this

Students and civil servants pay annual obeisance to the memory of King Chulalongkorn.

quotation sums up the historical relationship between king and commoner.

'If a boat founders, the boatmen must swim away; if they remain near the boat they are to be executed. If the boat founders and the royal person falls into the water and is about to drown, let the boatmen stretch out the signal-spear and throw the coconuts so that he may grasp them if he can. If he cannot, they may let him seize the signal-spear. If they lay hold of him to rescue him, they are to be executed. He who throws the coconuts is to be rewarded with forty ticals of silver and one gold basin. If the barge sinks and someone else sees the coconuts thrown and goes to save the royal person, the punishment is double and all his family is to be exterminated. If the barge founders and someone throws the coconuts so that they float towards the shore (i.e., away from the royal person), his throat is to be cut and his home confiscated.'

So extensive was Chulalongkorn's modernisation that European observers in the 1870s voted Thailand the Asian country most likely to industrialise. (The same observers thought Japan unlikely to succeed!)

King Bhumibol

Today, commoners may stand in the presence of the king and even snap his photograph. King Bhumibol (this is the usual English spelling; Thais pronounce the name Phumiphon, where the 'ph' is pronounced as a breathy English 'p', not an 'f') came to the throne in 1946 and has consistently built on the heritage of King Chulalongkorn.

Visitors who tend to see monarchies as relics of feudal times will be pleasantly surprised to find King Bhumibol very much a man of the 21st century. Far from being the cloistered monarch of the past, the Thai king of today covers an average of 50,000 km (31,068.6 miles) a year, much of it in jeeps he drives himself, visiting the people in the most dangerous and remote parts of the kingdom. He also initiates and leads development programmes and conducts experiments in Chitrlada Palace designed to provide renewable energy resources.

King Bhumibol—very much a modern monarch.

Few long-term visitors to Thailand leave without developing a deep respect for the Thai king. A man of many talents, the Thai king must surely be the only monarch in the world to play both the saxophone and the clarinet and have a recording of jazz compositions in the shops. Like King Chulalongkorn, King Bhumibol has been granted the title 'The Great'.

The Relevance of History to Modern Thais

Not all Thais in every corner of the kingdom will be aware of the historical names and dates that formed their nation and nationality; but all, with regional and ethnic variations, belong to Thai society and this society has been formed by the specific history of Thailand. Much the same could be said for the English, French and Germans. Ask an Englishman to comment on the 100-year war with France and he is likely to say, "What war?" He might also feel something of an ambivalent relationship towards the French that he cannot really explain. Thais perhaps feel a similar relationship with their Burmese neighbours.

Young Thais of modern and democratic Thailand are most unlikely to regard *sakti na*, if they have heard of it at all, as any thing other than a relic of history—like an English schoolboy might think of the Magna Carter or the Doomsday Book—but they will automatically *wai* first when meeting people older or people of greater status than their own, and will adjust their vocabulary depending on the age and status of the person they are talking to. When serving a Coke to a guest in a good hotel or to the head of the household, it remains quite normal for the server to go down on his knees to do so. When passing in front of somebody sitting, the passer-by lowers the body. When handing something, the right hand is often supported by the left, or both hands are used. Just habit? Of course, but habits which result from a long history. Thailand is sometimes referred to as a 'loosely structured society' (in comparison for example with Japan), and so it is. Plenty of poor Thais have risen through the wealth and status hierarchy, but the underlying principles, while no longer sanctioned by death and beatings, are still rigidly there, holding everything together.

RELIGION
The Wat
While the visitor's ignorance of Thai norms of courtesy involving one's fellow man will often be excused by the Thai as simply odd, or, at worst, rude, inappropriate behaviour in any religious context will not be easily forgiven, and deliberate or unintended insult to what the Thais consider sacred could land you in real trouble. Behaving disrespectfully in a Thai temple or to a monk is absolutely taboo.

The Thai Buddhist temple, the *wat*, can be very simple or extremely elaborate. In small villages, the *wat* may consist only of a simple *bot* (the central hall of any *wat*, which shelters

A *Chedi*

the main Buddha image and in which ordinations take place) and a wooden house for one or two monks. In larger population centres, a *wat* may also include a *sala*, where laymen gather for social functions, for ceremonies such as the *Sukhwan Nak* (the lay ritual preceding ordination as a monk) and funerals, and even for such secular activity as voting in elections. Somewhere in the *wat* grounds will be found a Bo tree and, to the west of the grounds of the larger temples, a crematorium. In addition, some *wat* grounds contain a library and one or more *chedi*, a massive structure usually erected over the bones of a very rich man who wills part of his estate to 'make merit'.

The *wat* grounds are cut off from the outside world by a wall. This preserves them as quiet, cool and green oases of sanity in the hot and noisy madness of Bangkok. Not surprisingly, *wat* grounds, in every part of Thailand, provide a place of peaceful recreation, and the *wat* functions as a community social centre as much as a religious centre.

Some *wats* in and around Bangkok are so large that they resemble little city states, with roads, paths, housing blocks for hundreds of monks, nuns and lay helpers, and shops and stalls selling refreshments.

Women

Women are permitted everywhere, although they should enter the monks' houses only under special circumstances. These houses may be grouped together or dotted around in the forest. There are no restrictions to prevent a menstruating woman from visiting a *wat* (as, for example, a Hindu would be prevented from visiting a Hindu temple).

Bot

Certain parts of the *wat* grounds are more sacred than others, the central *bot* and its Buddha image being the most important. You must take off shoes and hat before entering the *bot*, usually but not always to the *sala*, and before entering a monk's quarters. You should also respect the Thai custom of stepping over door thresholds, not on them.

Bo Tree

The Bo tree, easily recognised by its vast size and sprawling branches (also, it is often clothed in a saffron robe wrapped around its trunk), is sacred because the Buddha attained enlightenment while sitting under one, so please don't allow your children to climb it!

Dress

Normal dress—within the guidelines of Thai respectability—is usually quite acceptable in most *wats*. However, some of the royal *wats* in Bangkok will refuse entry to women in trousers and men or women in shorts and T-shirts.

Ambience

The ambience in the *wat* might surprise the Christian visitor, who is most likely to behave as he would in church. He should remember that Buddhist worship is primarily an individual activity and that people are likely to come and go at any time. Social activity is not clearly distinguished from religious activity and the visitor should therefore not be surprised to find some people, including monks, smoking cigarettes, drinking tea, chewing betel-nuts and quietly chatting during a sermon or ceremony, while others sit in devoted attention. Spittoons are usually placed around on the floor and should be used for saliva, cigarette ash and as general rubbish bins.

Sitting

One problem for the visitor is that very rarely will he find a chair to sit on. High seats, in traditional society, were reserved for royalty, and it remains the norm that most commoners live out their lives sitting, eating and sleeping on the floor. The most comfortable and healthy way of sitting on the floor is to sit cross-legged and this is the way monks sit. However, it is not the way a layman or a laywoman sits in the *bot*. There you should sit in the respect position, with the legs tucked under the body, facing the Buddha image. This position is inconvenient and tiring even for Thais and there is no reason why you shouldn't prop yourself up on one arm.

THE MONK

The same sitting position is adopted before monks as before a Buddha image. To sit cross-legged in front of a monk would be to suggest that you are his equal, and you are not.

Status

The superiority of any monk over any layman is very evident in the Thai language which has a set of special vocabulary to be used when talking to or about monks. It is also evident in all aspects of monk-layman interaction; laymen eat after, walk behind and seat themselves at a lower level than monks.

There are many obvious reasons, secular and religious, to respect a monk in Thailand. In the villages, many monks continue to fulfil an important secular function by providing basic education to farmers' children. Many aid development efforts directly by teaching crafts and trades to the adult population and mobilising cooperative efforts to construct wells, bridges and dams. There are, of course, a few monks in Bangkok and elsewhere who do not keep all of the 227 monastic vows, and a minority who behave in most un-monkish ways, but the vast majority stand as shining examples of virtue in an increasingly unvirtuous world. It

Traditionally, a Buddhist monk wanders with few possessions, living simply, spending his time in mediation, the quest for spirtual knowledge, and teaching the people. Today, monks continue these traditions. Many monks now possess teaching certificates and run simple village schools, bringing education to remote areas.

is surely healthy that the most respected people in society have taken a vow of poverty, which prevents them eating after noon, and a vow of celibacy, which prevents formation of a priestly caste.

During chantings, the monks sit in a row on a platform that raises them physically above laymen. In one or two of the *wats* frequented by tourists, the visitor may notice a sign in English saying 'reserved for monks' or 'monks only'; in most places, however, there will be no sign. Even if the monks are not there, you do not sit, or place anything, on this platform.

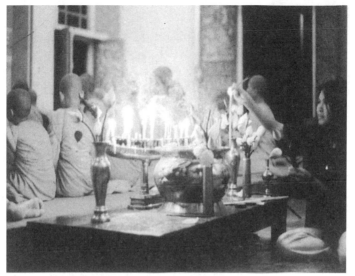

A platform raises monks physically above laymen.

You are welcome to attend chantings and to leave whenever you please, but while you are present, do not stand towering over everybody—sit down on the floor.

Abbot

All monks take vows of poverty and humility, but they are as much occupied with relative status within the order as are laymen outside it. Although all monks wear the same 'uniform', individual status is evident in the type of fan carried. The abbot of a large *wat* is at the top of the local hierarchy and is a powerful man in both religious and secular communities. Nothing should happen within his realm of authority without his knowledge and approval. If you plan to take photographs, you should ask his permission. (For obvious reasons, this is neither practical nor necessary in those Bangkok *wats* popular with tourists, where, unless you see a sign forbidding it, you may feel free to take any pictures you wish.) When approaching the abbot, it is not necessary for the visitor to go through the full respect procedure of the triple obeisance, but it is appropriate to lower yourself to beneath his height and give the most respectful *wai*.

Offerings

For those who wish not only to observe but also to participate, and make some merit, you may buy in the *wat*, or take with you, an appropriate set of offerings to the Buddha. The usual offering is three incense sticks (representing the Buddha, his teachings and the monastic order), some flowers, one candle and a thin piece of gold leaf.

The *wai phra* (routine for offering) is not rigidly fixed and you may notice quite an amount of individual variation (although it takes place in public, *wai phra* is essentially a private action between the individual and the Buddha). Usually, the candle is lit first and placed among the other candles in a row set in front of the image. The flowers are placed in water. Then the incense sticks are lit from the candle and held between the palms in a *wai* on the chest. Sitting quietly in the respect position, the Thai would recite in the mind some set phrases in *Pali* (the language of the Buddhist scriptures), praising the Buddha, his teachings and the order of monks that the Buddha created.

This would normally be followed by a wish, expressed mentally in Thai, of a general nature, 'Keep my family healthy,' etc. or a far more specific request, 'Please help me to pass my university exams' or 'Please make me win the

Offering candles and flowers to the Buddha.

lottery this month.' The incense sticks are then stuck into the container of sand provided, the square of gold leaf is pressed onto a Buddha image, and the individual concludes with the triple obeisance. The visitor is quite free to follow this procedure if he wishes, or he may prefer simply to sit in silent communion with the Buddha or his own god.

Following the simple ritual of *wai phra*, it is normal to donate some money into the box provided. This goes to the upkeep of the *wat*. The visitor with religious qualms about engaging in Buddhist ritual may put some money in the box (although he cannot escape the merit this action involves!).

If the visitor wishes to present monks with 'presents' and participate even more in Thai life, he should be aware that these objects (usually items of daily need) should be purchased especially for this purpose. You do not simply take some razor blades and toothpaste from the bathroom and give them to the monks; also you do not buy some packets of cigarettes intending to give them to the monks, change your mind, and smoke them yourself.

In the same way, if you choose to make religious merit by offering food, you do not cook up a good meal for yourself and then give a bit to the monks, you feed them first and then eat what remains. Even the flowers you present to the Buddha or the monks should be 'goal specific'. The visitor who innocently sniffs them before offering could find horrible things happening to his nose in the next life!

Safety with Monks

The presence of a monk on a vehicle, especially one as dangerous as a Bangkok bus, is said to ensure safety. During the 1973 revolution, a group of monks standing up in an open car drove slowly down Rajdamnoen Avenue through the crossfire of police on one side and student revolutionaries on the other and escaped unharmed. The monk is the most sacred of living beings. To kill one, even by accident, is the worst thing you could do in the world.

Meeting Monks

You will encounter monks not just in the *wat*, but everywhere. Many of them in Bangkok seem to be learning English and almost all of them would be happy to chat with you. Their English is likely to be very textbook and basic. If a smiling young monk greets you with "good morning, sir" (it happens all the time!) in much the same way as a doorman at an expensive hotel, please realise that this is purely a linguistic error (nobody has yet produced an English language grammar for such respected people as monks). You may well have a very informal chat with a monk and even exchange addresses, but it is really not done to shake his hand on taking leave, unless the monk insists (which he will not do for a female). This is the time you can be sure your *wai* is appropriate.

Women

Women present a special problem to monks, who are not supposed even to think about them except in terms of piles of skin and bones. The pile of skin and bones should keep as much social distance between herself and a monk as she possibly can—even if he is her son or fiancé.

Touching of a monk or the robes he is wearing by a woman is absolutely taboo and would involve the monk in elaborate purification rituals. It is also taboo for a woman to hand anything directly to a monk; the object should be passed via a man, set down so that the monk can pick it up, dropped into the monk's bowl or placed on the piece of saffron cloth every monk keeps handy for this purpose. Monks may tie sacred threads onto a woman's wrists, but he should do so without touching her—so keep that arm still.

The visitor should note that monks sit on the back seat of a bus and, for this reason, women avoid this seat. When a crowded Bangkok bus halts to allow a monk to enter, a place will be found for him on this back seat. (No such privilege is accorded the poor nun who must take her chance along with everybody else.) Taking a back seat does not indicate suspension of status. Simply, by using the back door the possibility of brushing past a woman is greatly reduced.

SACRED SYMBOLS

The most well known of Buddhism's sacred symbols, the one most respected by Thais and, unfortunately, the one most abused by non-Thais (and some Thais) is the Buddha image.

Buddha Images

These images are not 'idols'. They do not represent any god and, strictly speaking, are meant only as an aid to help the individual in his path towards the attainment of 'Buddha nature'—the complete elimination of suffering. However, the distinction between worshipping Buddha nature and worshipping the actual image is a fine one and does not change the sacred nature of that image.

It should be, needless to say, that these images must be treated with the utmost respect. In the past, severe punishments were handed down to anyone guilty of desecrating an image or scraping the gold leaf from its surface. Today, in spite of restrictions on taking images out of the country, they are openly on sale in tourist shops and even set out disrespectfully by the roadside. Many valuable images have disappeared from the country and turned up in museums in the West. These images are stolen by Thais (and if they can't carry the whole image, the normal procedure is just to take the head, since this is the part most valued by the buyer), but sometimes these Thais act in open connivance with otherwise respectable foreign museums and universities.

Such behaviour by a few Thais (unfortunately, those whom the tourist is most likely to encounter) stands in sharp contrast to that of the great majority of the population. To the average Thai, the Buddha image is not an object of merchandise. It is also not seen primarily as a work of art. In talking about images in Thai, special respect language is used, the ordinary term for 'it' is never used and the parts of the image's body are called by those terms used to refer to the king's 'arm', 'head', etc. The Buddha image is an object of veneration, not of decoration. Mistreating a Buddha image in Thailand is tantamount

Some years ago, a *farang* family was imprisoned for climbing onto a giant Buddha to pose for a photograph. Their plea that they did not understand Thai conventions and meant no disrespect was dismissed in court.

Merit for sale. Discount for ten or more images.

to going into a devout Catholic's house and turning the crucifix upside down.

Even when it comes to sacred images, there are degrees of abuse. Few Thais would object to a non-Thai keeping Buddha images in his home for decoration, as long as these are in a reasonably high place (certainly not at foot level). The Thais would also probably hold in their feelings if the visitor entered their home, picked up their image and said, "How lovely, where can I get one?" (A Thai should *wai* the image before moving or cleaning it.) However, the foreigner would have overstepped the tolerance line if he climbed onto one of the many huge Buddha images dotted around the country (the lowest, the feet, being placed upon the highest, the Buddha).

The King

Next to the Buddha and the monks, the king, although no longer officially 'sacred', is treated with such respect that the visitor might safely categorise him, his family and their images as sacred.

Pictures of the royal family are shown on the screen and the 'king's national anthem' is played before the film in Thai cinemas. If you are on your way in, you stand to attention, arms by your sides. If you are seated, you stand up. Actually, the music played is not the Thai national

His Majesty King Bhumibol Adulyadej during his Coronation (5 May 1950) pronounced the Oath of Accession to the Throne, "We will reign with righteousness, for the benefit and happiness of the Siamese people." As he said these words, the king poured ceremonial water symbolising dedication of his whole being to the task of reigning over the Thai nation according to the Moral Principles of the Sovereign.

The King blesses the people at the beginning of Buddhist Lent.

anthem, but a tune reserved for the presence of the king and queen or their images; the real national anthem is never played in the cinema. There is also a special tune for when the king's representative is present; the visitor should treat all three tunes with the same respect. And try to remember not to sit down during the pauses, which are part of the music.

Every Thai banknote and coin carries a picture of the king. It is acceptable to fold the notes, put them in your wallet and the wallet in any pocket, even the one you sit on. However, try not to make the same mistake as the poor Frenchman who disagreed with the amount of change given him after paying for his meal in a restaurant. He got into a heated argument and refused to accept the banknotes that the waitress held out for him. He grew so angry that he grabbed the notes, screwed them up, threw them to the floor and ground them underfoot. A foot on the king's head! A Thai drinking at a nearby table jumped up, smashed his fist into the Frenchman's surprised face and followed up with a flying kick to the stomach. The limits of tolerance had been passed.

Books

Several other objects of everyday life are not sacred in the same way as the Buddha and the king, but are treated respectfully by Thais. These include books and hats. Books, because, until comparatively recently, education was confined to the *wat* (it still is in many remote villages) and the only books were those containing the sacred scriptures. By extension, all books, as vehicles that carry man towards the goal of knowledge and understanding, should be treated appropriately and not defaced. Unfortunately, to judge from the scribblings in books at Chulalongkorn library, this norm of good behaviour requires some social reinforcing.

Hats

Hats are to be treated respectfully because of their association with the head. They should be hung up even if the only place to hang them is a humble nail, not tossed onto the back of a chair. When taking off shoes and hat before entering a *bot*, do not place your shoes outside the door with your hat resting on top of them because of the unlucky association between feet and head. It is also worth noting that objects of 'low' status should be treated appropriately: placing your shoes on a chair, whether your feet are in them or not, is as bad as placing your hat on the floor.

Elephants and Umbrellas

Many other items carry respect through association with royalty or religion. Rare 'white' elephants are always presented to the King; other elephants work for their living but are regarded as very special animals. Umbrellas have the same association with royalty—the greater the number of tiers, the higher a noble's rank. Ordinary single-tiered umbrellas may, of course, be used to keep off the rain and sun by anybody. But even if there is no rain or sun, an elaborate umbrella will be used to 'shelter' a young man on his way to become a monk, or a dead person on the way to cremation—two moments in existence when a commoner attains his highest status.

Rice

Rice holds a very special position in the hierarchy of animals, plants and objects because it is the giver of life both for the individual and the nation. Half of all Thais continue to work in the rice fields and Thailand is the world's principal exporter of this commodity. Rice is said to contain a spiritual essence of its own and everybody, from the king down to the humblest peasant, goes to elaborate lengths to keep the rice spirit happy. Planting and harvesting call for special ceremonies.

Rice dropped on the floor is carefully swept up. Some mothers even rebuke their children, if they complain of tummy-ache after overeating, that they are insulting the rice goddess. If the rice goddess is insulted, the rice crop will suffer. As long as the rice goddess is happy, the Thais will eat and prosper. So please don't throw your leftover rice down the toilet.

ECONOMY

The Thai economy in recent years has certainly had some very significant ups and downs. In the 1980s and 1990s (until the crash), Thailand was acclaimed as one of the Asian Tigers. By the end of the 1980s, the growth rate had reached 13 per cent per annum, property prices were almost doubling during the time it took to construct a property, new roads meant more access to markets and increased land prices along the new routes, shopping centres became more familiar than traditional markets, the eastern seaboard was industrialised, and the percentage of people working in agriculture fell from 75 per cent to 50 per cent (where it remains today). Young people became comparatively rich. All had motorcycles (built or assembled in Thailand) and some had cars. People bought rather than rented houses, in the firm conviction that they could always sell at much more than they paid. Every house had a TV, fridge and many had air-conditioners.

The under-developed Thailand of the early 1970s was galloping full speed towards prosperity, without time to look sideways and certainly without thought of putting something away for a rainy day. Everybody borrowed, repaying less than the gain in their capital. It was great while it lasted. Many educated Thais today owe their education to those prosperous and uncompromisingly optimistic days of the Tiger. Many buildings and communication systems were established during those years.

Then, suddenly, in mid-1997, the bubble burst. The baht devalued some 40 per cent against the dollar in just four months and individuals and companies could not meet their debts. The external debt, to be repaid in dollars, had reached over 52 per cent of the country's GDP by the end of the year. In 1998, during frantic attempts to restructure the financial and property sectors of the economy, many banks and finance companies went broke or closed their doors. In that year the Thai economy, instead of growing in double digits, shrank by 10 per cent.

The International Monetary Fund (IMF) provided short-term loans to a total of US$ 17.2 billion and, almost miraculously, Thailand repaid by 2000, when the growth rate was far from the dizzy figures of the 1980s, but had recovered to a healthy and maintainable 5 per cent. Some Thais were ruined in 1997 but most reacted philosophically, realising that what goes up must come down. They got to work rebuilding the economy, without incurring the tremendous debts that had marked the Tiger years. The result is a truly strong economy, based on various sectors and an exploitation of Thailand's natural resources (tin, petroleum and natural gas leading the way) with the government's economic strategy firmly focused on exports, particularly textiles, rice (Thailand is the world's largest exporter of rice) and tourism. The December 2004 tsunami disaster set back one of Thailand's principal tourist areas, but in 2005, rebuilding was already well under way, and Phuket's loss had been partly matched by gains in other resort areas on the Gulf side.

The Thais have shown an amazing resilience and determination in building up their country and, in spite of economic setbacks and natural disaster, Thailand remains the country which, in the entire world, has moved quickest from comparative poverty to comparative wealth. With a low inflation rate and a fair per capita income spurring domestic consumption, quality control that Vietnam and China can only dream of, and an export-led economy, the next decade looks bright for this Asian tiger.

PEOPLE

CHAPTER 3

'A friend to eat with is easily found.
A friend to die with is hard to find.'
—Thai saying.

POPULATION AND DISTRIBUTION

In 2005, the population of Thailand was estimated at some 62 million people. Estimating the various populations of Thailand's cities, where more than a third of Thais live, is more difficult; figures are sometimes given for the municipality and sometimes for the *meuang* (municipal district), and sometimes include extensive suburbs, and sometimes exclude them. We can therefore say that Bangkok has a population of six million (municipality) or eight million (*meuang*), or up to ten million if all suburbs are included rather than regarded (as they are officially) as separate population centres. If we consider *meuang* figures, Udon Thani and Nakhorn Ratchasima in the north-east are second and third in size, Hat Yai in the south is fourth, Chonburi in the centre is fifth and Chiang Mai is sixth.

This is not a very realistic way of looking at things since suburbs and satellites can be more impressive in terms of population than the municipality or the *meuang*. Chiang Mai, for example, has an official *meuang* population of 172,000, but estimates including suburbs, satellites and transient population, go up to one million—making it Thailand's second city rather than its sixth.

The demography of Thailand has changed dramatically over recent decades, largely because of the success of population control measures, and a change in values which now favours small families. (Much of this particular change can be attributed to the efforts of Meechai, a birth control campaigner whose name in Thai has become synonymous with condom.) The population growth rate is currently between 1–1.5 per cent, comparatively low in the Asia region. The population remains relatively young, with only 12 per cent over the 50 mark. Advances in health, education and modern medicine (now some of the best in the world) have raised life expectancy dramatically to an average of 70 years.

Thai education has greatly improved in recent years, although rote learning remains the norm in most villages. Thailand's literacy rate at 95 per cent is one of the highest in Asia. Most Thais complete nine years of schooling, and the two best universities, both in Bangkok, Chulalongkorn and Thammasat, rate among the top 50 institutions of higher education in Asia. Many Thais go abroad for further studies; this is particularly the case with Thai doctors, many of whom have studied in the US.

DIVERSITY IN UNITY

Some 75 per cent of the population are ethnic Thai. However, this percentage is divided into four major groupings which may be distinguished geographically, linguistically and to a varying degree, culturally. Central Thais of the Chao Phraya Delta (the main rice-growing area) form the majority and speak Central Thai (the Thai the foreigner is likely to learn). About six million Lao speakers (more than the population of Laos) live in the north-east and speak Lao, although this is referred to as Thai-Isaan in Thailand, a political rather than a linguistic distinction. Ethnic Thais of the south and of the north also have their own dialects/languages and traditions.

Because of the spread of education (in central Thai) and the use of Central Thai in the written system and particularly on TV, all Thais understand the Central Thai you will hear in Bangkok and the surrounding area. The same is not true in reverse and a Bangkokian transferred to the north-east or the south will only understand the local Thai if he has a length of intensive exposure to the language (this has been estimated by a linguistic expert who devised a course for Central Thai policemen who were to be stationed in the north-east and other provinces, as at least 100 hours)—the visitor is not alone in having language problems in Thailand.

Minorities

It has been estimated, without any pretensions of real accuracy, that ethnic Chinese Thais make up over 10 per cent of the population. It is certainly true that there are families which remain essentially Chinese, speak Chinese, follow Chinese culture in life cycle rites and go to Chinese temples practising Mahayana Buddhism rather than, or as well as, Thai Hinayana Buddhist temples. However, the real influence of the Chinese in Thailand is that most have not remained a distinct and separate group but have intermarried with Thais to the point where it is now more difficult to find a Thai with no Chinese ancestor somewhere in his or her past, than it is to find a Thai who can name a Chinese ancestor.

This integration has been possible because of the excellent and tolerant relations from both sides. There have been a couple of anti-Chinese periods, but these are now lost in history, along with the unfortunate statement of one of Thailand's most impressively tolerant monarchs, that the Chinese are the 'Jews of Southeast Asia'. The reality of the Chinese presence in Thailand is that the Chinese get on better with Thais than they do with any other group in any country of the region.

Such is the influence of the Chinese that many Thais can speak a southern Chinese dialect, even if they cannot read Chinese. This influence is often evident in physical features but not always. A southern Thai might appear far from Chinese but have a grandparent who is 100 per cent Chinese.

Second to the Chinese in terms of numbers but, in the modern world at least, not in terms of influence, are the Malays. They constitute 3.5 per cent of the population and almost all live in the four southernmost provinces, bordering Malaysia. Just about all of them practise Islam and dress in a Malay, rather than a Thai way. All speak Malay as their first language and practise Malay/Islamic rites such as circumcision and burial (which Thais generally do not practise).

While there have been long periods of peace where Thai Buddhists and Malay Muslims have lived side by side, for example in the small southern fishing town of Narathiwat where mosque and *wat* are equally evident, there has also been a simmering tension that has occasionally erupted into violence—more a violence between Malay liberation organisations and the Thai military than between Thai and Malay farmers and fishermen. The existence of a large Malay population in the south relates closely to the history of the region and shifting borders. (There are also Thai-speaking villages in the north of Malaysia.) It may be compared with the six million Isaan/Lao speakers in the north-east of the country. While the Muslim south has been marked by conflict and separatism, the Lao-speaking north-east, which shares Thai Buddhist customs and values, has been peaceful (ever since the Lao were beaten in a war with Thailand and forced to live on the Thai side of the Mekong River).

Pork or *Moo*?

A devout non-Thai-speaking Muslim from Malaysia, travelling up to Bangkok by train and forbidden by his religion to eat pork, ate nothing but plates of fried rice during the two-day journey. Before beginning each plate, he pointed at the little pieces of meat mixed up with the rice and, shaking his head, pronounced emphatically "No pork! No pig!" The waiter agreed with him "No pig" and added, emphasising the rising tone, "Moo". At least, the Malaysian thought, remembering his mother pointing out 'moo-cows', he had learnt one word of Thai; *moo* obviously meant cow or beef. But it doesn't, as our Malaysian friend found out when he got to Bangkok. *Moo* means pig. Culture shock is not just for the *farang* visitor.

Up to one million other minorities live throughout the country, ranging from the proto-Malay Sea Gypsies in the south, large groups of semi-integrated Khmer and Mon speakers in the east, and the hill-tribes of the north. These include the Akha, Karen, Lahu, Lisu, and, perhaps the most famous of them all, the Hmong, who traditionally live (lived) at high altitudes and grew opium poppy (no longer a problem in Thailand). There is some literature on all of these groups and most of what has been written is available at the Tribal

Research Institute located at the Chiang Mai University campus. The only group with an ethnography (description of their traditional life) available in the bookstores and online is *The Hmong*. (*Refer to* Further Reading *on page 342 for more details.*)

THAI VALUES AND TRADITIONS

As with all people everywhere, Thais are changing. Traditions, of course, remain what they always were, and I have covered some of this area in the chapter on history. Values, however, are no longer necessarily in step with traditions, and behaviour is no longer always in step with values (the way things should be). The transition from being an underdeveloped to a modern developed state was accomplished only recently, and at great speed.

This transition created movement of people away from the agricultural villages to urban centres, where education and jobs away from the traditional controls and coping mechanisms opened up exciting new horizons for many young Thais, but also gave them a rather different set of objectives, priorities and ways of seeing good and bad to those 50 per cent who remain in the villages. Even this latter lot now has access to education, good roads and a transport system for trips to town and, almost everywhere, TV. Every night, in the remotest villages, farming families turn on to Thai drama—two-hour episodes which might include some of the more gory aspects of belief in the spirits, but which almost entirely centre on modern middle-class, well-educated Thais who dress well, live in big houses, drive expensive cars and lace their correct Central Thai with words of English origin.

To put things simply, most Thais now no longer see success in life in fairly simple terms of having enough rice fields to ensure their family's welfare, having a buffalo to plough the land and having a house on stilts large enough to accommodate a large and extended family, preferably in the vicinity of their relatives. Thais now see the TV and VCD-player, the fridge and the fan as essentials, and the concrete house, with an air-con bedroom, as desirable. The average Thai will continue to give to support the Buddhist religion with food and money, and many young men become monks for a time before they get married (although somewhat fewer than a few years ago and for rather shorter periods than their fathers).

The King and the Peasant

In searching, unsuccessfully, for a nutshell to put Thailand into, I came across a Thai folk-tale which sums up something of the Thai way of seeing things.

In this tale, a king meets a peasant and asks what he does with his surplus. The peasant replies: "Your Majesty, all the money I am able to save, after paying the expenses of our frugal household, I divide into four parts. The first I bury in the ground; the second I use to pay my creditors; the third I fling into the river; and the fourth and last part I give to my enemy."

The king asks the peasant to explain his strange behaviour and is told: "The money I bury in the ground is the money I spend on alms and in making merit. The money I give to my creditors is what it costs me to keep my father and mother, to whom I owe everything I have. The money I fling into the river is the money I spend on gambling and drink and opium; and the money I give to my enemy is the money I give to my wife." (Translated by A. Le May, *Siamese Tales Old and New*, London, 1930)

The peasant spends his money on four things: religion, parents, enjoyment and wife. His views on supporting parents and wife are diametrically opposed. The remainder of his money is divided between the temporary pleasures of life and the permanent treasure of Buddhism. An investment in religion is the only insurance for the future. This ancient tale remains a favourite with modern Thais. Things have not changed too much.

However, in pursuit of material consumption and the trophies of modern life, many are prepared to allow or encourage their daughters (and their sons) to enter some form of prostitution. A prostitute can earn, in three days, more than a university professor gets in a month. Such is life; but not all Thais are university professors and not all Thais are prostitutes. It is still possible to find very traditional families, particularly in the established middle class, where girls remain virgins until marriage and where family values dominate all other. But things have changed and are still changing. It would not be helpful to the visitor to imagine Thais as conforming to Thai values, unless he realises the shifting nature of these values. Values—Thai ways of seeing—still exist, or I would not go into them below. But they exist more in public then in private. The visitor would do well to remember, as he goes through the following section, that Thais know full well this is how they should behave, at least in public.

THAI WAYS OF SEEING

If the Thai world of shifting values could be fully pressed between the covers of a book, it probably would not be worth reading. My task in the remainder of this chapter is not to provide the complete picture of this fascinating jigsaw puzzle called Thailand. That would be impossible because the pieces of the puzzle are changing all the time. I limit myself to considering those pieces which most intrigue, worry and please the visitor unfamiliar with Thai ways of seeing and doing. When the visitor understands something of Thai ways of seeing things, he will have learnt a lot about Thailand and a great deal about himself.

The Five Basic Precepts of Life

The five great commandments of Buddhism are as follows:
- Do not take life.
- Do not steal.
- Do not commit adultery.
- Do not tell untruths.
- Refrain from intoxicants.

All Thais know these commandments and almost all Thais are Buddhists. Thailand is one of the most Buddhist countries in the world, and yet a great many Thais break most or all of these commandments almost every day.

Taking Life

Few Thais deliberately take life, but all Thais love to eat. Almost all Thai food contains meat, usually pork, chicken or fish. Even the monks eat meat. This requires the killing of animals. It also requires some very Thai rationalisations which permit full indulgence yet leave the commanding principle intact. Monks explain that they eat meat because they must eat anything put in their bowls with neither enjoyment nor disgust; one famous monk is said to have calmly eaten a leper's thumb that fell into the bowl! Laymen resort to less convincing excuses: I just took the fish out of the water and it died without killing; the chicken was already dead when I bought it; the pig was fulfilling its destiny, that's why it was born a pig. Fortunately, very few Thai Buddhists find themselves in a position where they would have to take life since most are rice farmers and slaughter-men are mostly non-Buddhists.

Theft

Most Thais do not steal; the minority do. Unfortunately, the minority seem to be quite active and *khamoys* (thieves) abound. Any bus (but of course not every bus), even in the centre of Bangkok, is a potential target for the *khamoy*, who enters through the back door with knife or gun, grabs what wallets and gold chains he can, exits through the front onto his friend's motorcycle and flees the scene. Houses and pedestrians are also fair game, if rather easier to protect.

Apart from the professional *khamoys*, many Thais employ a 'fish out of water' rationale for keeping what is found: it fell off the back of a truck. Considering the number of things that really do fall off the backs of trucks, the explanation is reasonable. The practice of finders-keepers might be considered fair compensation for Thais who live in constant knowledge that any day, home and family could be smashed to smithereens by a ten-tonne truck.

Cheating

More subtle forms of *khamoyery* are performed on hapless visitors by those shopkeepers who sell jewellery constituting 50 per cent of the stated gold and silver value and which would be much cheaper back home. If you are staying some time in the country, make the fact known and you may get a better deal. This is because any reputable disreputable jeweller will give a guarantee of full refund if goods are found to be of less than stated quality. This guarantee is worth the paper it is written on and little more, unless you have several months to waste in legal inactivity. Not all jewellers are dishonest, but visitors should note that several laboratories will test gold, silver and gems for a small fee and that this service is provided to fulfil a need.

Sex

The third precept—to refrain from adultery—is kept publicly and often broken privately. The visitor may notice that many of the middle-range hotels not only have the strange habit of renting rooms by the hour, but also have very quaint basement 'car parks'. As every car pulls in, a young boy runs to pull a curtain and hide the car from the world. The purpose of this roof-to-ground curtain is not to keep the car clean.

Telling the Truth

The fourth commandment is very difficult to keep in daily life. Truth and untruth are, of course, relative and debatable concepts. The Thai does not necessarily deliberately lie, but also does not necessarily deliberately tell the truth. Norms of respect and politeness require flattery and exaggeration. Conflict avoidance is often achieved by the lie. If the boss asks why you did something stupid, say the first thing that comes into your head, fact or fiction. And if you are cheating on your spouse, what is to be gained by telling them about it?

Intoxicants

The fifth commandment is openly broken. Alcoholism is a problem and although the sales of the two major brands of Thai whisky, Mekong and Sang Som, report a 20 per cent drop in sales during the three-month Buddhist Lent, few Thais consider drinking alcohol to be particularly un-Buddhist.

Other intoxicants include marijuana, opium and heroin, all of which are illegal. Production and consumption have decreased in recent years, but Thailand perhaps still has one of the largest drug addiction problems in the world. All visitors are warned at points of entry to the kingdom that dealing in drugs can result in imprisonment, confiscation of property and execution—foreigners are in no way exempt and many languish for years in harsh Thai prisons because of drug related offences.

Flattery and Candour

Thais are masters of the 'sideways lie'—stepping aside from any possible unpleasantness by saying whatever is required. Sometimes, however, in circumstances when the westerner would tell a white lie, Thais can be embarrassingly candid, as I found out one night at the Bangkok Alliance Française, where I was treated to a superb exhibition of flattery and candour.

The Thai master of ceremonies stood on the stage for ten minutes, lauding, in textbook French, the praises of the film star he was to introduce to a packed audience. Having stretched the peak of flattery into a seemingly endless ridge, he finally came to "… and it is with the deepest honour that I am privileged to present to you the one and only Monsieur X." Silence. Monsieur X did not rush up and shake the outstretched hand. More silence. Until at last the MC whispered in Thai to a waiting auditorium, "Where is Monsieur X?" A Thai doorkeeper answered clear and loud from the back of the hall, *"pai hong nam"* —"in the toilet".

Ideal and Reality

Daily contravention of the five basic Buddhist precepts places them very much in the realm of the ideal, that which should be rather than that which is. Every society has contradictions between ideal and reality. Western societies could no more be adequately described by reference to the Ten Commandments of the Old Testament, than could the behaviour and feelings of most Thais be expressed by reference to Buddhist precepts. (Although the Western Christian might have trouble in naming all ten commandments, while each Thai schoolchild knows his precepts by heart.)

Making Merit

The Thai does not seem to have any great problems living with his contradictions. This is perhaps because of other aspects of Thai Buddhist philosophy which teach that the individual is responsible for his own destiny and that he can change it for the better by accumulating religious merit. Religious merit is gained by keeping the precepts but also by other actions which may be easier and much more fun.

I asked a group of monks to try and express the essential truth of Buddhism in one sentence. They unanimously agreed on 'all life is suffering'. They were sitting in front of a wooden wall on which somebody had written, in English, 'Life is very fun why quickly to go.' All Thais know that life is suffering, and almost all Thais seem to enjoy life to the full. If there is a contradiction in this, the Thais are not worried by it.

Merit-making in everyday life often means little more than giving money, or things bought with money, to the *wat* and its monks. This refers us back to the Thai folk-tale mentioned at the beginning of this chapter in which the peasant balances the amount spent on daily pleasures with the amount spent on merit-making activities. Most Thais seem happy to strike a balance. Just how effective this balance is in bridging the gulf between ideal and reality is uncertain. However, the idea of balance is essential to any understanding of Thai personality and behaviour.

FAMILY

The family is the first world. A safe world. A world which is, for the first few years at least, gentle, kind and good. It is the world in which an individual learns to obey and respect his elders and betters. The family makes a Thai. This is the way things have been traditionally for a long, long time and the way they remain in essence. However distant a Thai is physically from the family of his or her birth, mentally and morally they remain within the family for life, and after it. The bond is particularly strong between mother and daughter (anthropologists note there are significant matrilineal elements in Thai society). The daughter will feel obliged to support the mother in every way. This has resulted in a general belief among Thais that a bad mother inevitably means a bad daughter. So if you are thinking of marrying a Thai, it's worth knowing that you are marrying a whole family (perhaps a smaller one these days, and one more able to stand on its own feet), and certainly worth having a good look at the mother and her behaviour.

Rules of Respect

The child quickly learns that by behaving in a way that openly demonstrates consideration for the feelings of others,

Rules of respect extend to esteemed members of society. *Luang poh* (father)—a monk continues the tradition of teaching the young.

obedience, humility, politeness and respect, he can make people like him and be nice to him. This behaviour may be summed up in one Thai word, *krengjai*.

Krengjai is usually translated as 'consideration'. It is more than that. It is a feeling. A father might consider the welfare of his children but he would not feel *krengjai* towards them. His children, in considering his feelings and adjusting their behaviour to give him peace of mind, do feel *krengjai*. *Krengjai* is felt by the person who considers. In Thailand, the person 'who considers' is normally the inferior in any social relationship. Thus, *krengjai* has a lot to do with the hierarchical Thai system of status and respect.

Rules of respect, strongest in the relationship between children and parents, are also very evident between children. The younger should obey the elder, the elder is responsible for the behaviour of the younger.

Terms used between family members are often extended to the Thai community, a practice which indicates relative hierarchical status rather than the establishment of close, family-type relationships. A *phii* (elder brother or sister) is always superior to a *nong*. A *nong* could be a close friend or a complete stranger filling up the car petrol tank or waiting on tables. Even husbands and wives use *phii* or *nong* to refer to each other and they are, of course, very unlikely to be brother and sister.

In the same way, *luang poh*, *luang ta* and *luang phii* ('father', 'grandfather' and 'elder brother' with the respect prefix *luang*) may be used to refer to monks, *poh luang* is used in parts of Thailand to refer to the village headman, *mae chi* ('mother nun') refers to nuns and *mae khrua* ('mother kitchen') is used with a female cook. 'Uncles', 'aunts' and 'cousins' may have no biological relationship at all. Stop on a country road to ask the way from a complete stranger older than you, and you should call his attention with *lung*, 'uncle'. There is a family term for everybody in Thai society. They are at one and the same time friendly and hierarchically unequal.

Social and Economic Unity

The Thai village household is, by Asian standards, quite small and is usually confined to a couple, two or three children and perhaps an aging parent, aunt or uncle. Houses vary between the strongly built, ornately decorated, large houses of the wealthy and the frail bamboo boxes of the poor. Differences are much greater in town. Large, modern villas, with servants to run and open the gate at the master's tooting car horn and shacks of cardboard and tin can exist side by side.

Rural Thai families continue the long tradition of social and economic unity. Young children do household chores and look after younger brothers and sisters, older children help their parents in the family rice fields. Urban families lose the unity that comes from working together. However, low wages mean that all family members must contribute to family costs. In Thailand, 'housewives' are found only in privileged households. Wives and children of poor families in the city make cakes, thread flowers into garlands, recycle waste paper into paper bags, sell newspapers and flowers to car owners caught in traffic jams, or do one or more of the thousand jobs that support Bangkok's 'informal economy'.

Security

The family traditionally provided an individual with security against sickness and old age. This remains true in most cases, but in towns, an increasing number of old people find themselves spending their last years in the *wat* or in the anonymous and alien environment of an institution.

Children

The Thai reputation for pampering small children is well deserved. Unfortunately, it is tarnished by the media exposure of the fact that each year, thousands of children are abandoned in temple grounds where they are often raised by the monks and nuns, or abandoned in the street to be raised in orphanages. Newspapers frequently report a flourishing trade in child labour. Parents in town with no means of support and parents in the villages who want a new house or a pick-up or just a TV and motorcycle may sell their child's virginity or labour through 'agents'. These children are often set to work long hours in factories with guards at the door to prevent them leaving. Occasionally some are rescued in much-publicised police raids, but most grow up in an environment that is cruel and depressing by any standards and, in later life, enter the world as *khamoys*, pimps and prostitutes. Perhaps the amazing thing is that the strong bond between mother and child, particularly daughter, survives such mistreatment. The mother can do no wrong.

The Lucky Majority

The unfortunate lot of the unlucky minority must be placed in perspective. Most Thai children are not sold into semi-slavery. On the contrary, they are pampered and fussed over for the first few years of life. Studies of Thai child-rearing patterns suggest that this produces a pleasant, gentle personality but also tends to kill initiative and retard the development of an inquiring mind.

I am none too sure of this process of cause and effect. I am sure, however, that most young children are treated extraordinarily well. The visitor will see adults on a Bangkok bus giving up their seats for children; Western children

The lucky majority.

are told to give up their seats for adults. As for individual development: much smaller families now mean that parents can concentrate on education for their children, including early attendance at a kindergarten. In the old days, one of the first phrases a child learnt was *may pen rai*, which means 'never mind'. Not any more.

Avoiding Aggression

Pampering of small children does not last for long and all too soon, children are hard at work, either contributing to the family fortune or to their own education. If early childhood teaches self-indulgence, late childhood teaches self-sufficiency and responsibility. The adolescent Thai personality is often a mixture of these conflicting patterns of socialisation. An individual may provide for himself and sometimes for others, yet is never encouraged, as the western child is, to 'stand on his own feet'. The Thai learns how to avoid aggression rather than how to defend himself against it. If children fight, even in defence, they are usually punished. The only way to stay out of trouble is to flee the scene.

The Monsters

Some of the most horrible children in Thailand belong to expat families living in the country on a temporary or permanent basis. The expat child is likely to be bigger, stronger, better nourished and psychologically much more prepared to compete, defend and win than are the Thai children he is playing with. Some, but not all, expat children become impossibly pretentious and arrogant. They are aware of the Thai respect status system but are outside it and, in a sense, above it. Their hands are not brought together in a *wai* when an adult visitor enters the house, as are those of Thai children. The Thai adults of the expat child's world are usually servants who will spoil him to keep him quiet.

"Huh!" says the expat reader, "My children must be prepared to live in their society, not in Thai society." I agree. And having pointed out the problem, I offer no solution. To encapsulate them in an expats-only situation might produce even more arrogant monsters and would deny children the unique opportunity to understand Thais and learn the Thai language without tears. I would suggest only that parents be aware that their pride and joy may be another child's hate and misery.

AUTHORITY

The Thai child's world expands as he grows up and very soon it includes far more people than the members of his immediate family. In an agricultural setting, *krengjai* feelings and behaviour expand as this world grows. All elders receive something of the consideration and respect an individual demonstrates for his father and mother.

There comes a point in life when an individual needs to interact with people who are not family, neighbours, friends or even fellow villagers. He enters the world of strangers: the schoolteacher, policeman, *kamnan* (the head of a *tambon* or subdistrict, composed of 10–20 villages), *nai amphur* (district officer) and people who come in trucks and show movies on a big screen which they set up in the grounds of the *wat* and then talk about strange things or line up all the frightened children and stick needles in his arms, poke sticks down their throat and tell them to say "aaaaaarrrh".

This unknown world is potentially dangerous. It wants to be obeyed and insists on being obeyed. So, the most sensible way to deal with it is for the individual to behave in a way that obviously demonstrates obedience, humility, politeness and respect; to behave, superficially at least, in the way he would behave in front of worshipful parents, and hope that this will make strangers like him and be nice to him. By extending *krengjai* behaviour to the outside world, the potential dangers involved in temporary, unknown and unpredictable relationships are, hopefully, neutralised.

Fear

If, in spite of conforming to all respect procedures, the stranger (or a child's father!) does not respond with kindness but becomes hostile, the individual's external actions (the superficial world on view) remain the same, and humility may even be exaggerated to the point a western observer might call degradation. Inside, however, things have changed. The feeling of *krengjai* (consideration/respect) has changed to *krengklua*, literally 'fear'.

At this point, the most sensible thing for the individual to do is to get out of the situation as fast as he can before nasty things happen. Sometimes, the individual may literally flee the scene. More usual is to say and promise anything to placate this unreasonable force and, at the first opportunity, to break off social contact and make sure it is never renewed in the future.

Humiliation

If the individual is impossibly stuck in a *krengklua* situation, self-degradation will continue to the point where wild violence erupts. A wife continuously beaten, a civil servant humiliated once too often, a servant treated too contemptuously; all could eventually rebel, delaying urgent letters, adding a few zeros in the accounts, planting some drugs in a compromising place, or even running amok with a meat cleaver or hiring a thug to kill or maim.

EQUALITY

Few Thais are equal and many are more unequal than others. Twins born minutes apart and raised in the same family will still refer to each other in *phii/nong* terms. A man 34 years 29 days 5 hours 4 minutes and 3 seconds old is the elder of a man 34 years 29 days 5 hours 4 minutes and 2.9 seconds old. Other things being equal, the *phii* (elder) is superior. Of course, other things are rarely equal, but a surprising number of Thais can tell you, within the margins of accuracy of their father's clock, precisely when they were born.

If each Thai midwife was equipped with a stopwatch, it would be possible to rank the entire population from one to 62 million in terms of the age criteria. If it were possible to place an equally exact numerical value on all other attributes of status, add up each individual's totals, and arrange individuals in perfect pecking order, all social behaviour in any situation would be perfectly predictable. The anthropologist's dream and nightmare.

SENIORITY

Status and seniority are so much parts of Thai life, Thais rarely give them a second thought. The single file of monks on the morning almsround walk in abstract detachment from such worldly considerations as status and prestige—the senior monk at the front and the junior at the rear. The guests at

With the senior monk at the front and the junior monk at the rear, these monks would walk in abstract detachment from worldly considerations such as status and prestige,

a wedding, retirement, funeral and other ceremonies are pleasant, polite and *wai* each other at the same time (almost) and at the same height (almost), before lining up to bless the centre of attraction in order of status. It seems to happen naturally. No caste marks, no secret signs, everybody dressed more or less the same. The hierarchy is not perfect and there are areas of overlap, but surprisingly few. How do they know? How do they do it? And why? Few Thais would be able to tell you. A historian could give you some idea. (*Refer to Trailok and the* sakti na *system in* Chapter 2: Land, History & Religion *on pages 23–24.)*

CENTURIES OF RESPECT

Things have changed a lot in Thailand, as everywhere, but old habits change slowly in a predominantly agricultural society. Most Thais continue to think of the royal family as something more than flesh and blood, and land continues to be the major source of wealth, power and status. Equality in the sense of equal shares and equal status is an ideal yet to be realised in both the East and the West. Thais respect the ideal and are, perhaps, moving slowly towards it while managing to steer clear of much of the senseless bloodshed and suffering that result from forcing the pace.

Much of the charm of the Thai people, the *wai*, the smile, the consideration for the comfort of others, is a result of centuries of respect between non-equals. The visitor should try to remember that the most respected people in this country are those who have dedicated themselves to the pursuit of the spiritual and material ideal of overcoming suffering. Thais do not seek to gain the world, but they do wish to keep their soul.

The most respected people in Thailand are those who have dedicated themselves to the pursuit of the spiritual and material ideal of overcoming suffering.

UNDERSTANDING THAI SOCIAL STRUCTURE

The Western visitor used to simple upper/middle/working class distinctions may be confused by the individual way in which Thai society is stratified. The complexity and individuality of the Thai system will begin to be revealed if you begin the daunting task of learning Thai. Then you will be intrigued by the ease with which a Thai changes language and behaviour patterns, slipping in and out of positions of superior, inferior and equal.

Visitors from most non-English-speaking European countries will be used to manipulating two words for 'you'. In modern Europe 'inferior you' is decreasingly heard and may cause offence. Not so in Thailand. The Thai adjusts all of his language to suit the social situation. I give the 'status chart' below for the personal pronouns 'I' and 'you' only

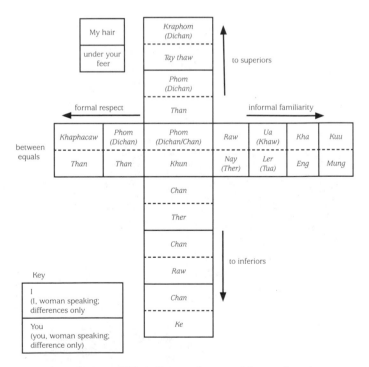

Status chart. The central box indicates safe respectful neutrality when speaking to strangers whose status is not evident or to dangerous inferiors, e.g. drunks and traffic policemen.

to indicate the complexity of the Thai deference system. On this chart alone there are 11 different words for 'you'. The chart is adapted from the one given at the very end of the AUA intensive 20-week Thai course—some Thais consider it an over-simplification!

Some people are very evidently at the top of the structure. The king, royal family and monks (and Buddha images) are all *phra* (excellent). They are excellent in every sense and stand as moral custodians of the Thai world. Almost every Thai household has Buddha images, pictures of monks and many pictures of the king and queen. The Thai world is simply inconceivable without these essential components. An individual status system must have a commonly agreed point of excellence at the very top of the system.

Guess the Status

For those of us who fall short of perfection and whose status is not immediately evident, there is the deceptively simple Thai 'small talk' to put each one of us in his place. Thus, outside of 'fixed status' situations like restaurants, taxi-cabs, etc. where the customer buys temporary higher status, first encounters establish as quickly as possible the relative standing of the individuals involved.

Guess the Status

A visitor may bear in mind the following seven points in this subtle game of guess-the-status. A Thai is likely to assess you on the following:

- Superficial appearance
- Age
- Occupation
- Wage and (intra-organisation) ranking
- Education
- Family
- Social connections

The last two of these points are the most important and tend to determine appearance, occupation, wage and education.

Most really important Thais are recognisable by their surnames. Because surnames were introduced as a legal requirement only in the 1920s, when each family had to pick a name that was different from any other name in the kingdom, you can be sure (with one or two exceptions) that people with the same surname are related in some way. Surnames are rarely used outside of form-filling and formal occasions, but there is nothing at all to stop you asking someone their family name.

Titles

Top families in the 1920s were given their surnames by the king and most top families then are top families now, a century later. With the qualification that there has been some cheating (imitation being the highest form of flattery), it would be a simple exercise to list the 'top hundred', but I refrain from doing so! The visitor may be guided, however, by the fact that a great many important people have titles: royal, civil service or military.

Apart from royal titles, you might come across some other titles which do not show royal descent. Civil service titles have not been granted since 1932 but by some sort of time warp, they are still frequently heard among older members of 'society'. These are, in descending order:

- Chao Phya (wife: Khun Ying)
- Phya
- Phra
- Luang
- Khun (spelt and pronounced differently in Thai from Khun meaning 'you' or 'Mr')

If somebody has a title, use it in place of 'you', 'he' or 'her' when talking to them or about them. You may like to follow the same practice with high military rankings, which are probably more important in Thailand than they are back home because prime ministers, and other very important people, have a strong tendency to be, or to have been, top army personnel. These military rankings are not specifically Thai and are usually translated into the nearest American equivalent on the English side of the name card.

Royal Titles

A surprising number of people in top positions have royal titles; these decrease in status and scarcity following a five-generation rule. The visitor should be aware of this ruling since any title is inevitably displayed in abbreviated form on namecards and invitations and provides an instant guide to status. These titles with their English abbreviations are as follows:

P.O.C.   Phra Ong Chao, grandchild of king

M.C.   Mom Chao, child of P.O.C.

M.R.   Mom Rajawong, child of M.C.

M.L.   Mom Luang, child or wife of M.R. and wife of M.C.

With the fifth generation, the title is lost. The king and queen, crown prince and the princesses stand in a category above all these ranks. They do not, of course, hand out namecards.

Knowing One's Place

The visitor might notice that the who-do-you-know game is not limited to top Thais. Establishing social contacts with people of standing is the aim of all middle-class Thais, who compete among themselves to curry favour with the powerful in much the same way as people did in the *sakti na* days.

Anthropologists have noted that Australian aborigines who meet on walkabouts sit down and go through their family trees until they find an ancestor they share. This common point in the past provides the basis for cooperation and interaction in the present. Versions of the same process of placing strangers exist in all cultures, particularly in Asia and especially in Thailand. (And, I might add, most clearly within expat communities!)

The main purpose of the status game, for most Thais, is not one-upmanship or social advance. On the contrary, the game is a part of knowing one's place and behaving accordingly. However, even when relative statuses are clearly evident, conversations between strangers have a strong tendency to follow the pattern established by the status game. The man who cuts your hair, the girl who sells you a packet of aspirin, the boy who brings you a Coca-Cola; they are all inferiors, they know it and you know it, but they still ask the same personal questions. In such situations, the purpose of the game is not really to establish relative status but rather to flatter the superior. The visitor who begins to learn some Thai will very quickly pick up the pattern, since everybody is a stranger. If you can say nothing else, you will soon be able to give name, age, marital status, occupation, wage, reason for coming to Thailand and the price of your new blue jeans in something approaching understandable Thai.

SUCCESS

When I asked ordinary Thais (the non-VIPs) the simple question, "How do you measure success?" I received a variety of answers. "If I'm still alive at the end of the day" (grinning *tuk-tuk* driver); "Five hundred baht a day" (lottery ticket seller); "Money, lots of it" (shopkeeper, office-worker, policeman); "Being a policeman" (schoolboy); "Having lots of friends" (schoolgirl); "Marrying a rich *farang* and going to America" (hotel waitress); "More of everything" (rice farmer); most answers were personal and subjective, involved money, were within the realm of possibility and emphasised immediacy and luck.

Success, for most people, is a day-to-day affair. Very few could imagine themselves moving up the social ladder and surprisingly few expressed their view of 'success' in a religious way, although almost everybody subsequently said that monks and royalty were the people they most respected. While few men can obtain a royal title, almost all can ordain and achieve the pinnacle of respect during their period as a monk. About 50 per cent or more Thai males do enter the monkhood, but most remain for only the three-month period of Phansa (Buddhist Lent), or less. Above the multitude of 'ordinary' people stands a comparatively small, extremely well educated and very 'successful' elite whose members fill the top echelons of the military and the civil service.

Paths to Success

The typical top government servant comes from a socially acceptable family. He would receive his first degree in an arts subject from Chulalongkorn or Thammasat universities in Bangkok and take an MA overseas, probably in America. Upon return from abroad, he would be ordained as a monk for three months, marry wisely, enter government service and prove himself loyal to a 'patron', often a friend of the family, who would take the protégé under his wing and repay obedience and loyalty by recommending promotion within the service.

Today, not everybody with a good education can be sure of a top position in the civil service, which is markedly 'top heavy', and many graduates now reply to advertisements in the English language press for managerial positions in large multinational companies. These advertisements often stipulate the Chulalongkorn/Thammasat/overseas university qualification, always require a high level of competence in English and, for top positions, sometimes state bluntly that candidates must have 'good social connections'. The reason for this last qualification is that the Thai manager, if he is to secure advantages for his non-Thai company, must be of recognised status and able to operate within the traditional framework of Thai social interaction. In this way, the successful Thai, although he may work for an international company, reinforces traditional Thai social structure.

Thais throughout the status hierarchy resist dreaming of the impossible and tend to think of success either in day-to-day terms ('cook only for today') or as something that comes from consistently staying out of trouble and thereby pleasing everybody. All agree that 'success' means more of what they have not got enough of, usually money.

CHANCE

The philosophy of karma—that good and bad things happen to an individual as a consequence of his good and bad actions in this and past lives—and the Thai inclination for present indulgence rather than long-term investment, provide the socio-economic base for the major Thai industries of gambling and fortune-telling.

Gambling

In Thailand, it is difficult to resist the temptation to gamble. National lottery tickets are on sale on every corner, each bus ticket contains a lottery number and even conscription into national service is determined by the luck of the draw—a black ticket and you are off the hook, a red one and in you go. Even the poorest paid workers periodically get together (especially after pay-day) to put a few baht each into a kitty and play a game of pure chance to allow one or two of them to go on a temporary binge of indulgence. Not to take part might be seen as anti-social.

Gambling, unless officially organised, is illegal but laws are not strictly enforced. For most people it provides a relatively cheap form of entertainment, is a favourite topic of conversation and, since winners inevitably treat their friends, provides endless opportunities for getting together and having a good time. Some forms of gambling, cock-fighting, fish-fighting and betting on the outcome of a Thai boxing bout, not only provide entertainment but also involve high degrees of skill and can become full-time occupations. There are, of course, some Thais who are addicted to gambling. Most of these seem to be women and most are losers.

Some accumulate huge debts that can only be paid by their children, or by sale of their children. Fortunately, this is a minority—although a minority large enough to keep debt collectors busy.

The average Thai spends as much on gambling as he does on religious activity, and the second expense is often directly related to the first. Some people *tham boon* (give food and other items of daily use to the monks) and then immediately ask a monk to give them two numbers; they later match these with the final two numbers on a lottery ticket before buying it. Others prefer a less overt but more direct request to the source of all knowledge and during the quiet moment of *wai phra* (offering flowers, incense and a prayer to the Buddha) will follow the set recitation with a request for a modest win in the next lottery.

CHANGING THE FUTURE

Frequently, Thais try to bribe the gods and spirits, offering to reward extra-human assistance if they are successful in a bet, an examination, request for promotion, job application, a courtship or in recovering from an illness, all things which involve an element of chance. The major part of the bribe is paid only after success has been achieved (as in the material world!). Not to keep such promises would be very dangerous.

One favourite object of votive behaviour in Bangkok is the elephant god at the Erawan corner. This shrine is constantly covered with mounds of flowers and a professional group of musicians and dancers in classical costumes earn a good income from a stream of people who fulfil vows by hiring their services for a fixed period of time to play and dance for the god.

In almost every *wat*, there is a monk to tell fortunes. Many laymen and women also engage in this activity. For some, this simply involves reading cards and hands, and rewards are small. For others, however, fortune-telling and manipulation of destiny can be a highly lucrative, if dangerous, profession. To prove real communication with the spirit world, a *khon song* needs to do more than simply

In fulfilment of a vow, this lady takes a walk through the fire pit in a Chinese temple.

go into a trance. The highest paid will demonstrate their powers periodically, often in contest with colleagues of the profession, by walking across fire, cutting the tongue or sticking knives and skewers through various parts of the body. Having demonstrated that he or she has the protection of an important guardian spirit, the spirit medium does not merely tell your fortune but may actively intervene in it, by enlisting the help of his familiar to solve your personal problems or satisfy your wishes. All, of course, for an appropriate fee.

A Chinese-Thai spirit medium demostrates that he has the protection of an important guardian spirit.

Intervention in individual destiny by a spirit medium or spirit doctor is usually specific and short term. It should always be accompanied by a more long-term balancing of individual karma through making religious merit, the only sure path to a brighter future.

PUNCTUALITY AND TIME

When necessary (in the context of Thai values), Thais can be extremely punctual. They will get married at a time set by an astrologer within an auspicious few minutes and note the precise time of a child's birth for his future use in fortune-telling. They can also move extremely quickly, as anybody who has travelled from Bangkok to Chiang Mai by bus will verify.

For most of the time, however, such punctuality is unnecessary, especially in the agricultural world where people get up at dawn, move off to the fields and stay there until the work is done, which may take two hours or may take ten, depending on the stage in the rice cycle. For these people, the traditional distinctions made in the Thai language are quite enough: dawn, morning, late morning, noontime, afternoon until about 4:00 pm, evening (4:00–6:00 pm), night (7:00 pm–midnight), and nightguard (midnight–dawn).

The rural Thai way of seeing time is not compartmentalised in the same strict way as it is in the industrial world. Eating, sleeping, working and playing tend to get mixed up. The idea of 'a time and place for everything' is very flexibly applied in Thailand.

Days for Doing

There may not be a time and place for everything, but there is (or was, since these habits are dying out today) a day for doing things and a colour for each day. Variations on colour schemes are the most common.

Thai days, like days in European countries, are named after planets. Thais associate a certain colour with each planet, and it is considered lucky to wear the colour of the day. The fashion conscious ladies of Bangkok in no way stick to this regime and though our postman likes the idea, government servants are not given seven different coloured uniforms to wear on appropriate days. Some restaurants still do just that and in Chiang Mai, civil servants were ordered to turn up on Fridays wearing traditional blue.

Superstitions associated with doing certain things on certain days are many; I give only those involved in the dangerous undertaking of having the hair cut. Again, people no longer stick to these beliefs—no more than westerners avoid walking under ladders. Few barber shops close on Wednesday!

Colour Schemes and Haircuts

Day	Colour of dress	Haircut on that day signifies
Sunday	Red	Long life
Monday	Yellow	Happiness and health
Tuesday	Pink, lilac	Power
Wednesday	Green	Great misfortune
Thursday	Orange	Protection of the angels
Friday	Blue	Lots of luck coming your way
Saturday	Mauve	Success in important undertakings

Calendars

The Thais recognise that Thai time is not quite the same as *farang* time. This recognition is not limited to questions of punctuality, it also involves different calendars. The Thais have three calendars, the Gregorian (the same calendar as in the West), the Buddhist Era and the Lunar, which is now used only to set the dates of religious ceremonies.

In true Thai fashion, New Year's Day on the Gregorian calendar (introduced in 1899) was celebrated on the first day of April until 1941. Thai New Year (the Songkran festival) continues to be celebrated on 13 April each year, although the first month of the lunar year (which Songkran marks the 'beginning' of) is in December!

Just to add to the chronological confusion, the Buddhist Era (BE) year in Thailand is one year behind that of Burma, Sri Lanka and India. The bewildered reader will be relieved to hear that BE and Gregorian calendars, the only ones used officially, now both begin on the familiar date of 1 January. Books and reports, even those written in or translated into English, often carry the BE date. To find out how recent they are, the visitor has only to subtract 543 to find the Gregorian equivalent. This easy to remember formula is important, since even those Thais who speak good English usually have a lot of trouble when it comes to translating years.

MONEY

Thais see themselves as a generous, tolerant and contented people lacking in worldly ambition and unhappy about entering into situations of direct competition. Foreign visitors, unless they are being tapped for a case of beer or a bottle of whisky, tend to see them in much the same way—a happy people whose material modesty is more than balanced by spiritual wealth.

Thais are certainly generous and love to treat their friends (and themselves). This apparently altruistic behaviour is not, however, without some self-interest. It increases an individual's status, builds up his entourage of dependent friends and, if he can be consistently generous, gains him a reputation which may bring positions of trust and access to money. This type of behaviour comes close to what anthropologists term 'sympathetic magic', of which plenty of examples exist among the Thais. During the hottest month of the year, April, when water is most scarce, it is squandered in orgies of water battles during the Songkran festival, which can last for weeks in the rural areas, and functions to attract water by throwing it around.

Thais often behave in much the same way with money. Songkran, coming at the end of the dry season, inevitably brings rain, but squandermania, unfortunately, doesn't always lead to wealth. If it did, the Thais would be a very rich people.

VIOLENCE

Violence in any form—physical, verbal or mental—and for whatever reason, is detested by Thais. Whenever possible, a sensible man avoids placing himself in a situation of potential violence and behaves in a way that prevents such situations arising or neutralises them if they cannot be avoided. That being said, not all men, or women, are sensible, and plenty

seem to end up backed into a corner with no escape except to lash out with whatever means are at hand.

Cool Hearts

Conflict-avoidance is conceptualised in Thai as *jai yen*, literally 'cool heart', the opposite of *jai rohn*, 'hot heart', characterised by overt acts of anger, displeasure and impatience. Whatever the situation, *jai yen* reaction is good and *jai rohn* is bad. The man who meets a difficult situation in a *jai yen* way is admired. If you lose your cool, you lose respect.

So strong is the social pressure to avoid conflict that injustice or abuse may be tolerated with an outwardly submissive attitude. If you listen carefully, you might hear the *tuk-tuk* driver, pulled over to the side of the road by a policeman who seems to be determined to ignore all rules of acceptable social conduct, muttering half to himself and half to the unreasonable force confronting him, '*jai yen nah, jai yen-yen*'.

Superficiality

At their best, *krengjai* attitudes and *jai yen* reactions produce a harmonious society. This can be very attractive to the non-Thai visitor who confines his world to the safety of first-class hotels and the sanity of royal temples. The longer-term visitor will come to understand that this harmony is superficial.

Superficiality or, to put it another way, surface actions of a relationship, are not seen in exactly the same way by a Thai and a Westerner. In the West, real 'meaning' is thought to lie some way below the surface. The surface has meaning, but it is not all there is to meaning. No doubt the same is true in Thailand. The difference is that the Thai would tend to accept superficial reality without looking for a deeper meaning. In a sense, the surface is the meaning and surface harmony, whatever the motives or feelings of the individuals involved, is real harmony.

Surface Harmony

There are very sound reasons for preserving surface harmony and avoiding conflict rather than trying to resolve it. Firstly, most Thais live in villages, in daily close contact involving periodic cooperation. Secondly, Buddhist dogma makes a virtue of the 'middle path' (avoiding extremes) and detachment; love and hate are recognised as two sides of a single coin and should be treated carefully. A third reason is provided by the spirit beliefs that coexist with Thai Buddhism; anger offends the household spirits and brings bad luck. Fourthly, in a village community, social pressures to conform to norms of conflict-avoidance largely take the place of written law and punishment. (Anybody interested in following up these four points could start with Klausner's book, *Conflict and Communication*, and continue with Mulder's *Everyday Life in Thailand*, refer to Further Reading on pages 342–343 for details.)

The last of these four reasons requires some explanation because it can be argued that social pressure is, if not a form of violence, a qualification of the assertion that Thais are tolerant of individual idiosyncrasies. In fact, this tolerance is real enough, but the well-being of the community takes precedence over individual liberty. This situation has been summed up by King Bhumibol in this way: 'individual liberty is restricted by the liberty of others'.

Anger and Conflict

Any individual who openly demonstrates anger threatens the community. The Thai explanation for this process of cause and effect involves reference to the spirit world. Human anger attracts the anger of the spirits. These spirits behave in much the same way as a drunk suffering from *jai rohn* who flings a hand-grenade into a crowd of innocent people in order to get the one person he wants to kill; the spirits heap their displeasure on the whole community in the form of floods, droughts, famines, epidemics or attacks by bandits.

The Thai worldview sees violence and tragedy, whether natural or man-made, as the effect of human anger. In an agricultural community, this way of seeing things is perfectly logical. Anger disrupts a community and reduces cooperation in important activities such as construction of irrigation systems which can control floods, bring relief from drought and reduce the possibility of famine, low nutrition and epidemics. Anger within a community also reduces its ability to defend itself against bandits. Social norms of conflict-avoidance, supported by an ideology of spirit propitiation, serve very real functions.

The urban situation releases individuals from many of the restraints of public opinion and modern explanations and solutions for disasters undermine belief in the power of the spirit world. Yet, although anger and violence are today part of daily life in any big city, *jai yen* behaviour and the belief in spirits are also very evident, even in the anarchy of Bangkok. The consensus of village community is lacking, but the man who keeps his cool still earns the respect of his friends and workmates.

Self-control

Jai yen keeps Bangkok from blowing apart. The calm faces on a bus packed and overflowing, the crowd sheltering for an hour waiting for the rain to stop, schoolgirls standing in a line in the thin shadow of a lamppost, the only shelter from a blazing sun. *Jai yen* is a people in control of themselves, a passive refusal to be ground down, a deep-seated individualism and existentialism; human dignity.

Jai yen has been likened to the French *sang-froid*. The latter is, however, an exceptional reaction in a nation known for (and perhaps rather proud of) its excitable citizens who often see open, public conflict as a virtue. The French musketeer could fight a duel, kill his enemy and retain his *sang-froid*. For a Thai, violence is *jai rohn*, he cannot fight and keep his cool.

I see *jai yen* more in terms of the English reserve, a studied non-involvement, a conscious avoidance of the unpleasant or potentially unpleasant. Both are self-imposed constraints on spontaneous behaviour and both are likely, at times, to break down. Perhaps the major difference between the two is that English reserve breaks down into friendship, while Thai *jai yen*, perfectly compatible with friendship, breaks down into violence.

Hot Hearts

When the mask breaks and hearts leap to boiling point, violence ensues. Unfortunately, it is quite impossible to predict at what point this will occur; each heart has an individual thermostat. Some indication is usually given of impending violence, although this may not be immediately evident to the non-Thai. Polite speech becomes less polite until the point of no return is reached when the pronoun for animals and objects, *ke*, is used for 'you'. Alternatively, if somebody is feeling very *jai rohn* but has the sense to remain *krengklua* (afraid), he may try to release his violence on any handy inanimate or animate object, slamming a door, 'accidentally' knocking a glass from the table, ripping the seat of a parked motorcycle, yelling at a child or kicking a dog.

Open violence is today all too frequent. Newspapers are full of reports of attacks by wives against husbands and workers against bosses. Many of these are a result of the sudden snapping of internal controls after a long period of brooding of which the victim might be completely unaware. In recent years there seems to have been a vast increase in the number of sexual organs chopped from sleeping husbands by brooding wives. Even more frequent, and something of more direct concern to the average visitor, is the habit of hiring a professional bully-boy who will poison a dog for a few baht, maim a person to order for a few thousand or kill for a few thousand more. Knowing and appreciating the limits of *jai yen* is important for any visitor who wants to live, and perhaps work, for some time in Thailand. The abuse of cool hearts will surely, somehow, bring the wrath of the spirit world down on your head.

SPIRITS

The Thai attitude to spirits is very similar to the Thai attitude to human beings. Some spirits can be trusted and respected; others cannot be trusted and must be feared.

Trusted spirits can be members of the family and live in the family home. They are known generally as *phii ruan* (spirits of the home). In the north, these spirits are thought of as deceased family members and are often assigned a special place to live in the house, usually a shelf high up on an inside wall. On this shelf fresh flowers and drink are offered to the family ancestors. Their duty is to look after the family's welfare and they will be asked for special help during difficult times (sickness, pending law suit, a job interview, etc.).

Spirit Houses

In central Thailand, the *phii ruan* have no specific place to live in the house and some young people in Bangkok may never have heard of them. In Bangkok and the surrounding ricelands, the *phra phum* (spirit of the land) is more important. This spirit lives in the spirit house constructed in one corner

Phra Phum with slaves, horses and dancers outside his spirit house.

of the compound. The exact place and time for erection of a spirit house is determined by consulting an astrologer. It is usually placed on top of a wooden or concrete post, high enough to show respect but low enough to permit offerings to be made. Spirit houses are also erected by the sides of roads at accident black spots or sites of past massacres. Individuals set them up in fulfilment of vows and, over time, a collection of spirit houses can grow into a 'spirit town'.

Spirit houses are usually shaped like a miniature temple. They look something like a birdhouse in the West, but no bird would dare occupy them because the *phra phum* will not allow it. A figure, representing the *phra phum*, carved from wood or moulded from clay, is placed against the far wall facing the door. If the *phra phum* grants a wish, he might be given elephants or slaves, represented by similar figures. Some modern *phra phum* even sleep on little beds and I know of one who watches television and drives a Mercedes.

Making Vows

The habit of making a vow and keeping it if the wish is fulfilled is extended to various shrines in Bangkok. This explains why a shrine you walk past every day is suddenly covered in flowers—somebody has won a lottery. The nicely carved little elephants that you see on such shrines are given to the spirit so that he can go for a trip to consult the gods in the sky on Thursday. To take one away might cause the spirit to land right on your head and bring you some very bad luck.

Spirit Types

Apart from family type spirits and spirits of the land, other natural spirits which are 'role specific' and respected are the spirits of rice, water, trees and wind. Each of these has specific powers over the environment and can provide help only within specific areas of influence. Thus, the rice spirit is propitiated on planting and harvesting in the hope of getting a good crop, but no matter how great the propitiation, the rice spirit can never protect the house. Such spirits enjoy an inviolable division of labour which might be the envy of a British trade union.

Unfortunately, many members of the spirit world are less predictable, more mobile and far more dangerous. These are the ghosts of dead people who failed to be reborn. There are some good ones, but most of them are rather nasty pieces of work who will wait a long time for rebirth. Some are more powerful than others, but hierarchies are not as established as they are in the human world. The absence of hierarchical norms of behaviour accounts for the unpredictability of these spirits. However, like human beings, they do respond to bribery. Generally, the rule is that the more you bribe a spirit, the more he or she uses power to your advantage.

Significantly perhaps, the *phii tai tang klom* (ghosts of women who die in pregnancy) are being edged out by the *phii tai hong*, ghosts of those who died violently! Particularly nasty are the finicky carnivores known as *phii gaseu*. These

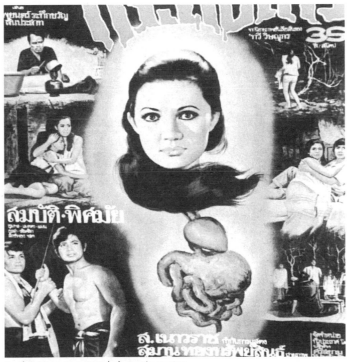

A *phii gaseu* on a Bangkok movie poster.

gourmands can digest nothing but intestines, preferably of pregnant women. As proof of the saying 'we are what we eat', they take the form of disembodied human heads, glowing as they float through the moonlight, trailing long tails of intestines.

Anti-ghosts

Fortunately, no ghost exists without its 'anti-ghost'. The difficulty comes in locating it. The first step is to identify the evil force that has been causing you to lose badly when gambling or has helped the young girl next door resist your natural charms for so long. For appropriate diagnosis of your problem and help in selecting a strong ally in the spirit world, you require the services of a *mor phii* (spirit doctor) or a *khon song* (trance medium).

Charms

Spirit doctors, trance mediums and some monks will provide (for a considerable amount) an appropriate amulet to protect against danger and misfortune or to ensure love, luck and power. These charms come in three categories: *phra khreuang*, *khreuang-rang* and *khreuang-rang pluk-sek*.

Phra khreuang are Buddha pendants, or likenesses of famous monks. These are worn around the neck, the more the better. *Khreuang-rang* are more specific in function, protecting or aiding within a specified area of influence. Most common of these are tiger teeth, pieces of elephant tusk or buffalo horn, boar tusk and adamantine cat's eyes. They are usually hung around the neck or worn as bracelets. Sometimes, charms with a function as specific as the moulded phallus are worn in other places!

Khreuang-rang pluk-sek are secret formulae. These are usually memorised but can be written down on an object and worn. If they are written, old Khmer letters are used. The memorised kind are usually very specific, one to be used when attacked by robbers, one to protect from accidents, one to help when a special favour is needed from somebody in authority, and so on. The trick

Full protection and high virility can be a weighty affair, but this man is leaving nothing to chance.

is to repeat the appropriate formula for the occasion over and over in your mind, silently sapping the power which threatens you, while keeping your cool. If attacked by bandits, however, the formula, yelled at full volume, might just stop them dead in their tracks—although it is wise to flee the scene at the same time.

Some *khreuang-rang pluk-sek* take the form of tattoos on the body. These serve many purposes. A bird pecking at a Bo leaf tattooed on a man's cheek ensures he can win a girl's heart. Hanuman, the monkey of the Ramayana epic, tattooed along with appropriate spells, endows the bearer with great strength and stamina. A girl who finds herself inexplicably attracted to a man and unable to resist his advances may suspect that he has caused a drop of magic oil (usually fat melted from the chin of a woman who died in labour!) to touch her skin. If she wants to retain her virtue, there is only one sure remedy—a magic tattoo on the forearm.

Whether measures such as these really work and whether the spirit world really exists are, of course, totally irrelevant to belief. Belief in an animated spirit world and the belief that an appropriate charm, spell or bribe exists to enlist the power of the spirit world in the manipulation of daily life are very important parts of Thai psychological make-up and relate directly to everyday behaviour. An amazing number of regular journals exist in Thai on charms (especially *phra khreuang* amulets) and lots of Thais buy and read them and may spend hours or days looking for an appropriate charm. This does not suggest this particular part of Thai tradition is in any way fading away.

How to Deal with the Spirits

The best way to deal with unfamiliar ghosts and spirits is exactly the same as the way of dealing with living strangers. Firstly, avoid attracting attention to yourself by boasting or doing anything that makes you stand out from the crowd. Secondly, if an unknown power is directed at you, promise it anything in order to get out of an unpleasant situation, and once out of it, employ any means to neutralise that power.

If, in spite of your modest behaviour, you find that you have a spirit on your tail, be prepared to try a double bluff. Make yourself really stand out by doing things in reverse. Have a bath with your clothes on, then take them off. Walk around backwards. Go to bed at dawn and get up at night. This should be enough to totally confuse the spirits (and everybody else!).

These deliberate 'rites of reversal' are, perhaps fortunately, very rarely necessary. Sometimes, however, I do them subconsciously. If you find yourself putting your left leg in your right trouser or putting your shirt on backwards, or your knickers on inside out, watch out, your pre-industrial psyche may have sensed something nasty lurking in the shadows. I hasten to add that the girls in banks and offices wearing cardigans back to front are trying to protect themselves from the air-conditioner, not from wayward spirits!

Such odd behaviour as wearing your clothes inside out is recommended only as a last resort. The best way to stay safe from the spirit world, as every Thai child knows, is to stay calm and stay out of trouble. Spirits love trouble. Any break in the façade of superficial harmony between living beings brings with it the risk of stirring up unknown and potentially dangerous powers. The best technique for keeping evil at bay is non-involvement. Smile, show respect, but don't show your feelings. If you hate somebody, cast a spell on him, but keep your cool. If you can't keep your heart cool, then flee the scene.

FITTING IN

CHAPTER 4

'To be true to Thai culture, any guest under
your roof must always be made welcome.'
—Thai proverb

From your first moments in Thailand, you will be interacting with the Thais, men and women. Open, receptive people they are; but don't expect to fit in immediately. Unless you have taken a language and culture course before arrival, which most visitors have not, interaction may initially be limited to those Thais who speak English, or another language you understand.

There are certainly plenty of Thais who think they speak English and are happy with any opportunity to practise it. Repeated interaction at this level can be tedious. Many of those people who really understand English and have studied it for years have a very limited ability to communicate verbally but may be almost perfect in the written language, to the point of using English on the Internet and texting your telephone number. Today, many Thais have specific English e.g. the pump attendant will know enough to ask you if you want a full tank, taxi drivers might understand simple directions, the check-out person at the supermarket counter will know at least the numbers in English.

While Thai is not an easy language for most foreigners, it does not take a protracted effort to bring your Thai up to something above the average Thai level of spoken English. The reasons for this are that you will have plenty of opportunities to speak Thai and your conversations will tend to be repetitive. Saying the same thing over and over again to different people is, for some reason, far less tedious in Thai than in your own language; and all the time your Thai should be getting better slowly (if you listen as well as speak).

BODY TALK

Initially, of course, you will not understand even the simplest things said in Thai. In Thailand, this does not mean you cannot communicate with people. Although Thais do not wave their arms about like French or Italians, they do use plenty of body language and this is easy to pick up. Most of it is associated with being polite, so even without speaking a word, you can establish yourself as a good person who knows how to behave. Nobody expects you to wear a suit and tie, but clean, sensible clothing also makes Thais prone to accept you. This initial period of dumbness should teach you that Thais value appearance and good behaviour. Maybe this is superficiality, but don't expect to get below the surface for quite some time and you will enjoy Thais from the first encounters.

This chapter begins with body talk—communication without words. Even if and when you become fluent in Thai, body talk will remain important in everyday life. There are at least a few visitors who got on better with Thais when they could only body-talk than when they could speak enough Thai to get themselves into trouble. This, of course, will not be the situation with you. Will it?

THE WAI

The *wai* is not just a way of saying hello without using words, it is an action of respect. As such, its use conforms to all that I have said and will have to say about Thai values and attitudes. It is the most significant of the many social actions that reinforce Thai social structure. It does so through public literal demonstration of what I shall call the 'height rule'. This basic rule is simple and clear: in any social encounter, the social inferior takes on a physically inferior position and the social superior assumes a posture of physical superiority. Height is right.

How to Wai

The *wai* may be thought of as a respect continuum. The lower the head comes down to meet the thumbs of both hands, pressed palms together and held fingers upwards, the more respect is shown. In daily practice, this continuum has four main positions (and many in-betweens).

- Hands close to the body, fingertips reaching to about neck level but not above the chin. This position is used between equals or between strangers as yet unaware of their social differences (although these differences usually are indicated in some way and a correct introduction by a third party should provide such information).

- Hands as in above example, or lower. Head straight or slightly inclined. Used by a superior returning the *wai* to an inferior.

- Head lowered so that fingertips reach above the tip of the nose. Used by an inferior showing respect to a superior

- Forehead lowered to base of the thumbs and lowering of the body from the waist. This is not the epitome of respect achieved by the *wai*. It is possible to flatten the whole body on the ground, while holding hands in a *wai* stretched out in front of eyes that are turned down to the earth. However, this fourth position is, for most visitors, all they are likely to see in regular interaction.

In Daily Life

The *wai* is used for objects as well as people and although the pace and conditions of modern times tend to restrict complete fulfilment of respect procedures, it remains a very meaningful part of Thai daily life.

On any long-distance bus, you will notice the passengers *waiing* sacred places as they speed by. And don't be surprised if your taxi-driver, having beaten the longest red light in the world at the Erawan intersection and screaming on two wheels around the corner, takes his and your lives in his hands and raises them in a *wai* to the elephant-god on the corner.

Buddha and Monks

Ideally, in making a *wai* to the Buddha, or to a monk (the Buddha's representative), the procedure is:

- Drop to your knees
- *Wai* while sitting in the respect position (men sit on their heels, women sit with their legs to one side),
- Maintaining the *wai*, bend head and body down from the waist while keeping the backside as low as possible,
- When the head almost touches the floor, and the top of the head is facing the object of respect, place the palms on the floor (strictly speaking, the right palm should touch the ground first)
- Straighten the body back to the sitting *wai* position. Repeat the whole thing three times if *waiing* a Buddha.

Origins

The position of the *wai* shows that your hands are empty of weapons and, in this aspect, the *wai* probably shares a common history with the Western touching or clasping of

Homage to a fallen comrade in the October Revolution of 1973.

sword-hands—what we have come to term the handshake. However, the *wai* does far more than the handshake. Handshakes are between equals, the *wai* is, more often than not, an expression of inequality.

When *waiing* a superior, the inferior places himself at the superior's mercy. The inferior always initiates the *wai*. (Learn this—it is one of the most common mistakes of visitors.) Historically, the weaker man would be the first to show that his hands contain no weapons. The lowered eyes and head further reduce the individual's ability to defend himself. The superior may, or may not, return the *wai*. If he is absolutely superior, as is a monk, he certainly will not do so. So, if you

The Wai

While waiting for the *wai* habit to come naturally, here are a few tips to avoid embarrassment to all parties.

- Do not *wai* servants, labourers, children and other people of an obviously lower social status than yours. If you insist on doing so, guided or misguided by an inappropriate desire to be equal and friendly instead of a more appropriate recognition that people can be unequal and remain friendly, you will create a situation of extreme embarrassment for the inferior which may terminate any chance for future social encounter. You will also make yourself look ridiculous.
- If you receive a *wai*, reply with an equal or more casual *wai*.
- The safest people to *wai* are monks and the very old (but not if they are your servants or street vendors!).
- The appropriate deference position is shown by lowering the head and body, not by raising the hands (holding your hands right above your head while standing straight up is not showing respect).
- Remember: a *wai* is not 'hello'. Overuse would devalue its meaning.

are lucky enough to find yourself in the company of the king or queen and you go through appropriate respect procedures, don't expect a *wai* in return.

Returning a Wai

The Thai king does not *wai* his subjects (unless they are monks). When the social distance between any two individuals is very great, the *wai* is not returned. Thus if a young child *wais* a senior elder, the elder may reply with a nod or smile; if a waitress *wais* on receiving a tip, the giver does not return the *wai*; if a junior employee meets the big boss, he will *wai*, the boss need not.

When to Wai

The question of when to *wai* and how to *wai* is learnt from the earliest days of childhood; it comes naturally for a Thai, but is a problem for the visitor. Having overcome preconceptions about proper democratic behaviour, learnt the rules and even got to the point where you can place yourself in the status structure, you will notice that many Thais, obvious juniors, will not *wai* you. This is not because of any feeling of racial or cultural superiority, but because the junior has seen enough western films and television programmes to know that *farang* don't *wai* each other.

The use of the *wai* to say 'thank you' is widespread among Thais. However, this is not an easy way through the language barrier for the visitor. Generosity traditionally moves in one direction, from the superior to the inferior; in return, the inferior demonstrates symbolically that he or she is at your mercy. Thus, although equals may use it, the thank-you *wai* from a superior to an inferior, even if a significant service has been performed, is most out of place.

As the visitor learns a bit of Thai and gets to know more about Thailand, the *wai* will creep into his social actions at the proper time. The best advice to the newcomer might be: unless you receive a *wai*, stick to the handshake with men and use a polite half-smile with women.

When the wonderful day arrives that you meet the right person at the right time and he or she naturally raises the

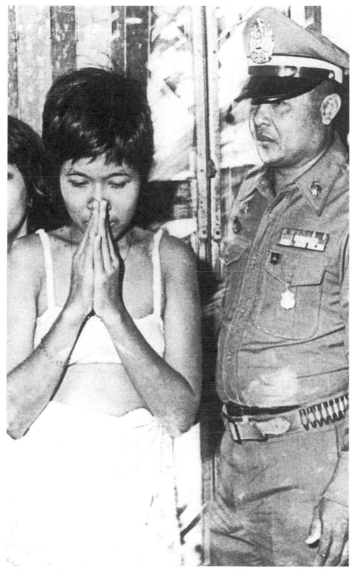

When caught in a comprising situation, a *wai* is worth a thousand words.

hands in a *wai*, you will probably find that yours are full of papers or that you have a whisky-soda in one hand and a cigarette in the other. In this case, don't worry, just place your hands as near together as possible and bring the whole bundle up to the appropriate position.

THE SMILE

One thing the visitor is sure to have heard before setting foot in the country is that Thailand is the Land of Smiles. He will quickly discover that this is true. Thais smile much of the time.

Surrounded by beaming faces, the casual visitor often concludes either that he has arrived in a land of imbeciles or that the Thais are a very happy, contented people. The second conclusion is nearer to the truth but is not all of the truth. While I would like you to go ahead and enjoy the smiles without thinking too much about it, a day will probably come when you will ask yourself what these people have to smile about. The majority of Thais are near the bottom of their own social deference ladder and have too much month left over at the end of their salary payment. So, what do they have to smile about?

Behind the Smile

The Thais do not necessarily smile 'about' something, but their smiles are not meaningless. In the West, people smile primarily to show amusement and in many situations, a smile would be out of place or even rude. Smiling or laughing at somebody's ungainly attempts to do something beyond his capabilities might, in the West, produce a feeling of insult and the hostile retort "what are you smiling about?"

In the West, a smile is about something. In Thailand, a smile is a natural part of life. It does, however, serve social functions and, at the risk of over-analysing and classifying this most beautiful and natural of actions, I offer the following basic list:

To Show Amusement

A smile—and often a laugh—may, for the Thai, as for all human beings, show amusement. However, while the Westerner generally would not smile on seeing a person slip on a banana skin (unless he was watching a cartoon), a Thai generally would. This does not mean he is unsympathetic; the Thai is just as likely to help the wretched banana-skin-slipper to his feet as anybody else. Rarely would a Thai smile or laugh involve ridicule, although it may sometimes seem that way to the visitor.

The Thai Smile

One luckless *farang* of my acquaintance was strolling the lanes around the Pratunam area of Bangkok when a bucket of sudsy water came flying through an open doorway and caught him full-frontal. Clearing the muck from his eyes, our hero found himself surrounded by smiles. Fortunately, he had been in Thailand long enough to catch a smile as easily as he caught the water, smiled back, and soon everybody was laughing and cleaning the *farang*. When it was discovered that he could speak some Thai, the water-thrower said "excuse me".

To Excuse

In the above story, the smile may have been prompted by amusement of the banana-skin variety, but it also served to excuse the perpetrator of an unintended inconvenience. When the smile was returned, it demonstrated the granting of pardon. A smile may be used for these reasons a thousand times a day (usually, the visitor will be relieved to hear, for incidents less serious than the example above).

You are in the slow moving queue at the self-service cafeteria at lunchtime and, having made your selection, you move around people still in the process of discussing the merits of the various dishes on display and join the queue further on. (Such 'queue jumping' is perfectly acceptable and, given the protracted negotiations that often precede selection of food, is somewhat necessary if the line is to move at all.) You accidentally step in front of someone you thought was still selecting, then realise he is waiting to pay. There is no 'get to the back of the queue, mate' and no need for an elaborate excuse. You smile, he smiles, and everything is all right. (You should, however, retake your correct place in the queue!)

The observant visitor will quickly realise that the smile

If the visitor thinks he is in a difficult cultural situation in Thailand, he can spare a thought for the poor Thai student in a London pub, standing at the crowded bar covered in identical pint mugs full of bitter beer. Unintentionally, he picked up the wrong glass and drank from it. Upon this fact being pointed out to him in very clear terms, he smiled...

is the correct mechanism for repairing minor breaches of etiquette. It may take longer to realise that the smile can also be used to excuse conduct that, in his own culture, would require elaborate explanations and, possibly, monetary compensation.

To Thank

The smile is often used to thank somebody for a small service. As I point out in the section on small talk, a verbal 'thank you' is used far less often than it is in the West. In Thailand a smile, perhaps accompanied by a slight nod of the head, means 'thanks a little'; the return smile could be translated 'oh, that's quite all right'.

To Side-step

The last two functions of the smile that I will go into here have to do with the *jai yen* (cool heart) philosophy of conflict avoidance, the motive for so much of Thai social action.

Some Thais can smile their way out of almost any situation, carefully avoiding any words or actions that might be regretted later. This kind of behaviour infuriates many *farang* but is respected by Thais. Perhaps the best-known master of the side-step smile in recent years has been General Prem, who was Thailand's longest serving prime minister and is now a member of the Privy Council advising the king. His survival and popularity owed at least something to his ability to smile his way through the most difficult situations and to get everybody smiling with him. More than anybody, General Prem who had the whole army to play with, demonstrated the devastatingly disarming and charming power of a simple smile.

The side-step smile needs no verbal accompaniment and could perhaps be best translated as 'no comment'; it functions to leave situations exactly the way they are while extricating the smiler temporarily from the scene.

To Show Embarrassment

The embarrassment smile also functions to avoid conflict, but indicates the smiler's guilt and his willingness to

In place of the usual giants, Wat Sutat in Bangkok has 12 stone figures like this one to guard the temple. They are said to represent the first *farang* to set foot in Thailand. All of the 12 are smiling.

make amends. Backing over somebody's motor-bike or accidentally shooting a bullet through the ceiling while you are playing with a revolver in a crowded restaurant are potential conflict situations in any country (they just seem to happen more often in Thailand!). A smile (but not a hearty guffaw) can demonstrate your embarrassment and defuse a potentially explosive situation. Of course, this is not an appropriate time for the 'excuse me' smile, the cringing embarrassment smile should be accompanied by a verbal apology and an attempt to rectify the situation and, if necessary, compensate your victim. An alternative, common throughout Thailand, is to take conflict avoidance to the extreme and 'flee the scene'. Not very sporting perhaps, but maybe safer if it looks as if you are going to be one against many. You can always return and pay for the damages later.

Smiling Makes You Beautiful

This is by no means a full treatise on the Thai smile, which has almost as much complexity as the *wai* (and indeed may be used by a superior to return an inferior's *wai*). Since smiling, like frowning and yawning, is contagious, the visitor will quickly find himself using it. Certainly, he will miss it upon returning home.

Don't worry about the smile; enjoy it. Do, however, remember that the wide smile from the lovely young girl selling flowers on the corner does not (necessarily) mean she is madly in love with you. But smile back anyway. Smiling makes you beautiful and keeps you young.

HEADS AND FEET

I have already mentioned the height rule in connection with the *wai*. Many other social actions conform to this basic idea that status superiority should be reflected in a physical high-low continuum. This hierarchical philosophy even permeates the way a Thai thinks of his or her individual body. The top of the head, inhabited by the *khwan* (spirit essence), is the most important part and the feet are the least important and dirtiest part.

Thus, in the not-too-distant past, when subjects literally crawled before royalty, they were demonstrating their humility by placing their most sacred parts (hair and head) below the level of the royal feet, which although low compared with the royal head, were a lot higher than anything non-royal.

In those days, the wretched subject could not look at the king and, being too low to speak to him directly, had to say words to the effect that 'my head beneath the dust under your feet addresses you'. From these humble origins grew the everyday male pronoun *phom*, meaning 'I' (literally, my hair) and used today as a term of respect when speaking to equals and superiors. (All personal pronouns change in Thai, depending on the status of the person you are talking to or about. At the end of your first 250 hours of instruction in the Thai language, you will have mastered some of them!)

The Improper Appendage

Heads being almost sacred and feet being something a Thai would rather not talk about, you must, of course, take care what you do with your extremities. As one Thai civil servant wrote, when asked to submit advice for American visitors to Thailand:

THE FOOT IS NOT CONSIDERED THE PROPER APPENDAGE WITH WHICH TO POINT.

Just about the worst insult you can pay a Thai is to point at his sacred head with your lowly foot. This, you may think, is not easy to do unless you are a taekwondo expert, a Thai boxer or a ballet dancer. You may like to reason that since you are very unlikely to find yourself accidentally committing this unforgivable social crime, you can safely ignore this warning about heads and feet. Not so. Pointing your feet at people or at sacred objects is easier than you might think.

Try to keep your feet under control. Absolutely taboo is to allow them to wander up onto the top of your desk, even if nobody is sitting in front of them. Equally vulgar is to sit in a temple with your back propped against the wall and your legs stretched out in front of you.

A little more subtle than the above examples is the taboo against sitting with your legs crossed in the presence of monks or respected elders. This applies whether you are sitting on the floor, in which case the feet should be tucked away out of sight under the body in the respect position, or if you have managed to find a chair to sit on, in which case the legs should not be crossed. A well-known Thai woman reformer and journalist was physically removed from parliament when she refused to uncross her legs.

Touching Heads

In the Thai social and physical environment, which is usually crowded and made for people considerably shorter than most *farang*, it is surprisingly easy to touch heads and misplace your feet. If you do accidentally find your elbows touching a head or two when hanging on for dear life to the ceiling rails of a speeding bus, never mind that your own head is constantly denting the low metal roof or disappearing into an air vent, the correct response is to say 'excuse me'—preferably, if you want to be understood, in Thai. Even when you need to reach over somebody's head and have no intention of touching it, to retrieve a bag from a rack on a train or bus, you can excuse yourself, although a smile should be enough.

Remember that Thais like to excuse themselves before inconveniencing people, if this is at all possible (thereby implying that the doubtful action is unavoidable rather than accidental). Even executioners excused themselves to the executionee before 'touching' the head with the sword. This charming old custom has been made redundant by modern technology but it is still possible to find a hairdresser who offers excuses before trimming your locks.

The taboo against touching heads is maintained even between close friends but, like all rules of this kind, it is not allowed to interfere with what people really want to do. It is not upheld between lovers. Old people may be seen placing the right hand on a young child's head as a mark of affection and parents in Thailand are not going to think twice before ruffling the head of their own children or even of your children. However, in this as in other social rules, the visitor should model his behaviour on the generally acceptable. Later, maybe, you will develop a feel for the way to do what you are not really supposed to do.

Stepping Over

Because a lot of traditional social activity takes place at ground level, you may find yourself developing a desire to step over people that you never had in your native land. Resist it.

When, having had a bit to drink in the *sala*, your path to the toilet is blocked in all directions by circles of people, each circle almost touching, don't step over two close backs (or any part of anybody). It's taboo. And be careful not to step over the food inside the circles; that's also taboo. You can, of course, make it plain that you want to get through urgently (it is not taboo to say you need to urinate), and a gap will be made for you. But your troubles aren't over yet. Don't simply rush through that gap. The height rule requires that you lower your body when passing in front of a seated adult. Ideally, you should show your respect and humility by not being at a higher level than anybody else—something extremely difficult for the average *farang* to do! In practice, bending the body when passing, to show that at least you are trying not to tower over everybody present, is much appreciated.

FRONT AND BACK

An extension of the height rule is the horizontal maintenance of social space between people of different status. Superiors sit at the front, inferiors at the back. So, if you are ushered into the front seat at an event, sit there even if you are long-sighted, otherwise everybody else will have to sit behind you. It is quite usual on occasions where rows of chairs are set up, for the front one or two rows to be empty except for

The walking order is no longer rigidly adhered to but the social order it symbolises is still very much a part of Thai personality; the junior is under the protection of the senior for as long as he follows behind. This is summed up in the Thai saying, 'Walk behind an elder, the dog doesn't bite you'.

a monk, an elder and any other important person.

Horizontal social distance is also evident in the order of walking—superior in front, inferior at the back. Taken to the extreme, this does tend to kill the art of conversation. In modern Thailand, this practice is therefore reserved for ceremonial occasions. However, you will make a good impression by not moving ahead of an old person.

HAIR
Hair, of course, is sacred when it is on the top of the head. This seems to have little effect on hairstyles which, for Thai men, are often all or nothing, the hair being either very closely cropped or falling onto the shoulders. The Thai of high status is likely to avoid both extremes and settle for something a bit more than a 'short back and sides'. The visitor, to play it safe, may like to copy him. However, convention on hair length, for men and women, is somewhat more relaxed in Thailand than in some other Asian countries. Moustaches are occasionally worn, but few Thai men can grow a beard and the visitor should be warned that many Thai women find beards unattractive and associate them only with old men! The major concern with hair, however much you have of it and wherever it is, is that it should be clean.

HANDS
Now fully conscious of your obnoxious feet, your towering height and your sacred head, you must also be careful about what you get up to with your hands. Ideally, do as little as possible with them. Leave them hanging down inoffensively by your sides. Certainly don't use them for slapping a chap on the back or tousling his hair! In fact, be careful about touching people anywhere, and never touch across the sex line (unless in an establishment built for that purpose). The safe exception is a polite touch at the elbow, usually to draw

In Thailand, hand movements have meaning.

attention but sometimes just for the sake of it, between friends and colleagues.

In the office, touching, like every other aspect of social interaction, is subject to the rules of the superior/inferior structure of Thai society. It is quite acceptable for a superior to put his or her hand on an inferior of the same sex, most often on a shoulder. In the office, this would reinforce correct work relationships: it can emphasise that an employee has done a good piece of work, it can soften any criticism, or it can suggest that the meeting is over and that the inferior should leave. Such touching is avuncular. It is like the friendly uncle putting his arm around a nephew's shoulders in the West and might at times come close to a master patting his dog on the head. Needless to say, the office inferior does not touch or hug in return.

Pointing
Pointing with a finger is less offensive than pointing with a foot and is acceptable for objects (except sacred objects)

but not for people, even very inferior ones. Unless you are picking somebody out at a police line-up or indicating to an indifferent public the chap who has just fled the scene with your wallet, don't point. If you really need to point somebody out to your companion and can't do it verbally, do so as discreetly as possible. A slight upward movement of the chin towards the person is permitted.

Sergeant-majors in the army and schoolteachers in the classroom are exempted from these finger pointing restrictions. But, so sensitive are the Thais to being pointed at, that even the girls in the massage parlours wear numbers, so that there is no need to point out which one you want.

All this sensitivity perhaps stems from the bad old days when a warlord would placate a quarrelsome village by assembling the population and haphazardly pointing to a few luckless peasants who would then be executed. Whatever the reason, and however it is done, a Thai does not like to be deliberately singled out.

Don't Wave Them About

Hands, of course, are not solely instruments for showing respect. Some people use them to work. However, the Thai makes very little distinction between behaviour acceptable at work and behaviour acceptable outside of the work place. Thus, even when preoccupied with a work-task, social relations and polite action take precedence over simple considerations of productivity.

Hands should remain tuned in to social protocol, whether engaged in the most thoughtless of menial tasks (like cutting the master's lawn with a pair of scissors) or in the pursuit of the most mind-taxing activities (like trying to decide whether to have *kwaytiaw nam* or *kwaytiaw pat* for lunch). Don't wave them about in an attempt to make yourself understood (special advice for French and Italian visitors); such action is likely to confuse rather than clarify and could give the impression you are angry about something—and even if you are, don't show it!

Getting Attention

Two actions that you need to do all the time are getting somebody's attention and passing things. The first does not require the hands, but the right hand may be used. The Thai way would be simply to call, in a quiet voice; in a restaurant you would use *nong* (little brother or sister), assuming the waitress/waiter is young, which most of them are. However, it wouldn't do to call the restaurant owner in this way, and therefore it may be safer for the visitor to use his hand, at least until he can say *khun khrap / kha* (depending on whether you are male or female). But don't clap, snap your fingers or hiss. The correct way is to beckon, palm down, moving the fingers rapidly towards you.

Passing

Having got somebody to come to you, the chances are that you wish to hand something over or take something from the person. These procedures are well defined in the deference system. Ideally, the inferior, handing or receiving, should use his right hand while supporting the right forearm with the

When passing to a superior, the left hand supports the right hand and the body is lowered slightly.

left hand and lowering the body from the waist. The superior should gently hand or receive, the supporting left hand being unnecessary. Equals may pass something without any protocol, but always gently; or both may touch the fingers of the left hand to the right arm. In practice, the full procedure is rarely evident in modern Bangkok—although a contracted version is still frequently enough seen, if you are aware of what you are looking for.

Always use the right hand when passing, even if you are left-handed. This is because the left hand is used to wipe the backside with water after defecation. Although an increasing number of Thais use toilet paper, the feeling persists that the left hand is not as clean as the right.

Throwing

Throwing things, even if it is only a box of matches, is considered quite slobbish; if the object is of the 'semi-sacred' category, e.g. food, it is rude. If throwing involves a sacred object, e.g. a Buddha pendant, then you are straining relationships, and perhaps asking for trouble.

Pockets

If by now you have decided that the safest thing to do with your hands is to keep them in your pockets, sorry, this is considered very bad manners. However, if you are really stuck for something to do with them then you might consider nose-hair plucking which, though behaviour which is hardly likely to endear you to the cream of Thai society, is not as taboo as it is in the West.

VOICE

The normal way of communicating with somebody, you will be relieved to hear, is the same in Thailand as it is in other places, through the use of the voice. However, since most visitors are unlikely to speak Thai, and most Thais are unlikely to speak anything else, this information doesn't help very much. If and when you begin to learn the language, you will find it fully conforms to everything you have learnt about Thai society.

These girls are dressed in traditional dress as they prepare for a dance performance.

The streets in Bangkok bustle with activity. Taxis are easily available on most streets and the more adventurous can try the *tuk tuks,* the three-wheeled taxis.

Picture postcard perfect with white sandy beaches and clear sparkling waters, surrounded by impressive limestone cliffs, Phi Phi Islands is one of the gems of Thailand and draws many visitors to its lovely shores.

Songkran, the Thai New Year, falls in the hottest time of the year in Thailand and is celebrated with water splashing and other festivities.

Exquisite crafts can be found throughout the country Here, a woman in Chiang Mai adds decorative touches to a handmade umbrella.

...quietly is best.

At least as important as what is being said is how it is said—using words and particles to suit the social situation and one's status position. Also important is to say it quietly.

Most visitors will have the time to acquire only a very basic Thai vocabulary and will never fully master Thai pronunciation. Even those who come to work in Thailand will spend most of their time using a European language, probably English. Fluent speakers of English are still rare, and the visitor will therefore need to be particularly careful to make sure he is understood. The best way of doing this is not to use familiar methods from back home. Ask the direct question "Do you understand?" and the reply will almost certainly be "Yes, sir."

As with most things Thai, the slow, indirect method may produce better results than the rapid, blunt, no-nonsense attitude that is seen as a virtue in many a visitor's homeland.

If you think somebody does not fully understand you (and the chances are he doesn't!) then repeat yourself and try using different sentence patterns, but don't raise your voice. There is a natural tendency to do this, especially in a city as noisy as Bangkok; try to avoid it. The loud voice is impolite and is also dangerous. To the Thai, it symbolises a potential anarchic power that could destroy him. He may act respectfully to you if you yell at him, but his mind will be working on ways of getting out of a potentially dangerous situation, not on trying to understand what you are talking about.

EYES

The Thais manage to do a lot of daily communication with the eyes and the eyebrows. Looking at the bus boy and raising the eyebrows is enough to call his attention to the fact that you are still awaiting your change. Taxis and *tuk-tuks* will jam on their brakes if you so much as look in their direction. And if your eyes, while trying to avoid looking at bus boys and taxis, happen to coincide with another pair of eyes, of either sex, they will probably get you a smile.

The *farang* is in rather a lucky position in Thailand, especially if he has blue or green eyes. Most people will look straight into them. This is, strictly speaking, against the rules, particularly where members of the opposite sex are concerned. However, this is one rule that everybody seems to break every day. Looking into eyes is a large part of the charm of the Thai smile, and the visitor need not fear eye contact. At the same time, most Thais would agree that it is impolite to stare at people (although some long-nosed *farang* are just so odd that Thais find it very difficult to drag their eyes away).

APPEARANCE

Self-presentation is one of the most obvious indicators of a person's status. In the West, it has become acceptable that an heir to the throne may appear in blue jeans and a coal-miner during his leisure time may wear the most elegant of latest fashions. Not really so in Thailand. Although a *phu yay* (important person) can more or less dress as he pleases, if you are a *phu noy* (little person) you cannot. A person's ranking, expressed through his actions, mannerisms and speech, is in most cases reflected in his physical appearance. However, this is changing fast. Fashion rules young hearts and if split-knee blue jeans are in, you will see them worn by the more fashion conscious; but not to go into the office, an official function, a wedding or funeral.

Uniforms
A surprisingly large percentage of the non-agricultural population is employed directly by the government as civil servants who wear uniforms which carry gradings every bit as obvious as those in the police force and army. All school and university students also wear uniforms. The sons and daughters of the Thai elite may have a reputation for student activism, but this doesn't stop them being proud of their Chulalongkorn and Thammasat University insignia.

If individual ranking is not adequately registered by the official uniform, a 'uniform' group may introduce conventions of their own to distinguish between degrees of standing. Thus, first year university students, by convention, wear white socks.

Upcountry
In the countryside, things are much more relaxed. Thai commoners might simply tie a *pha khao ma* (length of cloth) around the waist if they are men or wear a simple *sin* or sarong and blouse if they are women. This remains the daily dress for much of the agricultural population. In the north, Chinese-style cotton trousers reaching to the calves and collar-less shirts are worn by men. However, Western-style dress is taking over, even in the remotest areas. For one thing, Thailand's booming garment industry has made western-style clothing (initially produced for export) very cheap and available everywhere.

One unexpected effect of modernisation in Thailand has been the spread of the bra into country areas, where it sometimes replaces any other upper garment! The bra is, of course, hardly a traditional item of apparel in Thailand. While urban moralists worry about female liberation, many older Thai women in the countryside have yet to buy their first bra, while many of those who have done so seem keen to let the world know of the fact.

When it comes to dress, the visitor should think twice before 'going native'.

Modesty

I realise that fashion is becoming increasingly international and the respectable ladies of Bangkok like very much to be up to the minute. It is in the nature of fashion that it does sometimes get the better of modesty. My advice verges on the side of conservatism; if in any doubt, play it safe.

The visitor should be careful in 'doing as the Romans do'. The lady visitor in particular, if she wants to be thought of as proper and respectable, must keep in mind the image of western promiscuity rightly or wrongly projected through the

Short shorts and see-throughs will turn a head or two even during the 'anything-goes' atmosphere of the Songkran water festival.

(Western) media and not only wear a bra, but wear something on top of it! She should also avoid see-through dresses or too-short skirts. Ignore the fact that much of the night-time female population of the big cities are wearing tee-shirts bearing enigmatic messages such as 'I love sex in moon the night' or 'queen of the bad girls,' sexy short shorts or, as they come and go in fashion, mini-skirts. Unless you want to be the centre of attention, these are not for you.

Overdressing

There seems to be something of a general, if unintelligible, rule that the amount of clothing increases proportionate to status. Thus, it is not unusual to see the Bangkok executive and the university professor boiling under the tropical sun in a jacket and tie.

This, you might think, is taking things too far. Being polite is one thing, overdressing, particularly in Western clothing, is quite another. Plenty of *farang* visiting or working in Thailand manage to survive without the necktie and get by as long as they are neatly and correctly dressed (no shorts or rubber flip-flops but clean short-sleeve shirts are fine), but be warned that formal affairs always involve the status of the host and

therefore overspending and overdressing are the order of the day. Occasions like weddings, where official printed invitations are sent out, are times to air the suit and tie—you can always take off the jacket if others are doing so, but if the air-con is on full, you might appreciate keeping it on.

TALK

Well, by now you have learned that a smile can get you a long way, even if it can't necessarily buy you love. You will also find that using correct body language will encourage Thais to assume you have been around in the country longer than is the case. If they feel you fit in in some way, they are much more likely to speak to you in Thai, which is fine if you are learning the language. One of the greatest problems facing you is the language barrier; until you begin to learn Thai, you simply cannot talk to the vast majority of Thais.

For most foreigners, to learn Thai to any useful level would take a sustained daily effort for one or two years or more, and very few have the time. However, if you take a course in basic spoken Thai for 2–4 months, you can at least begin to engage in Thai small talk. (The best basic course is probably to be found at the AUA—American University Alumni Association Language Centre—on Rajdamri Road in Bangkok.) It will be small talk and full of errors that will make you laugh and cry, but you will be interacting with real Thais in real situations, and this is the only way to learn a language well and within a reasonable time.

In this book and in any book, English-alphabet transcriptions of Thai words are a double-edged sword. We could write, for example, that Thai for 'excuse me' is *khor thort*. If you know no Thai, the chances of you crushing a cute little thing's fragile little toes with your massive great feet, and saying correctly 'excuse me' in Thai are about the same as saying 'please fry' or 'please take off'. The wrong pronunciation would do very little to salvage the situation, however much you use the excuse-me smile. It is, of course, only good manners and good sense to learn as soon as you can the Thai for the few dozen words that will help you, and the Thais around you, survive. But learn them from a Thai, not from a book.

THAI ENGLISH

Given the language problem, you will most likely be communicating in English whenever you can, and your circle of Thai acquaintances is therefore likely to be limited to people met through the course of travels or work. Even when speaking English, be prepared to encounter problems in making yourself understood and in understanding. Part of the problem involves the standard of spoken English language learning, which is getting better all the time but is still not high. (Students need to pass a written examination in English before admission to university, but many, even those majoring in English, are unable or just too shy to speak English.)

One of the most frequent causes of misunderstanding is the Thai speech habit of never pronouncing two consonants without a vowel sound in between. Often the second consonant gets lost. This can be confusing; 'I can't go' and 'I can go' mean quite different things, but 90 per cent of Thais will pronounce both as 'I can go.' If you are wondering why your Thai friend constantly tells you 'I am Thai!', the chances are he is really trying to let you know that he is tired.

Other words are pronounced with all the consonants, but vowel sounds sneak in between them. Thus 'twenty' becomes 'tawenty', and since 'v' and 'w' are constantly confused in Thai and the 't' is rather different to the English, 'twenty' often sounds very much like 'seventy'—something to bear in mind when bargaining or paying a taxi fare!

The visitor will find that words that he grew up with, and that he thought of as essentially Western or international, are Thai-sised beyond recognition. 'Satem' is Thai for stamp; 'sanwit' is Thai for sandwich; 'bang' is Thai-English for bank and you take the 'lip' up to your 'aparmen'.

Time of Day

Another major cause of misunderstanding is that, although thoughts and words may be translated into English by a Thai speaker, his speech habits may remain very much Thai. Thus, if a Thai arranges to meet you at 'four o'clock', he might mean 4:00 pm or he might mean 10:00 pm. Everybody could be greatly inconvenienced because of a simple cultural misunderstanding.

Thais traditionally divide the day up into four sections of six hours each, instead of two sections of twelve hours. 7:00 am is 'one o'clock in the morning', 11:00 am is 'five in the morning'. In Thai, each part of the day has a special name, so mistakes are unlikely. In recent years, it has become normal to refer to morning hours in the Western way of counting time. Evening hours, however, remain inviolably Thai: 8:00 pm is, in spoken language, always '2 o'clock in the evening/night'. Fortunately, Thais are also familiar with the 24-hour clock (used on the radio and in timetables) and the visitor might be advised to stick to that when making appointments.

Please

The visitor might also be a little surprised to find that, in spite of the fact that they are obviously polite, Thais rarely say 'please' or 'thank you'. There are, in fact, a multitude of nuances of 'please' in Thai depending on the degree to which you are disturbing whomsoever you are asking a favour from. There are also polite and not so polite ways of saying 'give me' and many other request/order actions in Thai. The polite words already carry the 'please' element. Thus, in English, the Thai may sometimes appear to the visitor to be ordering or even demanding something when, in his own mind, he is making a polite request. While some Thais might be fluent enough in English to say 'Would you mind passing me the water?', some would struggle through a polite, if somewhat eyebrow-raising literal translation 'Help pass water a little', and some would settle for the equally enigmatic 'Pass water'.

Thank You

'Please' and 'thank you' are not used in Thai to the same extent as they are in English because alternatives exist. The most obvious and simplest of these is the smile, quite enough for most situations. 'Thank you' in Thai is reserved for situations where the words literally mean that you appreciate something that somebody has done for you. It is not usually used for minor favours like passing the sauce at dinner or where people are only doing their job. Thus a Thai would never think of thanking a bus conductor for giving him a ticket. The same Thai would, however, say 'thank you' when taking leave after visiting somebody at home. This is a sign of respect and might be accompanied by a *wai* or several *wais* or a bow of the head. It is also likely to be attached to other, less easily interpreted taking-leave phrases like, 'I go first'.

Hello

'Hello, how are you' would be an appropriate greeting for somebody you have not seen for some time, but is unnecessary for people you see every day. The English 'good morning' is expressed quite adequately in Thai with a smile, a nod or, if appropriate, a *wai*. Thai goodbyes can be equally brief and to drag them out might suggest a greater degree of friendship than is really the case.

Upcountry (that is an English word, at least the Thais think it is; it means just about anywhere outside Bangkok), you may find that everybody appears to be extremely interested in where you are going but nobody wants to say hello. 'Where you go?' is a direct translation of the most commonly heard Thai greeting. Think of it as 'How are you?' It does not require an elaboration of your plans for the day!

Speech Habits

Speech habits, of course, have very little to do with sincerity. The foreigner who goes around greeting everybody, thanking waiters, liftboys and bus conductors and excusing himself when he hasn't inconvenienced anybody, may be conforming to speech habits considered polite in his own culture, but he is likely to confuse the Thais, embarrass his social inferiors and could even make himself appear ridiculous and thereby lose respect and status. If you really want to thank somebody of low status, put your money where your mouth is. Tipping a few baht is appreciated (but a one baht tip is to be used only as an intended insult).

Offending

Meeting English-speaking Thais, the visitor is likely to find himself engaged in 'international' small talk. People will ask him if he likes Thailand, the food and the people. Polite answers are usual in any country, but you need fear offending nobody by saying the weather and food are too hot for you, complaining about Bangkok traffic, the number of thieves, pollution and mosquitoes (topics Thais complain about all the time). You are also on fairly safe ground if you complain about the police, unless you are talking to a policeman. However, the kind of 'plain speaking' that may be viewed positively in the West could be interpreted as impolite in Thailand.

The safest way of joking (when you are getting a bit bored with repeating how lovely everything is) is to tell obvious lies—no one would take you seriously if you say Thai girls are fat and ugly! When asked your age, knock off 30 years.

If you do get into any deeper conversation and onto the swampy grounds of criticism, make it absolutely clear your remarks are not meant personally. This is often very hard to do; it is difficult (but not impossible for Thais) to have an impersonal conversation on the subject of social inequality with a chap whose maid is walking across the room on her knees to serve you a beer on a silver tray. By all means talk about the king and Buddhism if you appreciate these most important Thai institutions; if you do not, keep your criticisms to yourself. Remember that even the poorest Thai considers that he was lucky to be born in Thailand.

Meaningful Conversation

'Meaningful conversation' is really only possible when you have got to know a Thai well. Even then, it is likely to be very different from the version back home. Although inferiors might seek the confidential advice of superiors in the office, even on personal matters not work-related, it would be unusual for a Thai to burden his friend with the kind of personal problems many Americans consider healthy (and perhaps even fun) to 'talk through'. For this reason, many of your social encounters with Thais will seem to take place on a very superficial level and stop before they really 'get going'. This does not mean they need be over formal. The Thai is a master at appearing relaxed, but relaxation requires conformity to rules of social conduct.

Flattery

One of the most pleasant aspects of Thai small talk is the Thai zest for flattery. Try to keep your ego within limits when everything about you is being praised. Height, hair, eyes and skin colour are all acceptable subjects for praise. Having admitted to being over 40, you will be told you look 30. Such flattery can cross the sex line (within limits), but try to remember that it is only small talk!

Establishing Status

It is, for the Thai, difficult to get onto anything more interesting until superior/inferior roles have been agreed upon. This agreement is the function of much of the initial small talk. The visitor may be a little taken aback at such frank questions as "How old are you?" and "How much do you earn?" Such questions as these are not impolite in the Thai social context. They offer a quick, sure way of establishing a person's status. You may prefer to give a vague answer, "I earn enough to get by on," but this is likely to be interpreted as modesty and could be followed by the further question "Exactly how much?" You, of course, are free to ask the same kind of questions and, if you really do not want to answer a question, smile and say *mai bok* "I'm not telling"; you are unlikely to offend anybody.

Names and Titles

Whatever the size of your talk with Thais, you will need to call them something. In Thailand, as elsewhere, friendly and polite conversation usually involves the use of names and titles.

All Thais have two legal names, a personal name which comes first and a family name which comes last. Here the similarities with English end. You will find Thais are introduced to you by the first name only, however important they are.

This first name is normally preceded by *Khun*, the equivalent of Mr, Mrs or Miss, unless the bearer of the name possesses a higher title. Even when speaking English, Thais will use the polite formula, title + first name. Thus, you will find yourself referred to as *Khun* Peter or Misater (Mr) Robert or, if you have a PhD, as Dokter (Doctor) Fred.

Most foreigners (particularly Australians) like this first name habit; for one thing it means there is no need to remember or try to pronounce Thai surnames. Unfortunately, in our opinion, ways of referring to foreigners' names are today becoming quite confused. A growing number of Thais, aware of English speech habits, tend to use a foreigner's surname (with the correct title, of course). This is undoubtedly an attempt to show respect while demonstrating correct cultural use of English. If you like things this way, fine, but you must still refer to Thais by their first names (even to your obvious superiors) in spite of the fact that you are speaking English. If you prefer things the original Thai way, you can point out that to avoid the confusion of being known by two different names, and it can be confusing (ask Elton John), you would prefer everybody to use your first.

No visitor will learn all Thai first names. There are simply too many of them. Fortunately, it is quite in order to refer to somebody as simply *Khun* or you. It is also perfectly acceptable to use a person's nickname. This is usually a one-syllable name of early Thai origin. Most proper names have three syllables and originate from Sanskrit.

The visitor should be aware that the use of first names carries with it none of the implication of friendliness or familiarity that it does in the West. He should also bear in mind that the wife of *Khun* Somboon is not Mrs Somboon; married women, as married men, are addressed by the first name.

Nicknames

Nicknames are simpler, easier to say, and there are fewer of them. Most Thais have one and use it for all occasions except the very formal. These names mean things like frog, rat, pig, fat and tiny and are also preceded by *Khun*. The visitor will soon get used to calling somebody *Khun Moo*—Miss Pig.

The important thing to remember is to use the *Khun* for all adults, even when speaking English and even when talking about somebody as well as to somebody. When you become close friends with a Thai, the *Khun* is dropped and *-ja* is usually tagged onto the name—listen and you will pick this up.

Introductions

If you are not introduced to people in the same room or to your friend's friends at the same table, don't worry about it. Introductions are not traditional Thai convention. Thai protocol in no way prevents you from asking for somebody's name or giving yours. A more formal introduction by a third party is normally used only if there is a good reason for the people involved to know each other. Such introductions conform to status rules. Thus, a young person visiting his friend's home for the first time would be told 'These are my parents' and would then know who to *wai*. Relative status positions are always immediately evident because the inferior is addressed first, 'Somsak, this is my mother'. This ordering is the reverse of polite convention in Western cultures, where the most important person would be addressed first. Although you are speaking English, use the Thai ordering; so, if you are introducing your wife or husband to an important Thai, the spouse's name is mentioned first. That way you can flatter both your spouse and the Thai big man at the same time!

VISITING HOMES

Thais rarely invite just one or two people to eat at their homes, unless you happen to be there when they are about to eat, in which case an invitation is essential etiquette. Polite refusal and insistence is normal.

The usual style is lots of people and a relaxed buffet with people coming and going as they please. Under these circumstances, it doesn't matter very much if somebody turns up late or not at all. If you intend to invite a very small number of people to eat a sit-at-the-table dinner at a fixed time, make it very, very clear that you expect them to come. Be aware also that Thais might bring along a friend or friends without necessarily informing the host.

The visitor might feel uncomfortable calling on somebody at home without an invitation, particularly if that person is a social superior; the Thai does not. However, Thais do distinguish linguistically and socially between what we might call 'formal' and 'informal' visiting.

The first type of visit involves people of marked status differences or equals who do not know each other very well. Inferiors might call on their boss without prior invitation, bringing fruit or some other small gift. This would be regarded as a mark of respect and the guests would be well received, although the visitors are unlikely to move outside of the 'guest room'. The second type of visit would be more informal and between friends. Both types of visit may be made with or without invitation and specific invitations are rare

If one guest is prominent, make it evident that he is the guest of honour. Fawn all over him; other Thai guests will understand and not expect you to divide your attention equally between them. Do not be surprised or offended if your big man takes leave as soon as he has finished eating.

unless something fairly grand is planned. Far more frequently heard is the noncommittal, "Why not drop in and visit me sometime?" To which the answer is usually, "Yes, I'll try", not "How about Wednesday at 7:30 in the evening?"

When making a more specific invitation, it is quite usual among Thais to invite to eat in restaurants. Such invitations will not always include wives. The easiest way to find out who is included in the invitation and how to dress appropriately is to ask another guest, not the host. (If you ask the host how you should dress, he will inevitably say 'as you like' and you could find yourself the only sports shirt in a row of bow-ties!)

Wearing Black

One taboo on dress for the visitor to bear in mind when invited to a party-type gathering is that Thais never go to a party dressed in black. This is because of the association of black (and white) with death. A Thai who is in mourning and wants to go to a party will change his clothes for the occasion. To turn up at somebody's house party looking as if you are attending a funeral will not win you many friends. This being said, when black became fashionable for a time, even this taboo was overruled among the smart set in Bangkok. No taboo is absolute. And even Thai tradition says that wearing black on Sunday will bring you good luck.

In the Home

When you do get into a Thai's house, you will most likely find yourself in the 'room to receive guests'. While you are not obliged to remain in that room, the usual movement is to the space outside the house. Although Americans often like to show visitors all over the house, even into bedrooms, such behaviour is not normal Thai. However, if you do manage to achieve 'real' friendship with a Thai, you can more or less treat his home and family as your own. He, of course, will reciprocate.

However grand or humble the home of your hosts, shoes come off at the door unless you have been asked to keep them on. To deliberately enter somebody's home with shoes on would be a sign of the grossest superiority and would certainly offend, although, of course, nothing would be said. The visitor might, as many have done before him, rationalise the shoe taboo by reference to the bringing of communicable diseases into the home or simply dirtying the floor. (The origin of the practice may well lie in the fear of epidemics.)

Having convinced yourself that Thais are spotless around the home, you might be a little surprised to notice the reaction, or lack of reaction, when a small child defecates in public. Although some wealthy Thais with deep-pile carpets may be tempted to adopt *farang* norms of toilet training, the average Thai would never think of rebuking a young child for such a natural practice and would be rather surprised if the foreigner did so. The Thai reaction is simply to take a cloth and clean off both floor and backside. Thus, be wary of trying to over-rationalise Thai behaviour: your child could happily relieve himself on your host's floor (and even on your host's lap!) without causing any bad feelings, but if you walk into the house with shoes on, however clean they are, you have insulted your host.

Thresholds

The shoes-off rule is as absolute as anything is; even if your host, aware of Western norms, says "Never mind, keep them on", you take them off (unless your host is wearing shoes!). Other customs and taboos are often no longer upheld. There is, however, no harm in knowing that nine spirits live in and around the house, one of them in the door threshold. Thus, if the main door of the house you visit has a threshold, it is polite to step over it, not on it.

A few important doors in Bangkok now have notices in English to request you to 'Please step over the threshold'. This is not simply an invitation to enter. Apart from a desire to save wear and tear on historic buildings, there is a deeper, spiritual reason for such signs.

House Spirits

It used to be customary for visitors invited to stay overnight to ask permission to stay from the host's *phra phum*, the spirit of the land upon which the house is built, who resides in the compound's spirit house, and to thank him when leaving. This custom is still followed in some places, although the visitor would not be expected to conform to it.

If you do stay overnight in a poor person's house in country or town, you will be treated hospitably, but you must be ready to sleep on the floor and to cope with the mosquitoes and simple toilet facilities.

MAKING FRIENDS

Neils Mulder, a Dutch social scientist who spent six years in Thailand, spoke and read Thai and was in daily interaction with Thais, concluded his book *Everyday Life in Thailand* with the words, 'I shall leave without having developed a single deep friendship.' Most visitors, if they are equally honest, would say the same at the end of their stay.

Even for Thais, deep friendships are not easy to find in Thailand. Every Thai would like to have a 'friend unto death', as they call it, but all Thais recognise the truth of the proverb, 'A friend to eat with is easily found, a friend to die with is hard to find.' This is not to say that Thais do not form deep friendships; many manage it, but for many others, family apart, quantity seems to take precedence over quality.

Thai society is structured in such a way that almost everybody is superior or inferior to almost everybody else. This restricts development of the kind of deep friendships that can only exist between equals. The norms of Thai society further limit the opportunities for friendship that might be considered 'meaningful' from the *farang* point of view. It is rare for one Thai to bother another with his personal problems, even if, deep down inside, he is crying out for help. The imperative of all social interaction—the maintenance of superficial social harmony and the avoidance of any word or action that could create a conflict situation or embarrassment—makes Thais polite, pleasant, flattering and friendly but does not encourage deep, lasting friendships.

Insincerity

Both sides, Thai and *farang*, tend to see each other as insincere when it comes to friendship. The *farang* who is very, very friendly, invites a Thai to his house, shows him all over it and sits down and talks on a very personal level seems to be baring his very soul to the Thai in what can only be an

invitation to real friendship. When the Thai next calls at the same person's house at an 'inconvenient' moment, he is sent away. The *farang* involved in the relationship might complain that the Thai show of friendship was not sincere and only preceded an abuse of property (perhaps borrowed and never returned) or an abuse of generosity or privacy.

Slow Start

The Thai much prefers a polite and fairly cool start to a relationship. Such a start allows any deeper friendship to develop only if the conditions are right. Once such friendship has developed, however, a Thai would not hesitate to ask a friend for a favour, perhaps a big one, and a real friend would grant it. A real friend becomes one of the family.

Thais can also make mistakes in timing and ask for a favour, possibly borrowing money, before the visitor feels a sustainable friendship has developed. Asked to lend US$ 2,000, the visitor might feel he was being taken for a ride; that might be the case, but it could also be that the Thai wanted to establish a material basis to the friendship. Whatever the truth, I would advise the visitor to refuse such loans in a Thai way "You caught me at a bad time. Got to pay Junior's school fees", "Ask me next month". No need to be offended or to offend. But if the Thai does not take the hint, feel free to terminate whatever friendship has developed. Again do this in a Thai way. Don't answer the phone. Don't turn up when invited round. He will get the hint. What not to do is to quote Shakespeare, 'Never a borrower nor a lender be'.

Blood, or perceived blood relations, are always thicker than water. Real trust and social obligation, as in most Asian societies, is found within the extended family network. Unless you marry in, or become otherwise attached—which is possible, with time—you remain outside this loosely structured but all important family unit. In spite of the tremendous changes over the past decades, Thailand remains one of the least Westernised of South-east Asian countries in many ways. The patterns of behaviour and cultural values of her people differ greatly from those of the West. Both Thai and visitor might be wise, therefore, to take things slowly, to avoid any value judgements of each other and to maintain personal relations at the level of 'friendly', rather than attempting to rush headlong into friendship.

Gifts

Thais like to give and receive presents. These are almost always wrapped up beautifully. Do not be offended when the Thai thanks you for your present and puts it aside unopened. It is bad manners to open presents in front of the giver. Ripping the carefully prepared gift package apart to see what is inside is rude. Put it aside until you are alone. It is good manners and saves you having to say 'how lovely' when your face registers 'how awful'. It's the thought that counts.

SEXUAL INTERACTION

Ideal female behaviour (ideal, that is, in the eyes of a Thai man) may be best described by citing at some length translated pieces from *A Maxim for Ladies* (*Ovaht Krasattri*), written in 1844 by Sunthorn Phu, a famous Thai poet who continues to form part of the school curriculum and whose 'advice to women' continues to be wistfully cited by Thai romantics.

> 'Walk slowly. While walking, do not swing your arms too much … do not sway your breasts, do not run fingers through your hair, and don't talk …
> Do not stare at anything, particularly a man, to the point where he can tell what's going on in your mind … Do not run after men.
> … Love and be faithful to your husband.
> … Be humble in front of your husband.
> … When your husband goes to bed, *wai* him at his feet every night without fail. When he has aches and pains, massage him, then you may go to sleep.
> … Get up before your husband and prepare water for him to wash… While your husband is eating, sit and watch him near by so that when he needs something he does not have to raise his voice. Wait until he finishes before you eat.'

Unfortunately, or fortunately, depending on your point of view, slavish devotion by a Thai woman to her man is now (and perhaps always was) but a man's dream and a woman's nightmare. However, it remains generally true that the position of women throughout Thai society is one of social and economic inferiority to their men, and they are still frequently referred to as 'the hind legs of the elephant'—which implies that they are just as important as men in terms of economic contribution but that their proper place is at the back, behind their men and supporting them.

This inferiority may not be immediately evident to the visitor, who is likely to come into contact with efficient career women whose pay scale gives them an exceptional amount of independence and status. A top executive secretary, fluent in one or more European languages, a Chinese dialect and possibly with a working knowledge of Japanese can command a salary well above that of a university professor or an army general.

Courtship

Many foreign men get married to Thai women, but few foreign women marry Thai men. How do Thai men feel about this? In many countries, men might feel jealous and possibly antagonistic towards foreign men taking away their young girls. Not so, or at least not obviously so in Thailand.

I asked a selection of Thai men, including the only two I know married to non-Thai women. Their response, once they had understood the question (most said at first they had never really thought about it) was almost unanimous. Rationalised, their reasoning went as follows. Thai girls are either *prio* (sour) or *wan* (sweet); unlike Thai cooking, the two tastes should not be combined (although in reality there is always a bit of *prio* in all women). Thai men have a distinct preference for the *wan*. Foreigners, however, seem to find the *prio* more interesting. Thus the foreigners, particularly the *farang* (white foreigners), usually end up with the sour. So why be jealous? I should feel sorry for them!

The *prio/wan* dichotomy, when applied to women is understandable in Thailand and is almost a class thing. Middle class, or aspiring middle class, parents insist their daughters be sweet and passive. Working class girls, or village girls, are more likely to be *prio* (and, Thai men recognised, more independent and sometimes more interesting). Norms are changing fast; many Thais think too fast. But the preference for sweet over sour is a current reality. And sour girls are still regarded as inferior in the sense of not knowing or caring how to behave. The dichotomy is not precisely whore/virgin, but at times Thai male thinking seems to come close to an equation.

Foreign women should be aware of this. And while Thai women are not fanatical about covering themselves up, a good and sweet girl will not show off her body too obviously. Thai women escorted by *farang* should take extra care if they want to be thought of as something other than what a Thai boy would anyway reject. If you are a foreign man, and you want your girlfriend to dress within the wide limits of respectability, but your girlfriend thinks it cool to go braless and show off her legs up to the crotch, you might want to tell her that you would prefer her to dress differently, as you want everybody to respect her. This is a compliment rather than a criticism; if you meet argument, why not just change your girlfriend? What goes for Thai women with *farang* men goes equally, or more so, for *farang* women with Thai men. Why embarrass your partner if you like him?

Compared to the rest of Asia, courtship norms are very free and easy in Thailand. They were not always so easy, and families with middle-class aspirations are still more likely to uphold traditional patterns of courtship, where for the first few dates, a girl is accompanied by a friend or relative. Many foreign men invite a girl out; she accepts, and turns up with one or two friends—that expect to eat and be treated with almost as much attention as the object of the encounter. On the other hand, today, a mature girl might go alone, and that does not (necessarily) make her a whore, although she is unlikely to be a virgin.

Foreigners are not excluded as marriage partners, either by the girl or boy or their parents, but a subject of concern is how much they will bring to the family, since there will be no marital alliance to strengthen the family's social and economic position. It might seem to many foreigners that in Thailand, money can buy you love. If courting a girl, the progression of the relationship in terms of time, commitment and intimacy may, at least in part, be determined by the presentation of gifts, principally to the girl, but also to her mother, with smaller indications of generosity to younger siblings and even, occasionally, to the father. Such gifts will usually not be money (although that is unlikely to be refused too strongly), but something the girl wants—a mobile phone, a set or two of *sin* (traditional long sarong-type skirt and blouse), and a gold belt (not silver, unless you want to show how poor you are) to hold the *sin* in place. Many a bad girl knows enough to capitalise on traditional norms—so if she asks for a gold belt, do not presume she has marriage in mind.

If you marry a Thai girl, you marry her family. So if you can't stand them, think again. On the other hand, if you really like them and enjoy drinking with the father, don't marry her just for that reason—although it's not such a bad one. Periodically, you will invite the whole family out to a good restaurant and foot the bill. You will bring little things to the house, flowers and fruit or some delicacy. If the family has no TV, or only a poor one, you can become very popular comparatively cheaply with a large-screen TV.

After the first dates have gone by and you are trusted to take the girl out alone (this advice is only for 'good girls' and standards will differ depending on the girl's age, desire to get married and independence of personality), you will sit and chat for a while with her parents on picking her up and dropping her off. Gradually, you will get to know everybody in the family, some of whom will be no blood relation at all, and their spouses and children. Before you ever get around to asking for the girl's hand in marriage, family members are likely to ask you—at first in a playful way—when you will become a son-in-law. With the presentation of the gold bracelet and necklace, and one for mummy, your intentions are obvious and really the rest is detail. If you back out, expect none of it back.

Wedding Rings

Gold wedding rings do not have the same significance as in the West. So if you fancy a girl who wears a little band of gold on her wedding finger, don't ignore her on the assumption she is married. On the other hand, the absence of a ring does not indicate freedom. If you want to know, ask her. Gold 'wedding' rings are worn much as any other jewellery. By all means give a ring, if it makes you feel good (or if your parents are visiting Thailand and will meet your wife). You can give it before or after marriage, and don't be too offended if your chosen one sells it to buy something she likes better. What goes for women, goes also for men, and you should avoid reading something into the presence or absence of a ring.

Prostitution

Many male visitors are likely to spend at least part of their leisure time in the company of some of those Thai women who work in one form or another of prostitution. It has been variously estimated that between 1–5 per cent of the female population pursues this oldest of professions. This means, of course, that at least 95 per cent do not, a simple and obvious point that should be remembered.

The fact that women of easy virtue naturally gravitate around the male visitor's world—where the money is— means that many visitors get an impression of Thai women that is no more true than the impression of Western women held by many Thais. Men learning Thai will not learn much from these girls, as the great majority speak the north-east Isaan dialect, which is Lao by another name.

Prostitutes lose face and status within Thai society as a whole, but not necessarily within their own family and village, the two places that really count. This is because her family is often complicit in making her a prostitute and because sometimes, whole villages or areas are linked to prostitution networks (never in the village itself, always far away). In return for any loss of face, they make money, which can easily buy back many of the superficial daily actions of respect that are essential to a Thai's mental well-being. While making the money, these girls often compensate psychologically by a brash disregard for Thai norms. Sometimes they almost completely leave the Thai community, while continuing to live in Thailand, and live together with others of their kind, that accept only the company of *farang*, Arab or Japanese visitors and include Thais within their group only if they are *tom* (lesbian—from the English 'tomboy') or *khatoey* (cross-dressing transsexual). Their money provides a certain independence and their behaviour is usually the complete opposite of that advised by Sunthorn Phu.

Propriety

Thai women were probably never enslaved by their men to the same extent as their Indian, Chinese and Japanese sisters, and today many are an obvious success in their profession. But, however successful, broadminded or 'liberated' a woman is, if she walks down the street hand in hand with a man, even if he is her husband, she will lose face. Public displays of affection, common among the playgirls of Bangkok, are not widely accepted. If a woman, Thai or non-Thai, ignores sexual protocol, she is likely to be avoided by decent women and approached by men with one intention.

All of this has to do with the public realm of life; what goes on in private is often very different, and none of my business in writing this book! The Thais are quite capable of not seeing what is not made blatantly obvious. Thus the daughter who 'works' in the big city, but continues to send money home, may, when past the age of fancy, retire to her village, even carrying the baggage of a child or children of unknown paternity, without too many problems. But public impropriety forces people to see, and therefore to react accordingly.

The boundaries of 'impropriety', a changing concept everywhere, in Thailand include any form of physical contact between members of the opposite sex. Even if contact is avoided, it is not really proper for a woman to approach a man directly on an individual basis. It is, for example, the usual practice in Thailand's universities for a female student who needs to see her lecturer in his office to take along a girlfriend, who says nothing and whose only function is to be there. It is also normal for a 'decent' girl to turn up on her first, and probably first several, dates with a female friend, who not only acts as chaperone but gives her opinion on the man's qualities.

Taboos on physical contact do not apply between members of the same sex who may, if they wish, walk arm in arm in public without raising any eyebrows. Many Western men find this difficult to adjust to. They are not, of course, required to change a lifetime's behaviour, but they should try to understand that the hand on the knee is more an act of friendship than of homosexuality.

Restrictions on social encounter between the sexes present special problems to the non-Thai female visitor, as they do to the Thai professional woman. Social occasions are very often informally segregated into groups of men, usually seated around the alcohol, and groups of women, often structured around the preparation of food. The Western wife probably does not want to spend all of her time with the women, and, acknowledging the strange ways of the *farang*, nobody will really mind if she accompanies her husband. Tolerance of *farang* habits does not mean that a Thai male will not be offended if his wife is cornered by Mr West for an unduly long time, even if he is only doing what he thinks is polite by spending some time with the hostess. She will be too polite or embarrassed to break off social contact and her husband is most unlikely to express his displeasure in public. Of course, things are changing among the Thais. Also, many of the functions the visitor attends will be overwhelmingly expat, or at least hosted by expats, in which case norms of the *farang* culture may be more appropriate.

The visitor is largely on his own in deciding how far he can bend or break the rules of sexual interaction in any particular situation. However, he or she might like to bear in mind that many things may be going on under that phlegmatic Thai exterior and that a large proportion of Thailand's excessively high murder rate is made up of crimes of passion—very often committed some time after the event that germinates them. If the Thai social scene has lost some of its relaxed atmosphere for the visitor, now intent on avoiding unintended insult, then this is as it should be and as it is for Thais much of the time. The relaxed surface of social encounter is held up by a mild tension of self-conscious aggression avoidance.

Knickers

A minor but pragmatic point about sexual interaction. Taboos against touching across the sex line often (but not always) extend to undergarments, even when off the body in question. So if your clothes are washed by a man, do not expect him to wash women's undergarments. While being a 'washerboy' involves no more loss of face than being a male cook, washing a woman's knickers would hurt his self-esteem. A female maid may also object to washing a man's underpants, but the ruling seems to be more flexible here.

FITTED OUT?

Well? Having read this chapter do you feel more equipped to fit in to Thai society? Perhaps I have turned you off the whole idea. Perhaps I have suggested that fitting in is incredibly difficult and perhaps not worth the effort. I have certainly not presented the usual view of Thai society as seen through rose-tinted glasses. That is available, minus the warts, on some package tours. If you are here for the longer term, you should be prepared to accept a more balanced view of Thai society. Not that you have to agree with every aspect of it—most Thais don't, so why should you?

As I have suggested, there are difficulties to be encountered and quietly overcome. I have also suggested you do not rush in where fools fear to tread. Try to remember that even those bits of modern Thai culture you might not like exist because of the marked tolerance of the Thai people. This is exactly the same tolerance extended to you, the outsider. The Thais will let you into their most respected institution (the monkhood)—providing you're a man, of course. But nobody will even suggest you change your religion. If you want to fit in, you can, and remain more or less as you are. If you want to fit in a little way, you can do that instead. If you want out of most of it, that's up to you. Nobody will force you to become Thai. It's your life. Enjoy it.

THE PRACTICALITIES

CHAPTER 5

'Judge an elephant by its tail; a girl by her mother.'
—Thai saying

THERE IS NOT MUCH POINT in learning the finer, or the cruder, points of Thai culture and finding your way in Thai society if you have no knowledge of the material culture of the country and cannot find your way to a bank or your workplace. Initially, you will be less interested in learning the Thai language and Thai ways, then in finding somewhere to live, getting your documentation in order, opening bank accounts, enrolling your children in school and the hundred and one things that have to be done before you can realistically consider participating in your cultural adventure. Unfortunately, most of these things have to be done before you have any knowledge of Thai ways or language, which would certainly help you cope.

Employers differ greatly in the amount of help they are able or willing to give. The best are the embassies, and if you are lucky enough to be a diplomat or otherwise on embassy staff, you can almost sit back and let somebody do almost everything for you. For normal mortals, it is hoped this chapter will help you come to terms quickly with material musts and provide a reference for any future needs related to health and education.

The most useful tool you should have at your side throughout your stay is an up-to-date telephone *Yellow Pages*. There should be a copy in your initial hotel room; if the hotel won't sell it to you, you can get a copy from the Public Telecommunications Service Centre, in the main post office on Charoen Krung Road. Second is the English-language daily newspapers. Third is the advertising boards at expatriate-frequented supermarkets and occasional advertising magazines, available in those supermarkets. But, before doing anything at all, let's at least get into the country.

VISAS

If you are coming for less than 30 days and come from one of 57 countries, including most of Europe, Australia, New Zealand and the USA, you do not need visas. Visitors from Brazil, Korea and Peru come within diplomatic agreements that allow them 90 days without a visa. Visitors from other countries, if there is no Thai embassy in their country of origin, need a visa but can obtain it on arrival. Your short-term tourist visa cannot be changed into any other kind of visa, or extended for more than a few days, unless you land in hospital or prison. However, visitors from countries with no Thai embassy may pop out to a neighbouring country—all of which do have Thai embassies—and come back in with the appropriate visa to allow them to reside and work in Thailand.

Thai embassies are currently to be found in all ASEAN (Association of South-east Asian Nations) countries, which is now every country in South-east Asia. They are also in Australia (Canberra, Adelaide, Brisbane, Melbourne, Perth, Sydney), Canada, France, Germany, UK and USA (Illinois, Los Angeles, New York, Washington). Applications can usually be made by post or by going directly to the embassy. In addition to the application forms, passport with at least six months' life remaining, identification relating to employment or retirement (if applicable), you will need photos for visas and all other forms, so keep a good supply on hand.

If you are coming to work in Thailand and your employer does not handle arrangements, apply for either a Non-immigrant Visa, which is valid for 90 days and may be extended, or the Non-immigrant Business Visa, which allows multiple entries for one year, although you have to leave the country every 90 days. This re-entry need involve no more than a turn-around visa run to the Cambodian border and back in one day (see advertisements in the English-language press). An alternative is to pop up to Vientiane in Laos, but this takes longer and a Lao visa on arrival, valid 15 days for US$ 31. Those in Phuket and the south can see their local papers or ask any expat living in the area about the visa boat trips to Langkawi island in Malaysia, where they can get a new visa. Of course, if you have a reasonable job in a good company, none of this should be necessary—somebody will do it for you, all by magic.

Retire in Paradise

Special arrangements have been put in place over recent years for those who wish to retire to Thailand. They get a 90-day Non-immigrant Visa in their home country before departure and extend it one year at a time. You need to be at least 50 years of age and bring (or have somebody bring for you) the following documents to the Immigration Bureau, Soi Suan Phlu, Sathon Thai Road, Bangkok:

- Passport + copy of information and visa pages
- One photo
- Proof of income of at least 800,000 baht/year (bank statements, pension payment notices). Note: it is no longer necessary to deposit this money in a bank in Thailand.

If you are 50 +, have an average pension and do not intend to be doing any formal work in Thailand, this is the one. Great for writing your memoirs.

TAX CLEARANCE

Anybody without special privileges who receives income while in Thailand should obtain a tax clearance certificate from the Revenue Department in Bangkok [tel: (02) 281-5777] or in every provincial capital office. Provincial capitals are easily identified, as they all have the same name as their province, thus Nan is the capital of Nan Province, Khon Kaen is the capital of Khon Kaen Province. *Changwat* (province) offices tend to be more conveniently grouped in a single place, unlike Bangkok.

ELECTRICITY

Electricity supply throughout Thailand is 220 volts, as in most of Asia and much of the world. Accounts are billed monthly and costs are reasonably high, particularly if you use air-conditioners continuously and have a giant refrigerator. Sockets are two pin round or flat. Nothing is earthed, so insulated appliances are recommended. While supply is much better than it was, power surges can still damage sensitive equipment, but a UPS with surge control (available locally at a small cost) will protect your computer and prevent data loss whenever the lights flicker.

GAS

Many houses are equipped with cooking appliances that run on bottled gas (LPG). Bottles are delivered and usually fitted in place very promptly after you phone the supplier. If there is not already a company serving your house, suggest before signing contracts that the house owner buy a gas bottle, which remains his property. If this does not work, get a supplier from the neighbourhood—they advertise in the supermarkets and in the English press. Since the gas always runs out just as you are cooking for the boss and 50 people from the office, it's a good idea to keep two gas tanks, one big and one small (or two small if that's all you can get into your kitchen).

TELEPHONES, TV AND INTERNET

Fixed line services are available through the TOT (Telephone Organisation of Thailand) or Telecom Asia. Make sure you have one in your house or that it is installed before you move in, as you might have to wait some time for installation, depending on where you are. Do not accept any type of party line with the house owner or another tenant. Owning a mobile phone is illegal unless you have a work permit or residency, although nobody seems aware of this law and any visitor can now buy a mobile over the counter at the supermarket very cheaply. You can also buy secondhand phones at the same outlets. These are about 25 per cent cheaper but identical with new phones, and will even be put in a correct box. Fill up your phones easily almost anywhere. Some visitors don't bother with a fixed-line phone and some even disconnect this to remove the temptation for the maid to call her relatives long distance. Bills on home phones come in monthly for local calls and twice monthly for international calls. As long as you pay by the due date, these bills can be settled through your bank (if your bank doesn't provide this service, consider changing banks). Even though you pay the bill, you are not likely to get listed in a Thai phone book because the number remains attached to your landlord's name.

> If you experience faults with your phone line, dial 17 followed by the first three digits of the number experiencing problems.

Cable and satellite TV gives you the chance to follow news in your own country and the world in a language you understand. Several permutations of programmes are available quite cheaply. The phone book will give you numbers to call, or if you buy a TV made in Thailand (cheap and good), a deal or reduction on cable services might be thrown in.

Once you have a phone line, you might wish to have an internet connection at home. This is easy stuff and several local alternatives exist. One of the best Thai ISPs offering temporary internet accounts is WebNet by Loxinfo. In any of the many internet shops, go to http://www.loxinfo.co.th. You can buy blocks of so many hours of Internet use, valid for one year at prices about the same as the charge in the very cheap and good internet shops found just about everywhere in Bangkok. In fact, at 1–2 baht/minute, Thailand's Internet cafes are among the cheapest in the world.

WATER

Never, ever, drink tap water unless boiled or well treated. That said, tap water is no longer the poison it used to be and you can happily give it untreated to any pets. Bottled water is available in all sizes and it is easy to arrange a regular delivery. The bigger the bottle you buy, the cheaper it gets, and big suppliers are reliable. If you really hate the idea of paying for drinking water, make sure you boil tap water well. Some people get by very well on water boiled and kept hot in large (3 or 5 litre) electric water heaters—the maid drains out the boiled water and puts it in the fridge; while there is probably not much difference, some expats swear they will only drink home-boiled water, not the treated bottled kind. Such water boilers are also convenient for your tea and coffee (and instant noodles); they are available at any electrical goods shop. Those working on a push-button principle are a lot more convenient than the cheaper pump action type and can reboil at the touch of a button. You will be charged for your tap water on a monthly basis. Some landlords pay on the tenants' behalf and require reimbursement.

Two of the biggest bottled water companies are:
- **Boon Rawd** [tel: (02) 241-1361] which will deliver in the Sukhumvit area
- **Mincre** [tel: (02) 676-3588] which will deliver most places.

ACCOMMODATION
Temporary
Bangkok has a ready supply of good accommodation for reasonable rents. You should be able to find a place very quickly. However, because much is on offer and there is always room for negotiations, it pays to take your time. Zero in gradually on an area and a particular house and make several visits before you finally decide—after negotiating a lower price than that asked, plus additional furniture and a kennel for the dog. Should you need temporary accommodation during this time, there is a plentiful supply at a variety of prices.

Hotels are worth considering even if you have a family, as rooms are large. Many hotels have connecting rooms and many also have distractions like swimming pools and exercise rooms. Most also include a good breakfast. The big advantage of a hotel is that you can leave immediately once you find more permanent accommodation. Never accept the rack rate. Whether you are staying just a few days or a few weeks, expect a substantial reduction. Be aware that some very good hotels offer very substantial corporate rates, which often include excellent breakfast for you and your spouse (and with a bit of wangling, for the children too).

You might begin to pick up intelligence to help price negotiations by clicking 'Thailand' on your Internet search facility. This will give you numerous sites offering cut-price rates. Two sites worth a look are:

Temporary Accommodation

If you are paying out of your own pocket and want a good and safe hotel at a cheap price, try the following centrally located places:

- **Bangkok Christian Guest House**
  123 soi 2, Sala Daeng, Convent Road
  Tel: (02) 233-2206; fax: (02) 237-1742
  Email: bcgh@loxinfo.co.th
  Always full. Contact as far ahead as possible. You don't need to be Christian, but missionaries get priority. Because of demand, long stays are discouraged. You are also expected to eat your breakfast. Nice and quiet but not for night owls or naughty girls.
- **Bangkok YMCA**
  27 Sathorn Tai
  Tel: (02) 287-1900; fax: (02) 287-1996
  Email: bkkymca@asiaaccess.net.th
  Essential to book ahead.
- **Holiday Mansions**
  Vittayu; Tel: (02) 255-0099.
  Right opposite the side gate of the British Embassy and conveniently located for the sky train, Central Department Store, shopping malls and the inner reaches of Sukhumvit. They usually have rooms but

- http://directrooms-thailand.com
  This does not list the cheapest hotels/guest houses but gives substantive reductions on daily rates and has good information on seasonal discounts.
- http://www.the-b-and-b-registry.com/thailand/
  May sometimes have very good information and discounts.

For a longer temporary stay, or if you are in Thailand for only six months to one year, there is a range of serviced apartments which you may want to look into. These usually

phone first and ask for a 30–40 per cent discount. Good-sized rooms, a very good deal with the discount rate. No breakfast, but good eating next door.

- **Tower Inn**
  533 Silom Road
  Tel: (02) 237-8300-4; fax: (02) 237-8286
  Email: towerinn@box1.a-net.net.th
- **Souk 11** (Souk Sip-et)
  soi 11, Sukhumvit Road, Bangkok 10110 (behind 7-11)
  Tel: (02) 253-5927/253-5928; fax: (02) 253-5929
  Email: suk11@suk11.com;
  Website: http://www.suk11.com.
  One of the best deals if you are in Thailand teaching or as a student. Much better accommodation and location than the majority of guest houses around the Khao San Road area. The owner, Khun Somjet and his son, Anil, the manager, have created a very unique architecture and décor. Not for the hippiephobe as most of the clientele are young backpackers. Good restaurant in sit-on-mats style. Good breakfast included. Excellent and friendly staff. Near skytrain and Sukhumvit attractions. Already cheap for what you get, but ask about cheap rates for extended stays. One of Bangkok's bargains.

have maid service and in many ways run like a hotel, but generally have more space and rooms, and include a small kitchen and basic cutlery, crockery and sheets (useful if waiting for your personal effects to arrive). A refundable deposit is usually required. Do establish if this is only for loss or breakages, or if a deduction will be made if you leave early. Rental is usually on a one-month basis, payable in advance. Expect to pay less for a 6–12 month lease and more for fractions of a month (not always available). Rates usually include most things but check for extras. The following list is only a very small selection of what is available:

A Home

In viewing your potential dream home, apartment or house, check all the following points before arriving at your decision:

- Do you really feel good in it? First reactions are important but not paramount.
- How is the noise level? (Traffic during weekday rush hours, neighbours' children, school and construction works in progress or planned.)
- What is the time taken to travel to work at the time you would normally be travelling?
- What is the time taken to get to the children's school at the time they would normally be travelling?
- Does the roof leak or the area flood in October? As this is difficult to judge in the dry season, ask the neighbours which will give you a chance to see how friendly they are.
- Does water flow in the taps all day? Is pressure okay? Is there an annoyingly noisy pump? (No matter what the agent says, you will not get used to it, and it is likely to break down or be inefficient).

- **Cape House**, 43 Ang Suan, Ploenjit Road, Bangkok 10330
  Tel: (02) 658-7444; fax: (02) 237-8300-4
- **Centre Point** has four sets of apartments in Silom, Sukhumvit, Petchburi and Lang Suan.
  Email: cpsales@centrepoint.com
- **Emporium Suites**, Sukhumvit soi 24
  Tel: (02) 664-0000; fax: (02) 669-990
  Email: info@emporiumsuites.com
- **Palm Court**, Sala Daeng soi 1, Sathorn Nua
  Tel: (02) 267-4050; fax: (02) 267-4080
  Email: siri_santhorn@a-net.net.th

- Are there security bars on all the windows? Check fire escape routes, door locks and security guards. Some streets have community guards to whom you contribute a small amount of money as payment.
- Are the mosquito screens in good condition?
- Is there a telephone installed? Waiting for installation can try your patience. The advantage of a fixed house phone is that you can contact the maid and keep some sort of check on her use of the phone for private purposes. You will particularly need a phone in the initial days, but a mobile is more useful.
- What does the price include? In Bangkok and increasingly in Chiang Mai, you can expect to get furniture, air-conditioners, ceiling fans, a kitchen with stove and a refrigerator. Services are not usually included. When bargaining, remember you can ask for extra furniture at no additional rent (or for unwanted furniture to be removed). Hold back a small amount of rent until promises are met. Some house owners will want you to sign a contract that stipulates a lower rent than you actually pay; this is for tax purposes.

Housing Agents

These advertise frequently in the daily English press. Large companies often tend to deal with one agent in particular but if you are paying for yourself, take on as many as you have time for. Agents are generally friendly and will pick you up and drive you, and charge the landlord for a successful let, not you. You will frequently find different agents taking you to view the same house. Don't stop them. You can learn a lot from two different descriptions and the rent quoted may not be the same in both cases. This is because some agents are willing to pass on to you part of their commission in the hope of a let—go with them.

As in every place, location is the vital factor. You may have to balance convenience in getting to work with the time your children must rise and spend on the bus (non-learning time). If you intend to rely on public transport, including taxis, remember that a centrally located house at the end of a long *soi* can mean long, unpleasant walks in the heat.

When you have found your place, bargain over the price. Here an agent might be able to help you by driving down a landlord (and driving down his own fee) in the hope of an early lease. There may well be a fixed amount of rent payable in advance (often six months). Far from being housing-agent sharks, most agents are very friendly and charming and may offer genuine advice, even on the rental price. But remember you are not renting from them and are unlikely to meet them again once settled in. Be friendly, enjoy your home hunt and enjoy the company of the agent(s), who might well be the first Thais you spend time with outside of work and bureaucracy; but business is business.

It is possible, particularly if the house-owner has placed his property with more than one letting company, to double-cross the agent and deal direct with the owner. You might get a reduction, but both you and the house-owner have shown you are untrustworthy. If shown the same property by more than one agent, it is quite acceptable ethically to phone the agent you are not going with and tell him you are renting through another—this might result in a further reduction, so make the call before final commitment.

SERVANTS (DOMESTIC HELP)

Be wary of agencies offering cheap domestic help. Recommendations from Thai and non-Thai colleagues at your place of work are most likely to obtain you someone you can trust. Patterns of domestic work are changing as Thailand becomes a developed country. Young people often prefer to work in a factory, where social life is better than six days a week working for foreigners. However, it is no longer essential to have full-time servants. You can go to the supermarket yourself just as the maid can go to the traditional market. If you wish, you can have somebody come in three or four times a week to do the cleaning.

Expect to pay more for your maid, gardener or driver than the Thais do (although if you take them over with the house, this difference may be smaller). This is reasonable. Your servants have no long-term career prospects with you, and while you might treat them well, life with a *farang* family can be very boring to Thais, unless you have a community of domestics (which few foreigners can afford or need these days), and unless you tune into Thai TV. The servants who move from foreign household to foreign household report that working for Americans is best, for Europeans and Australians a close second and other Asians and families from the middle-east last. This is, in their words, because of the amount of work expected (less is best), the time off given without too many questions, the salary, the friendliness shown, and the chance to practice English or another language. Some even add the chance to meet foreigners as a positive point, but these are usually young ladies on the lookout for husbands or boyfriends ('secondhand' doesn't seem to matter).

The best place to find a maid, apart from word of mouth, is through expat organisations such as the British Club, American Woman's Club and Community Services of Bangkok. All have noticeboards and some organise maid markets. Servants are also advertised in the newspapers and in the notice boards of supermarkets. When interviewing domestic staff, clarify clearly face to face:

- Past experience or references from previous employers. Check them if possible.

- Working hours and leave day(s). One day off a week is normal, plus the Thai New Year and absences for family funerals and marriages.
- Work to be done.
- Live-in or live-out. Is accommodation provided?
- Food to be provided. Food not to be touched.
- Pay. Usually given at the end of the month, although advances are often requested.
- Disposition. It is much nicer to have a friendly person in the house and it is also easier to give orders to a smiler.

Before finally giving the OK, it is most advisable to take the servant to your house, and go through the work and rules and let them view the place and meet your children and/or dogs, etc. If that checks out, go to the servant's house (if they are to live out) and see what it is like. Judge the distance from your home (the nearer the better) and acquire a means of contact when the servant doesn't turn up (perhaps a nearby shop with a telephone). Count on incurring small costs for help during illness and larger costs if bitten by your dog or child, and a '13th month' salary, given mostly just before the Thai New Year (13–15 April). Keep a copy of the servant's identity card and make sure you know his or her full name, nickname and address. Any dismissal should be on the spot, face to face, with a reasonable settlement (unless in the event of theft or gross misconduct) and get your keys back immediately.

Maid Services

Agencies providing servants should charge you, not the servant. There are many bad ones but two good ones that charge appropriately are:

- **Maid to Order,** P.O. Box 14115, Ratburana, Bangkok 10140; tel/fax: (02) 874-0210; website: http://www.maidtoorder.net. Mr John Ellis, who runs the agency, has also written a book on how to manage your maid and will help you out with any trouble you might experience, including firing.
- **Team Up Services**, mobile tel: (02) 630-2052. You will be able to look for full-time or part-time maids and drivers here.

POOJA

If you find a small room in your new house that cannot be accounted for as a bedroom or anything else, it is probably a *pooja* room, built to accommodate Buddha images and to allow quiet meditation while the rest of the family watches Thai drama on TV. The images are likely to have been removed. If they have not, and if you are into a little meditation, you might suggest the landlady (house rentals always involve ladies rather than landlords) leave them in place. She might not; she might be delighted. Treat them with respect.

TRADITIONAL POOS AND BATH

In your modern Thai home, you will of course enjoy wall-to-wall marbled luxury, with Japanese-designed bathtubs and low-line toilet suites (all made in Thailand to good quality). But one day, you might find yourself with an irresistible call of nature when travelling in remote areas, or roughing it in a cheap hotel in Fang. Being a sensible person, you will of course have gone to the bathroom before leaving home. Being sensible, you will also know that if ever you are to get that mother of all diarrhoeas, it will strike upcountry when all you can do is stagger out to the wooden shack and peer into the fly-infested triangular hole, cut in the wooden planks and wonder what happened to the toilet. A cleaner version might well be under your very nose, so to speak, in the maid's quarters of your modern home. The thing is, many Thais prefer the seatless squat toilet.

Instructions for using one are most unlikely to be written on the wall beside you, so best commit to memory what follows. One day you might just need to know.

- Work out which way you are to face by relating the size and position of the raised ceramic foot pads, if any, to the hole. This being done, squat, or come as near as you can to squatting, with the backside over the hole, not on it. Crouch if you must, but whatever you do, do not sit or stand.
- Males should bear in mind that trousers pulled down a familiar distance to cope with a sit-down toilet, will

leave your pocket openings pointed straight down the hole of a squat toilet. Retrieval of coins, comb and wallet could be a new experience.

- The more sophisticated of the traditional bathrooms will have a rusty nail banged into the wall at a convenient height for you to retrieve scraps of Thai newspaper. This is not for you to read. If using, please remember there is a hole in each piece where it was jammed into the nail. After use, throw in the basket provided in the far corner, or get as near to that goal as possible while remaining in full squat. Under no circumstances attempt to force it down the hole. This practice is not to allow recycling but to prevent the drainage system blocking up.
- At times, there may be no paper but a bucket, or little tin can of water and a scoop. You pour the water from the scoop onto the left hand and wipe yourself clean, washing the hand afterwards and flushing with what remains, if anything.

If you feel a little damp after your attempt at getting close to nature, why not continue with a bath? The traditional Thai bathroom is a bit spartan, but it is a liberating experience. Hang all your clothes on the single nail. Scoop the water from the reservoir with the plastic or metal *khan* (a sort of bowl) or bucket provided, and throw it over your naked body. Soap up and repeat. The water will flow out through a small hole in the wall designed for the purpose. If you forgot your towel, I hope you brought a hankie. If not, the average drying time in lowland Thailand is 40 seconds. Enjoy.

FAMILY PETS

It isn't much trouble bringing cats or dogs into Thailand, but taking them back to your country may be problematic, so many expats decide it is not worth the expense and the distress to owners and animals. Thailand has no established quarantine period, but does sometimes impose quarantine on animals from certain countries or individual animals that look a bit sickly. Have your pet vaccinated as fully as possible, including for rabies, and contact the Thai Embassy before departure to be informed of any restrictions of the moment. If you can have the animal fly with you as excess baggage (some airlines allow small animals in proper containers in the cabin with the owner), you can obtain an entry permit on arrival at the airport. This may be best if you have accommodation to move into. Cheaper hotels and restaurants are not likely to complain if you take your dog in with you, as long as it is well-behaved. Most temporary and some permanent accommodation have no restrictions against pets, though some do, including some of the most popular, so check it out.

When in Thailand, be aware that dogs and cats face a new range of diseases, including mange, which is hard to get rid of. Veterinary services are mostly good and are listed in the phone book. Do not be tempted to adopt cute little monkeys, lizards or snakes unless you are prepared to live in a cage or a forest.

SCHOOLS

There exists a wide variety of educational possibilities for the children of expats in Thailand. I will start with that which is least likely to enter the minds of most foreigners coming to Thailand.

Thai Schools

It is not really legal for foreigners to send their children to Thai schools, but nobody minds, particularly if one parent is Thai and particularly if you pick a fee-paying school. Fees are tiny when compared to international schools, but they provide that extra resource which allows a school to attract the best teachers, buy some equipment and keep the buildings in reasonable repair. For some foreigners, e.g. missionaries in the remotest areas on small salaries, there may be very little choice other than a local school. Increasingly, expats in Thailand are to be found in all areas of work activity. Some of these offer close contact with Thais, but pay very badly. Teaching is the best example of this. Very often, foreign language teachers in Thailand are couples, getting by on two small incomes. When children come along, the Thai school is really the only place they can afford to send their children.

Thai schools tend to be old fashioned in teaching methods and rather crowded at 30–40 to a class. Students spend much of their time in rows behind desks and teachers stand mostly in front of blackboards. Teaching, especially during the early years, is largely by rote. However, this is not necessarily a bad thing when a foreign child is learning the Thai language. And he will not be alone. In the remotest areas, many or most of the students in a school might speak Khammuang or Isaan dialects, or a tribal language at home, and be learning Thai at the same level as the foreign child.

The younger the child, the more the alternative of a Thai school is a possibility to consider, even if you do not live in a remote area. Standards in some of Bangkok's Thai nursery schools are very good. Your under-seven-year-old can play and learn Thai and English alongside the children of rich Thais. Your company or agency might pay for secondary schooling, but many do not pick up the bill for nursery school. Fortunately, in Thailand, that bill will not break the bank.

If your child has been to a Thai nursery school, he is likely to be able to cope with Thai primary. The curriculum at primary level is national and the language of instruction is Central Thai. Grade One is for six to seven year-olds and starts from scratch with a large element of language learning during the first year, beginning with learning the Thai alphabet by heart. All children must conform to the system and things are done very much by the bell and the rule book. There is not much hint so far of Montessori methods. Uniforms are worn and the days are long, usually from 8:00 am–3:30 pm. Children generally bring their lunch and eat together.

Home Schooling/Correspondence Courses

One option rarely considered is for parents to teach their children themselves. If your child is over seven years old and Thai school is not practical, if your time in Thailand is one year or less, and if your company is not paying the huge enrolment and tuition fees associated with international schools, consider do-it-yourself. However, assistance is needed from the child's school in the home country and preparation is essential. The child will want to move up

with his cohort upon return and it is therefore important to maintain regular contact with the class. Gains in such an arrangement can be two-way. A good teacher will use your child's letters, photographs, tapes and such as a teaching resource. The teacher must also help you prepare before you leave by making sure you obtain all set books for the year and a general framework of targets, essays and tests. If your child is at secondary level, correspondence courses exist in English, French, German and Spanish in most subjects. Information on correspondence courses for the various countries may be obtained from:

- **USA**. **AUA Library**
  179 Ratchadamri Road, Bangkok 10330
  Tel: (02) 650-5040-4; fax: (02) 254-4338
- **UK**. **British Council Library**
  254 soi 64, Siam Square, Phayathai Road
  Tel: (02) 252-6136 ext. 504; fax: (02) 253-5311-2
  Website: http://www.britcoun.or.th

- **Australia**. **IDP Education Australia**
  4th Floor, CP Tower, Silom Road
  Tel: (02) 231-0531-3; fax: (02) 231-0530
- **New Zealand**. **The New Zealand Education Centre**
  New Zealand Embassy, Vittayu, Bangkok
  Tel: (02) 254-2530 ext. 46; fax: (02) 256-0129
  Email: nzecbkk@loxinfo.co.th.
  For languages other than English, contact the appropriate
embassy or consulate.

International Schools

Most expat children in Thailand will attend an international
school. However as there are so many, it is advisable to
contact a number of them before your arrival. Some allow
entry mid-year or mid-term and some do not. Ask questions
like these direct if you don't get the answers from the glossy
brochures that each school will send you. If you know where
you will be working or living, and all other things are equal, go
for the school nearest home. Not only do schools start early
with long bus rides, they also have significant after-school
activities which your child will want to attend, and to which
you will most likely have to travel by car in the perpetual rush
hours. (*For a list of international schools, refer to the* Resource
Guide *on pages 332–336.*)

BIRTH, MARRIAGE AND DEATH

These are all life cycle events that come under the
responsibility of the consular section of your embassy. All
require some involvement from the embassy, so have it
involved from the beginning. Let's start with marriage.

Getting Married

Many foreigners marry Thais and almost all such marriages
involve a foreign man and a Thai woman. Many embassies
provide a certificate of non-impediment, which means you
are not already married as far as is known. With this and
a small fee, a marriage may be registered at the *amphur*
(local district) office. Traditional Thai weddings may or may
not take place, depending on the wishes of both partners.

It is traditional for the man to make a gift to the woman's family. Anything from US$ 500–US$ 2,000 is normal, with more for an educated member of the middle class, especially if she remains a virgin (in addition to the gifts mentioned under 'courtship' above). Bar girls and divorced women with children in tow may be considered outside this traditional requirement (depending on the woman—some will demand very high payments and some have been married several times). If the woman leaves the man, this money should, theoretically, be repaid, but the foreigner can forget that.

A Thai woman loses many of her rights when she marries a foreigner. She cannot, for example, own land; but this being Thailand, there are ways around this problem—she can keep the land she bought before marriage and can pass it on to her heirs, presuming they are Thai.

Divorce requires a similar trip to register at the *amphur* where you got married. If both parties agree (which generally means a monetary settlement has taken place), it is very easy.

Many couples, whether both partners are Thai or a non-Thai is involved, do not bother with marriage and simply live together. Other couples, if legally married, do not bother with divorce. If his wife disappears, it can be a problem for a foreigner who registered his marriage at his embassy. He is advised to get a Thai lawyer to obtain for him a divorce certificate.

Having Children

Facilities for giving birth in the major towns are good, especially in Bangkok and provincial capitals. Birth certificates are provided at the hospital and state the nationality of the parents. If not officially married, it is important the father's name appear on the birth certificate or it will be marked 'father unknown'. You must register the child's name—so get it right—at the province office and get the appropriate stamp. Take the certificate, together with passport-sized photographs of the baby, to your embassy, register the birth under your law and obtain a national passport and, eventually, a national birth certificate. This will prevent many problems when taking the child out of Thailand and into your country. If the parents are of two different nationalities, the Thais will generally regard the children as of the father's nationality. If one of the parents is Thai, the children may be given Thai nationality. If your country allows dual nationalities, the child may under Thai law, hold two nationalities, at least until age 18 (although Thai law is lax on this and as long as passports are maintained every three years no questions are asked—an advantage for the growing number of *luuk khrung*, children of mixed parentage).

Death in Thailand

As soon as a death occurs, request the assistance of your consul in Thailand. Bodies may be embalmed and shipped home for burial but costs are high, and cremation at a temple crematorium is a common option. Foreigners married to Thais are advised to get a will written in English or their home language, and Thai, particularly if significant property or money held outside Thailand is to be inherited by a second Thai wife, living in Thailand, who has only Thai nationality.

Getting Legal Help/Advice

Consular offices of embassies hold selected lists of attorneys in Thailand with whom you can communicate in English, whether in a criminal or civil case. Embassies and consulates are listed in the telephone book in English.

MONEY MATTERS
Banking

Banking is well developed throughout Thailand, services such as automatic teller machines (ATM) are everywhere, and telephone and computer inquiry facilities are available. Foreign banks are well represented and this might help international money transfers, although these are readily available to and from Thai banks. The charge for a bank transfer is currently 3 per cent. Money may, however, be drawn from an ATM machine using a debit card without charge. Use of a credit card within a bank to take out money is possible up to the limit imposed on the card; charges are currently 3 per cent. A cabled transfer takes about three days and costs more. Western Union (person to person) is quickest and most expensive. For the sake of convenience, most expats bank with the Bangkok Bank, Bank of Ayudhya or the Thai Farmers Bank. These are large and solid institutions which are likely to have branches near where you will be staying or working, with plenty of ATMs upcountry. You may open accounts in Thai baht and in US dollars, and have your salary, or part of it, paid directly into either account (but the bank can only pay you foreign currency up to the variable

Banks in Bangkok

- **Bank of America**
  Bank of America Center, 2/2 Vitthayu
  Tel: (02) 251-6333/250-0775-6; fax: (02) 254-4003
- **Bank of Tokyo-Mitsubishi**
  Harindhorn Tower, 54 Sathorn Nua
  Tel: (02) 266-3011; fax: (02) 266-3054-5
- **Chase Manhattan Bank**
  Budhajit Building, 20 Sathorn Nua
  Tel: (02) 234-5992-5 /238-1720-4; fax: (02) 234-8386
- **Citibank**
  82 Sathorn Nua
  Tel: (02) 232-2000; fax: (02) 639-2560
- **Credit Agricole Indosuez**
  152 Vittayutel
  Tel: (02) 651-4590-2; fax: (02) 514-586-8
- **Deutsche Bank**
  Wireless Building, 208 Vittayu
  Tel: (02) 651-5151
- **HSBC**
  U-chu Liang Building, 968 Rama IV
  Tel: (02) 614-4000; fax: (02) 632-4818
- **National Australia Bank**
  16th Floor Sathorn Thani I Building, 90 Sathorn Thani
  Tel: (02) 236-6016-7; fax: (02) 236-6018

limit stipulated by the Exchange Control Act). Local (VISA) credit cards are available, but these are limited to use within Thailand. International credit cards are widely accepted, but a surcharge of 3.5 per cent is often added.

The status of the baht is changing. It is not really an international currency, although because of the great amount of tourism to Thailand, it is often quoted at European banks and readily available at Thomas Cooks in Europe. Be aware that changing your money into baht outside the kingdom will get you far fewer baht for your currency than changing inside Thailand.

Exchange facilities exist at the airport and inside the arrival and departure lounges; they offer the bank rate and there is no black market. Changing money at hotels generally gives a poor rate. In tourist areas, there is usually some exchange facility somewhere open 24 hours a day providing the official rate. You often get slightly more for large denomination notes and traveller's cheques. Although acceptance of debit cards in ATM machines has made traveller's cheques redundant in Thailand, it is useful to have some as a fail-safe in case of card loss, but also useful if you are crossing into a neighbouring country for visa or tourist purposes.

Banking Hours

Bangkok: 10:00 am–4:00 pm

Elsewhere: 8:30 am–3:30 pm

Banks are closed on Saturdays, Sundays and all public holidays.

You may want to ensure your credit card from your home bank has a healthy life span before leaving home, to avoid the need to get a new one via the post. You are not really supposed to open a bank account in Thailand until your work permit and residency status are in order; in practice, there is rarely a problem if you are putting money in, although the account opened in your name will carry no interest. Bring a letter from your employer and your passport and visa and an interest-bearing account just like the one back home may be opened with minimal formalities.

Taxation

Except for diplomats and UN personnel, expats are required to pay income tax on the same basis as Thais for any income derived from activity within Thailand, whether or not the income is actually paid in Thailand. Employers have the responsibility of withholding income tax from all salary and other benefits paid to employees. Tax relief operates for those resident in Thailand for at least 180 days in any year, and currently amounts to 30,000 baht each for the taxpayer and his spouse, and 15,000 baht for each child in full-time education. Here's an example of what you might pay before any relief. If you earn 500,000–1,000,000 baht per year, expect to pay around 142,000 baht. If you earn up to four million baht, your tax bill could be 1,042,500 baht.

Many countries, including the UK, have rules against double taxation, so if you are British, you will not be expected to pay tax on income derived from Thailand. Other countries allow only so much to be earned tax-free from Thailand before national taxes are levied. This is the case with the US, and the US expat might like to check his tax situation before coming to Thailand (some expat companies agree to cover all taxation costs, but not all behave so generously).

Currency Exchange

The dollar is still king in Thailand and may be exchanged almost everywhere. It is not, however, an alternative currency and payments are almost always in baht. Dollars, pounds and other major convertible currencies are easily changed in most large banks in urban centres. They may also be changed at hotels and some shopping centres, but the rate will be significantly less than at the bank. Traveller's cheques are best changed at a bank, where they attract a higher rate than cash. There is no black market in Thailand, but the Thai baht is not readily convertible overseas.

Foreign Chambers of Commerce

Any country can set up a Chamber of Commerce in Bangkok, and many have done so. Most are situated in the Vitthayu–

Sathorn–Sukhumvit area. Your embassy can give you details, or simply look in the *Yellow Pages*.

SHOPPING

Thailand is a nation of shopkeepers and stallholders, and just about everything is for sale at a price that is lower than in most other countries. Westerners who are quite used to seeing 'Made in Thailand' on their clothing and household products back home can now get the same thing at a fraction of the price. It means you need to bring very little with you, with the exception of shoes for those with big feet. Though they may be made in Thailand, large-size shoes (European 45 +) are not on sale here. But anything else that you can't find in your size, you can have made to measure.

The whole of Bangkok seems at times to be one huge sales complex. There is, however, an area often called the 'Central Shopping Area', where most of the big stores are found. This runs the length of Rama I, from Siam Square and Siam Centre, past the great complex of upmarket shops within the World Trade Centre, and crosses Rajdamri, where a short detour brings in Peninsula Plaza, to Sogo and Central Chitlom on Ploenchit. In the complex which houses Central Silom (conveniently right at a skytrain stop), there is a DHL delivery service which seems to be open all the time, and a small but useful 'export' clothes shop, where you can buy large size clothing intended for export at bargain rates, even winter coats if you need to travel to colder climes (look for small flaws and if you find any get a further 10 per cent off). All shopping malls have 'food courts', a good selection of other restaurants, fast food and supermarkets. They are all comfortably air-conditioned, although they can be crowded at weekends.

Outside of the shopping complexes, the pavements are open-air counters for the sale of clothes, watches, CDs and many things that might be illegal in your country (and even in Thailand). Other major shopping areas include the Chatuchak Weekend Market, where you can buy most things old and new or alive and dying. That's near the Saphankhwai station on the northern reaches of the skytrain. If you want to avoid heatstroke and stand a chance of a bargain, get there early in the morning—by 7:00 am, traders have almost completed their unpacking—then go one more station to the end of the line, or take a walk in the Bangkok heat to Central Lard Prao where the air-conditioned mall opens at 10:00 am.

Outside of Bangkok, every town has some form of market where clothing, electrical goods, watches and such, are on sale cheaply. The most well known of these is Chiang Mai's night market on Chang Klan Road which is open in the evening until around 11:00 pm. There is now hardly a town without a supermarket, including the familiar Tesco, which also has lots of appendages in terms of places to eat and buy cheaply. These might be located a little outside town, but every taxi or *tuk-tuk* driver will understand 'supermarket', and might take you there even if you say 'cinema' (and indeed, the cinema might be in the supermarket, which never stands alone).

Two floors of genuine Asian antiques, at genuinely negotiable prices, are to be found in the air-conditioned complex known as River City, next to the Royal Orchid Sheraton Hotel. Shop owners will provide authenticity certificates, arrange shipping or crating, and obtain permits to take antiques out of the country (usually by stating they are not Thai in origin—which many are not). Then there are things Chinese, particularly traditional medicines in Chinatown on Yaowarat, which will lead you to Thieves' Market and across the canal to Old Siam, a surprisingly pleasant crafts market.

Books and magazines are readily available in many English-language bookstores and secondhand bookshops, but perhaps not the books that you want. Of course, if some books are important to your work, bring them with you. Otherwise, the Internet bookstores can deliver as well to Thailand as to your home country.

About the only places you do not usually bargain are the

The answer to the question, "What shall I bring with me?", can be answered very simply. Unless you need special medication or have extremely large feet, bring as little as possible. The clothes you stand up in and your documents are really all you need. Even the suitcases you will fill on return visits home are made in Thailand and much cheaper here.

upmarket department stores (although if buying expensive items, ask for a discount or *khong thaem*, free gift), restaurants and the entrance to tourist attractions (which usually charge non-Thais many times above the price for Thais, and where 'don't bargain, don't buy' is the only sensible rule).

VAT can be refunded at the airport if you stay less than 180 days in any calendar year. Goods must be moved out within 60 days of purchase. In reality, this only applies to the larger shops where prices tend to be higher (partly because they pay the tax in the first place). At the time of purchase, ask for a VAT refund form (PP10) and attach original receipts showing transactions of at least 2,000 baht on each form. You should have your passport on hand for inspection. If your total receipted expenditure is over 5,000 baht, present this at the airport (with the items) and you will get a 7 per cent refund minus a hefty administrative charge. Getting a refund is only worthwhile if you have spent a lot in upmarket stores. As a general rule, the more you get back in VAT refunds, the less successful you have been in bargaining. Even at the computer superstore Pantip Plaza (nearest skytrain station Rachatevi, then walk), you can buy your computer and printer inside the smart fixed-price shop and get forms for a 7 per cent VAT refund, or at the small shops in the same complex at least 15 per cent cheaper, with no VAT forms.

The sensible thing to do is to go to the comfortable large outlets and check out exactly what you want and their price, then go just outside and, with a minimum of bargaining, buy the same thing at 15–20 per cent cheaper. The smaller outlets are able to offer cheaper prices because they pay less in overheads, keep less stock on the premises, and perhaps pay less tax than they should—not because they are trading in deficient products. All places will demonstrate that what you are buying works and most have the same guarantee. Sometimes, you will be quoted one price with guarantee and one price, significantly lower, without guarantee.

Payment is usually by cash. Many shops and supermarkets add a 3–4 per cent surcharge for payment by credit card. Acceptance of cheques varies. Where payment is accepted in dollars or other currencies, you usually get a poor rate.

Parking is available free at most big shopping centres. But many of these shopping centres are on the skytrain route, and a car is not necessary (although bulky packages are discouraged on the skytrain and humping them up the steps might make you wish you had brought the car). Taxis are, of course, available, but you might have to queue in the sun carrying your purchases.

In the unlikely event of your having some complaints about particular shopping outlets, or in the more likely event of wanting to know where to get what, try the Tourist Hotline. Dial 1155 and press ext 1 for complaints and ext 2 for information.

HEALTH AND HOSPITALS

It does not take a genius to discover that most of Thailand is very hot most of the year. Germs like heat, so keep yourself, your clothes and bed linen clean and eat only fresh food. There are some infections that spread quickly like fungal infections, which can be easily treated with a good wash and anti-fungal cream. Some people get prickly heat, others never do; again, there is prickly heat powder to control this problem.

Evenings bring mosquitoes, but these are malarial in only one or two border areas of Thailand. The usual advice is to cover up—pretty stupid advice when the temperature tells you to strip down. More sensible is to use roll-on mosquito repellent when eating outdoors at night and to sleep in an air-conditioned room; if necessary you might add a plug-in repellent that lasts up to 90 days before you need to replace the bottle (there is a shelf at the supermarket selling all this stuff, so don't bring it with you).

There is very little chance of being bitten by a malaria-carrying mosquito, so these precautions are more to allow you to enjoy your evenings rather than a health precaution. However, some mosquitoes can carry other things (but not AIDS) so take extra care if there is a dengue outbreak, which usually only happens in the rainy season. Dengue is spread by the larger, striped mosquito which thrives on the traffic pollution which has driven most other mosquitoes off the roads of Bangkok. Dengue mosquitoes are particularly nasty and unsporting because they feed during the day. If you get dengue, the initial signs are not alarming. You get a fever, occasionally vomit, and usually develop a rash on the arms or sometimes the chest, which goes away after a few days. Then, up to ten days later, wham! It hits you with a very high fever; you can't eat, and feel so weak you want to die. The treatment is essentially to let it take its course, which can be several weeks, while under hospital care in an air-conditioned room and on a drip. The danger lies in the fatal, non-stop bleeding (usually in the final stages), so stop taking any blood-thinners like warfarine or aspirin.

Mosquito-borne diseases are spread by the mosquito drawing blood from one person, then, before it has consumed all the blood, going onto the next victim. This occasionally results in epidemics. Take sensible precautions, particularly mosquito repellents and sprays, but the danger is small and panic serves no purpose.

Other possible, but unlikely, dangers such as snake bite, rabid dog bite, etc. are dealt with under the Resource Guide at the back of this book. There is also an annotated guide to Thailand's hospitals which, on the whole, are equal or better than most in other countries, and a lot cheaper. Most of the big hospitals have a special office to handle insurance claims. Having decided on a hospital to use if necessary, ask this insurance office to recommend some insurers. Check out the services and fees. Remember, hospitals are used generally as family doctors in many countries, and contain spectacle and dental sections, making a 'one-stop shop', whatever your problem

If your employer provides insurance, you must usually go to a certain establishment, otherwise select what your budget and needs require. In the event of hospitalisation, having insurance makes things a whole lot easier. Once you show your card or give the name, the hospital contacts the insurer and obtains a guarantee to cover your stay. Don't be surprised if you are visited by an agent of the insurance company and do not expect confidentiality between doctors and agents—indeed you are likely to have to sign a release for medical information on taking out an insurance policy.

There are many insurance companies catering for different needs, family groups, companies and time periods. Nothing would be served by listing these here. It is, of course, good advice to get the best insurance that you can afford, but in practice you might not need some of the services included e.g. if you are living in Bangkok, you are unlikely to need medical evacuation, which is expensive, but if you are travelling a lot in the region, you might.

If you have yet to sign the employment contract, try to get insurance included. Large companies generally get better deals from insurers and if your company cannot give you precisely what you want, ask about the cost of topping up payments yourself to provide for extra needs.

Talk of medical insurance should not suggest that people in Thailand are more at risk than elsewhere. Probably the opposite is true. But in any country where good medical care must be paid for, insurance makes sense.

TRANSPORTATION

In a large crowded city famous for its traffic problems, it is worth giving serious thought to getting around with the least aggravation and expense. In other cities, even Chiang Mai, transportation is not likely to be a very significant budgetary item; in Bangkok, it is. Let's consider the alternatives available. The visitor should be prepared to use a combination of everything to get from point A to B.

Buses

Air-conditioned buses offer fast connection between major cities. From Bangkok, buses for the east leave from the Eastern Bus Terminal (soi 40, Sukhumvit) and buses for the north go from the Northern Bus Terminal (Kampaengphet 2 Road, Mo Chit 2). Those for the north-east depart from the North-Eastern Bus Terminal (same location as the Northern), and those for the south go from the Southern Bus Terminal on the Phra Pinklao-Nakorn Chaisi intersection. Tickets can be purchased from the terminals, or through travel agents or

Within Bangkok, economy-class foreigners with a bit of adventure in the soul will find that buses have a character all their own. The festoons of flower garlands swinging in front of the driver's face, the conductor's ticket-clipping ritual, and the bus race are all a daily part of Bangkok culture.

hotels. Most travel is overnight. You get a couple of stops with at least one meal thrown in and some have services such as soft drinks and blankets provided by a hostess. All air-conditioned buses have toilets and many have video screens (sit towards the back to avoid the noise, towards the front if you want to follow the movie). Seats recline and are comfortable.

A journey from Bangkok to Chiang Mai takes eight to nine hours including stops, and it takes about the same time to get to the north-east and Hat Yai in the south. Be aware that some advertisements are incorrect, for example the Nongkhai-Bangkok bus should arrive at 6:00 am according to its advertised schedule, but it always arrives at 4:00 am, an inconvenient time to check into a cheap Bangkok hotel but a convenient time to cross Bangkok by taxi to your home, if you have one.

If you have a small group of people, there are plenty of mini-buses for hire. Check them out in the *Yellow Pages* or at a travel agent, since those from hotels are usually more expensive. You will often be asked to pay a fixed price for the driver and vehicle, and cover the cost of fuel. If you have half a dozen people, this works out to be quite cheap and will allow you to control your route and stopping points. Such vehicles, and even ordinary taxis, will often agree to go long distances, pick you up at home and deliver you precisely to where you want to go. Verbally agree the fare in advance.

Visitors should know that drivers and bus conductors work largely on a commission basis. This explains why they are happy to pack as many people as possible into the bus, scramble around inside and outside collecting fares, and zoom past stops with few clients when trying to beat the competition to the next major stop.

Stick your hand out to flag down a bus and signal the conductor when you want to get off. The bus driver works on two Thai words from the conductor, *pai*, which means go and *pai*, which in this context means stop (actually 'bus stop'). Confusing as this might be for the foreign visitor, it works perfectly even on the most crowded and noisy buses. Watch your pockets and handbags and remember, monks sit on the back seat.

Trains

Timetables and fares are available in Thai and English on the Internet (http://www.srt.motc.go.th). You can also book specific seats and sleepers online, although most people prefer to go to an authorised travel agent, who can provide a ticket on the spot.

Many foreigners love Thai trains, which move at a leisurely pace and have a regular service providing food and drinks. Washroom facilities, whether on trains or buses, are understandably better at the beginning of the journey than at the end. Air-conditioned second class will give you a wide, comfortable seat to yourself facing one other person. On long hauls, these convert into sleeping bunks, which will be made up for you at a reasonable time.

Rates are cheap. For example, a second class air-conditioned sleeper will take you the 11 hours from Bangkok to Nongkhai for just over 500 baht. For 1,000 baht on the same route, you can have one of the two berths in a first class compartment, and for 1,500 baht you can have the whole compartment and washbasin to yourself—that's cheap, but approaching the airfare, which is also cheap. The route is slow and you get a good sleep. It is, however, one of Thailand's unsolved mysteries how a train travelling so slowly can consistently arrive two hours late every time.

If going north or north-east, you do not have to leave from the central Hua Lamphong Station. You can get on at any convenient stop. One of the most convenient, especially if you come in by plane and don't want to go into the city, is Don Meuang, right opposite the international airport. You can walk across the bridge with your luggage trolley. It will take you to the platform.

Be on the lookout for excursion trains. These are special and very cheap trains rides. An example is one which leaves from Hua Lamphong at 6:30 am on Saturdays, Sundays and public holidays, and arrives at Hua Hin at 10:40 am. And don't forget that the Thais use their word for express to refer to the slow trains, but not to the incredibly slow (rapid) or the unbelievably, scarcely-moving, slow (normal).

Trains within Bangkok are almost unused by visitors. While the stations are hidden away and trains are infrequent, they do leave on time. And even the unbelievably slow can be a lot faster than the inner-city road transport; and it is easier to know where to get off than on the bus or boat, since station signs are written in Thai and English. Timetables are available from the central train station and some travel agents and hotels. Don't be afraid to take an overnight train heading to Udon if you only want to go to the international airport, or the train to Aranyaprathet on the Thai border with Cambodia, if you want to get off on New Phetburi or King Mongkut Institute of Technology. But check the timetable to ensure that the train stops where you want it to.

Boats

River and canal transportation in the 'Venice of the East' tends to get overlooked by foreigners. Although Bangkok's *khlong* (canals) are fast disappearing, a network of waterways continues to connect many parts of the city. With a bit of

planning, many of the worst traffic jams can be avoided by taking to the boats. River buses go up and down the Chao Praya River with reliable regularity. There are 21 stops 'in town', three of which are on the Thonburi bank (so don't panic when the boat suddenly zooms across the river).

River bus fares are cheap and fixed, but vary according to the distance travelled, so you need to tell the conductor where you are going (or show him the *tha* or pier written in Thai). Once you have a map, count the stops to know where to get off, although the conductors have uncanny memories and many let you know. There are other river bus routes on canals throughout the city. Particularly useful is the route along the New Phetburi side of Sukhumvit that passes Phratu Nam. Highly recommended in a city as crowded as Bangkok,

Boat Stops

Useful stops for you to know from upriver north, to downriver south are: (*tha* by the way means pier)

- Tha Theves and Tha Wisut Kasat, a short taxi or bus ride to the UN building and government offices.
- Tha Phrachaai, a short walk to Thammasat University, National Museum and National Theatre.
- Tha Maharat and Tha Chang, an easy walk to Thammasat and Silapakorn Universities, Sanam Luang, the Grand Palace and the Temple of the Emerald Buddha.
- Tha Ratchawong, to alight in the heart of Chinatown.
- Tha Wat Muang Kai and Tha Orien, for the main Post Office on New Road, French Embassy, Oriental Hotel and the Silom-Surawong business district.
- Tha Sathorn, for Sathorn Road.

For a full list of stops, check out Nancy Chandler's map, *The Markets of Central Bangkok* (March 2001).

river transport provides cheap convenience and opens up a whole new world. Definitely a great way to start the day.

Driving

Many Bangkok-based foreigners manage to live without a car for the following very good reasons.

- It is very cheap to take public transport.
- Domestic aircraft, buses and trains, skytrains, taxis, *tuk-tuks* and motorcycle taxis go almost anywhere you want to go.
- Cars or taxis can be hired as required for day trips with or without a driver quite cheaply. See the *Yellow Pages* or talk to taxi drivers.
- Unless you have diplomatic status, you pay 200 per cent import duty on imported cars (but not on locally assembled ones).
- The cost of having an accident.
- The horrors of the Bangkok traffic jam.

If you can't live without your own set of wheels, comprehensive insurance is advised. Bring with you a no-claim letter from your last insurance company and

Obtaining a Thai Driving Licence

To obtain a Thai driving licence, go along to the driving test centres at Sukhumvit soi 1 or Chatuchak. Bring:

- Your national licence / valid licence from your country or your international licence.
- Verification of your address in Thailand (your embassy, not knowing you from Adam, will do this for you in return for 1,500–2,000 baht).
- Your national passport with a non-immigrant visa.
- A health certificate from your doctor.
- A letter from your employer or an important Thai to support your application.
- Two 3 x 2 cm photographs of yourself.

you should get the usual discount. Legally, you need only third-party cover, which costs 1,500–2,000 baht per year. Comprehensive insurance kicks off at over 11,000 baht but is worth it if you back up over a motorcycle or come out of the supermarket to find your bumpers crumpled. The car owner is regarded as a well-off being. If a car driver puts a cyclist in hospital, it is the car owner who pays the bill (or his insurance if he has any). Minor accidents are often settled on the spot between the two parties. The driver (car or motorcycle) who accidentally runs a red light, may similarly settle on the spot by discussing things with the nice policeman who wants only to save you the effort and time of recovering your licence from the police station by having you pay your fine there and then.

If you have to take a driving test, don't be too worried. You simply have to be able to read a car number plate from a distance, pass a multiple-choice test, start a car and drive around the car park without hitting anything. Upcountry, tests are usually not this difficult. The official cost of the licence is cheap but you might like to have a supply of hundred notes in your wallet to show appreciation to some of those officials who will help you through things quickly. This is important since the application forms are in Thai.

Once you obtained or ordered your vehicle, gets quotes for insurance. Many expats go to one of the following companies:

- **Alexander Forbes Wattana Insurance Brokers**
  127 South Sathorn Road
  Tel: (02) 213-2000; fax: (02) 287-2329
  Website: http://www.alexanderforbes.com
- **AXA Insurance Public Company**
  1168 Lumpini Tower, Rama V Road
  Tel: (02) 679-8277
- **Thai-Zurich Insurance Co.**
  126/2 Krungthonburi Road, Klongsan, Bangkok, 10600;
  Tel: (02) 439-4800; fax: (02) 439-4840
  Email: tz@zurich.com

Taxis

Taxis come in three basic kinds. Firstly, there are those with a 'taxi' sign on the top and a meter inside which work in much the same way as their counterparts in New York or London, except that no tip is required or expected. Secondly, there are those which spin around going 'tuk-tuk', and where it is necessary to bargain over the fare. *Tuk-tuks* go for shorter distances than taxis, and are significantly noisier and theoretically cheaper—fine if there are only one or two of you, you know exactly where you are going, it's not raining, and you can negotiate a price in Thai. Lastly, there are the motorcycle taxis which hang around in packs at the mouth of long *sois*. Some just run passengers up and down the *soi* for a fixed fee of a few baht which includes the legally compulsory use of a helmet (some women carry a light scarf to protect their hair from the grease). Others will take you anywhere for an agreed price. Their popularity is evident from the number of businessmen who abandon a taxi or their chauffeur-driven car, to mount a motorcycle and get to that meeting on time.

Not all taxis will want to take you where you want to go at a price you want to pay, or a price set by the meter, but there are plenty of taxis to chose from, so if you don't like the look of one, or he doesn't like the look of you, never mind, take the next.

Skytrain and Underground

The central routes and stops of the skytrain are to be found in Nancy Chandler's map *The Markets of Central Bangkok*. A fuller but less expressive version is available at every skytrain station, which also includes the brand new 'metro' or underground sectors in the process of opening as this book is written. The skytrain was built principally to get residents to work and back, and not for tourists, although the system couldn't be simpler, and you can see much of where you are going, so taking the skytrain requires no knowledge of Thai and no intellectual effort greater than making sure you are going in the right direction. It does, however, take something of a physical effort. Stairs up to stations are steep and lifts and escalators are rare. There is talk of improving access, but for the moment at least, the skytrain is more or less impossible for the handicapped, aged or infirm—a great pity since this tends to exclude the very people who could most benefit from a quick and comfortable ride, above the horrors of Bangkok's traffic.

Trains are frequent, but stations are quite far apart, often requiring a long walk or *tuk-tuk* ride to reach your destination. The authorities have missed a tremendous opportunity to place toilets at stations, so like the rest of Bangkok's transports of delight, you might find yourself crossing your legs as you climb the stairs.

Trains run from 6:00 am to midnight. Have plenty of five and ten baht coins to get your single journey ticket from a machine. Fares are clearly shown, from the point where you are to any destination, and currently range from 10–40 baht. Children under 90 cm (35.4 inches) travel free. If you are using the skytrain frequently, get a stored value ticket from the ticket office for 100–2,000 baht, plus a 30 baht charge for the ticket itself. This doesn't give you cheaper fares, but helps you avoid queues. You simply pop your ticket in the reader at the gate, which is clever enough to deduct your fare as you exit and display your remaining balance. The ticket can be topped up at the ticket office. A word of warning though. You cannot use one, go in, and pass the ticket back for a friend to use—the system of calculating your fare can't cope with that and you could screw up your ticket if not the system.

If you happen to work near a station, this is a strong incentive to find accommodation near another station, and the Skytrain has revolutionised many Bangkok commutes. There are even some park and ride facilities being put into place, and further lines and stations on both skytrain and underground are planned. If interested in an update on the Skytrain, contact the Bangkok Mass Transit System (BTS), BTS Building, Paholyothin Road, Chatuchak [tel: (02) 617-7300; fax: (02) 617-7133].

Two Wheels

Many an expat has experienced the delays of car travel and the difficulty and expense of parking, and bought a motorbike. Bikes are considerably cheaper than the cheapest car and riding a bike, even a pedal bike, can reduce travelling time by half or more. The great advantage is that at every traffic light, you can wriggle your way to the front and be off as soon as the lights change. Disadvantages are the rain in the June–September rainy season, the need to wear a crash helmet in the tropics and resultant greasy hair, grime, a high accident rate, the need to ride in certain lanes or get fined, and the police game of stopping motorcycles to have a chat in the evenings, particularly during those difficult times before the next payday.

Walking

Bangkok and most Thai cities were not made for leisurely strolls. If walking, please look out for potholes along the way, motorbikes on the pavement, pointed iron awning poles at eye level, beggars at foot level, and things you don't want to have stuck to the soles of your feet for the rest of the day. 'Plasticated' shoes are a good idea, as they look smart enough and are reasonably waterproof. Another idea in the rainy season is to waterproof your jacket's shoulders and carry either a floppy hat in your pocket, a light cycle cape with hood, or a humble plastic bag to cover your head.

If you can bear with all the inconveniences of walking in Bangkok, it might actually save you time, and it will certainly give you a bit of exercise and a sense of being in Bangkok (right in it). But the thing is to be sensible about it. Study a map carefully and know your limits. Hop into a taxi outside the British Embassy on Ploenchit to go to Phetburi New Road and you are in for some long jams and a comparatively high fare. Instead look at the map and you will see that there are main *sois* going across between the two one-way roads that will take you where you want to go on foot and against the flow of the traffic in five minutes.

Crossing roads in Bangkok is not the life and death game that it is in Hanoi—Thais prefer to try to drive around you rather than through you—but knowing the roads can make walking much easier. A few nice places let you walk across the road at traffic lights, but increasingly, you are expected to mountaineer up sweat-inducing steps, review the static traffic and clamber down the other side. If you are familiar with the road, and if it hasn't got an assault course in the middle to prevent you crossing, you will often find that the easiest place to cross is far from the overhead crossings (usually at crossroads). Instead wait for the cars to pile up in front of a distant traffic light and simply cross between them. Learn also to make use of shopping malls. These sometimes offer a short cut between roads, but more importantly, they allow you to cool down in the air-conditioning before hitting the road again.

Reading the Signs

Whether walking, riding or surfing, there will come a time, when you desperately wish you could read those signs around you. Some you can. These are the really important ones like BEWARE OF THE PEDESTRIANS and BETTER LATE THAN

NEVER which are translated into English. The unimportant ones like STOP! and DANGER are written only in Thai.

Road users will notice little signs tacked onto traffic lights. Unfortunately, they all look much the same to the non-Thai reader. 'Turn left whenever you like', means you can ignore the red light and turn left, if you are in the left lane. 'Turn left only when the lights change', doesn't quite mean the same thing. If you don't read Thai, or decipher too slowly for the drivers behind you and the cop on the corner, try to fix a photographic image of these signs in your mind, or at least spot the differences between them and remember which is which. If you follow the same route to work every day, you will learn this and more. The time spent waiting at traffic lights can be very educational.

Road names are written in Thai but if you train a powerful telescope on them, you will find English transliteration in small fonts underneath the Thai. It's better to try to read the Thai. The transliteration sometimes represents the sound (as a Thai would say the word) and is sometimes a literal transliteration of all the Thai letters into the closest English letters which might match up on an alphabet chart but not in real life, where Thai letters carry different pronunciations depending on their place in a syllable, or are sometimes not pronounced at all. There is no official transliteration of Thai into English, as Thai has 44 written consonants and 24 vowels! Picking an English equivalent always involves a margin of flexibility.

Just to add to the confusion, some names are translated rather than transliterated, or both. Thus, Thanon Vittayu (Wittayu) can become 'Wireless Road' in English. All Bangkokians will know Vittayu, an important street housing the US and British embassies and Lumpini Police Station. But very few Thais will understand where you want to go if you ask for 'Wireless Road'.

If that's not enough to confuse, know that some places have been given an English name which is neither a transliteration nor a translation. This includes Charoen Krung, meaning 'prosperous city' and one of the oldest roads in Bangkok, which has the English name 'New Road'. And while Chiang Mai, Udon, Phuket and Pattaya have kept their names in Thai and English, the capital city Krung Thip, has been renamed 'Bangkok' in English. It's not much of an explanation, but 'Bang Kok' is the name of a little muddy village about 30 km (18.6 miles) from Krung Thip at the mouth of the Chao Praya River.

EATING IN THAILAND

CHAPTER 6

'From the curry you prepared,
I smell the aroma of kumin.
Any man who tastes your food
Will desire you so passionately
And dream of you only.'
—Poem by King Rama II,
translated by the author

THE JOY OF EATING

Eating is a national pastime for Thais, most of whom manage to stay delightfully slim in spite of giving in to temptation at every opportunity. And opportunities are many. Almost every street corner and doorway offers something. Cakes are carried on the tea trolley at workplaces, and Thai friends are constantly meeting up after work for a snack before dinner. Entertaining in Thailand presumes food, and good food. Invite Thais to come for drinks and they will drink, and wait for the food to arrive. Invite them to come after dinner and they may show up, if you are the big boss, but you will think you are being nice by giving them the best alcohol and nibbles and they might well think you mean. In Thailand, food leads into drinking and drinking leads into dancing, and, if you can bear it, karaoke.

Thai cuisine is now famous throughout the world, but Bangkok also boasts restaurants from every culture, and the prices are often a fraction of the cost in the expat's home country. Most eating places do not add service charges and in the simpler restaurants, no tip is expected, although a 'keep the change' remark is appreciated anywhere. In hotels and higher class establishments, you will often see prices quoted with ' + + ' after the figure. This means that a 10 per cent service charge and a 7 per cent VAT will be added to the bill. There remains a strata of restaurants in between, where nothing is added, but judging from the silver tray or velveteen folder supporting your bill, something is expected. Where tipping is up to the customer, 10 per cent is fine. Thais will often reduce this to around 5 per cent if a large amount has been spent (unless they like the waitress/waiter, in which case they might give more). Bookshops are full of guidebooks to eating out in Bangkok and Chiang Mai, and therefore no suggestions are offered here. One book that more than pays for itself is *The Best in Bangkok*, which contains comprehensive listings and offers significant discounts on dining and entertainment.

In addition to the three meals a day, you might enjoy a taste of luxury at a hotel like the Oriental where afternoon tea by the river is an experience that could become a habit. You will also find excellent (Thai, Western, Japanese and others) eating facilities in Central Department Store and other shopping malls. These malls usually have a 'food court' on the top floor, or in the basement, at which you sit at any table and carry the food yourself (no waitress service) from the many stall-like shops arranged around you. You see exactly what you are getting and how it is cooked, so a pointed finger can accomplish as much as a verbal discourse. Sauces are available at the outlet and trays, spoons and plastic cups of water are to be found in one or two places. You have to pay with coupons, which you obtain from a kiosk. One person will find that 100 baht is easily enough, including coke and dessert; take any unused tickets back to the kiosk for instant refund in cash.

Such food courts are ideal if you are eating alone or are in a hurry, as you can put several things on top of rice on one plate and not wait for service. They are probably the cheapest good food you will find in Thailand, good basic Thai food at less than a dollar (US$) a plate and with free drinking water. At the other end of the luxury spectrum, a cruise dinner will cost the same as eating in a fast-food restaurant back home but will probably cost little or no more because you are sitting on a boat. And after the nightlife, there are plenty of early hour markets serving late suppers/early breakfasts.

THAI FOOD

Thai food does not fit neatly into breakfast, lunch and dinner categories. Lunch and dinner tend to offer the same choice of various foods, while breakfast is either rice with yesterday's leftovers or *johk* (rice porridge), a bowl of ground rice well cooked with slithers of ginger in it (which you need not eat) and minced pork or chicken. This is served alongside 'horses urine eggs' and various other things that you may add or not as you wish.

Johk is the food least likely to upset the stomach. Indeed, it can have a calming effect and for this reason is a favourite last activity, or penultimate activity, for night owls, and is often served from 3:00 am in market areas, or for normal breakfast in Thai hotels. The basic *johk*, without accompaniments, is the ideal food for a runny tummy. Some people, particularly if they stay alone, keep a few packets of *johk* in the kitchen. These may be bought very cheaply in advance of an emergency in any supermarket/foodstore. They are instant; just pour into a mug, add boiling water and cover for a couple of minutes. While *johk* is not on most menus—of places that have menus—your hotel or guest house restaurant may be sympathetic if you make your wish known: explain that you have *tohng dern* (lit, walking stomach) or *jep tohng* (sick tummy) and that you want to eat some *johk*—for some reason this is a difficult word for many *farang* to say, it's nearer to joke, but almost rhymes with clock. You may be surprised at how people respond and if they have no *johk* on the premises might be able to send somebody somewhere to find some.

Condiments

Salt and pepper shakers are reserved for Western restaurants. Normally, on any table, you will find *nam pla* (fish sauce) and *prik-i-nu* (small red chillies), or both mixed together. You might be advised to spoon out the liquid and leave behind the chillies which, although small, are the hottest available.

Depending on the food being served, you might be provided with various *nam jim* (sauces you dip the food in) or the ingredients to make up your own—finely chopped *gatiem* (garlic), *manao* (limes) plus sugar and ground peanuts.

In the simplest places, you might find the fish sauce in the large bottle as you would buy in the market, usually with a squid picture on the front. It takes the place of salt and it is widely used (not only on fish). *Si-nyew* (soy sauce) is only used for Chinese food and is not likely to be on the table, but you can ask for it. While everything is already cooked with MSG (monosodium glutamate) to improve the taste, this is sometimes served separately—those fine white granules are not heroin but MSG, if you want to add it, especially to noodle dishes.

Daily Fare

The daily fare of the average Thai is rather different to that of special occasions. These 'special' occasions are very frequent and offer the chance to invite comparatively large groups or to be invited. Any Thai should be familiar with the special dishes—similar to the ones you might find on the menu of a good Thai restaurant overseas—and might well decide, if budget and preparation time allow, to include one, especially if a friend has dropped by. Even daily fare is therefore likely to be varied. Daily eating habits do not include courses— everything is there in front of you, pick as you wish and in any order. They also do not include desserts or coffee or tea (all of which is restaurant/special food). Ordinarily, a family drinks plain water with the food, alcohol or beer being drunk separately (usually, not always). There are a range of snacks for accompanying the drinking of beer and alcohol (the Thai distinguish between the two: beer is not considered alcohol). Very often drinking and eating sessions get merged. Again, Thai flexibility and tolerance at work (and play).

Even the plainest of meals should contain the essence of Thai food, which is a combination of (yin/yang type) opposites, and plenty of rice. This means that food can be both sweet and sour, spicy and salty at the same time or that one spicy curry dish will be offset by a 'tasteless' soup. The rice in the north and north-east is likely to be *khao niao* (sticky rice), while in the centre and south it is usually *khao jao* (also called *khao suway*), the kind of rice you are used to and which forms one of Thailand's principal exports.

Khao niao is eaten with the right hand, a less than mouth-sized piece being broken off and wadded into a soft flattish ball in the palm of the one hand. It may be dipped into the various foods, or sauces, or used to scoop up the more substantive food. If you cannot reach what you want, just ask for it and the various plates will be reorganised for access. *Khao suway* usually comes in a central container with a serving spoon or on a large plate. You spoon what you want onto your rice plate, rather than directly into the mouth. Do not hesitate, if your plate is temporarily empty, to serve yourself or to ask for more rice.

Protocol at home is minimal. However, the presence of a foreign guest will change things a bit, and probably increase the menu—unless you just happen to drop in as people are about to eat, in which case it is normal to be invited (and to refuse with thanks, and wait for the invitation to be repeated). Compliment your host on the food, but don't overdo it or you will get more than you can chew or begin to sound a bit hollow or sarcastic. Of course, if the family is eating alone, no compliments are necessary. Eat enough of your food to show you really enjoy it, but do not empty your plate entirely, or the hosts will blame themselves for not providing enough. It is good manners to say that you are full, *im layo*, several times if more food is pressed on you than you wish to eat.

If you are present at a typical family meal, it will almost always mean sitting on the ground, cross-legged. If you find this difficult, say so, and a small stall will normally be found which raises you a little above the company but increases the pleasure of the meal. Some Thais, particularly the old and infirm, Chinese-origin and hill tribes always use such small stalls.

Having eaten with a family, you have the perfect occasion to suggest a continuation in a restaurant or cafe for ice cream and beer. Perhaps not everybody will come, but the gesture will be appreciated. You do not send a thank you card the next day!

At the risk of oversimplifying and in some ways being Bangkok-centric (e.g. I do not include *lap*, the most common dish in the north-east in our two sample menus), everyday Thai food may include the following examples.

Daily Fare

In general, the daily fare of the Thais consist of the following courses:

- Plain, cooked rice, and plenty of it.
- A spicy dish of some sort, often a Thai curry (different from an Indian curry) or chilli dip.
- A salty or sweet dish, or fried or grilled fish. This complements the spicy dish by giving an essentially non-spicy alternative.
- Vegetables, either in the form of stir-fried and/ or simply uncooked and fresh, to accompany the dip.
- A plain non-spicy soup (*gang jurt*), which is essentially water with some tofu, sprigs of vegetables and perhaps some pork balls.
- Finally, fresh fruits as dessert. The fruits are said to clean the palette after a spicy meal.

Here are some examples of meals that the Thais will prepare for themselves at home:

Meal A:
Rice
Green chicken curry
Sweet crispy noodles
Stir-fried vegetables
Tofu and vegetable soup
Fresh fruits

Meal B:
Rice
Chilli dip with cooked vegetables
Fried, salted beef
Tangy vermicelli
Tofu and vegetable soup
Fresh fruits

Try These Out

Here are two simple recipes that you might like to try. After a while, you might want to make some for your Thai friends!

Som Tum (Papaya Salad)

Ingredients:

    1 cup grated green papaya
    2 cloves garlic
    2 small hot chillies
    2–3 cherry tomatoes
    1 tbs dried shrimps
    1 tbs palm sugar
    2 tbs lime juice
    2 tbs fish sauce
    1 tbs roasted peanut
    (Add small crabs for a refined version)

In a mortar, preferably a wooden one, crush the garlic and chillies together. Add the grated papaya using the pestle to pound this gently. Mix in the rest of the ingredients. Papaya salad should be served and eaten immediately.

*   *   *   *

Tom Kha Kai (Chicken in Coconut Soup)

Ingredients:

    Chicken fillet, sliced thinly
    4–5 galangal slices
    2 cups coconut milk
    2 tbs lime juice
    2 tbs fish sauce
    Small chillies, chopped
    Coriander leaves to garnish

In a pot, cook the chicken fillet, galangal pieces and coconut milk quickly until the meat is cooked. Remove from heat. Season with fish sauce, lime juice and chillies. Garnish with coriander leaves. Serve with rice.

Ten Popular and Traditional Dishes

- Tom Yum Goong
  Spicy and sour soup, usually made with prawns and/or other seafood. Flavoured with lime and chillies, it is a refreshing soup if a little spicy in the full Thai version. Remember that most of the things in there are to add to the flavour, not to be eaten. Tom Yum Goong has become a national dish, liked by most Thais and foreigners.

- Yum Woon Sen
  Clear noodle salad. Like Tom Yum Goong, it is flavoured with lime, fish sauce and chillies, and topped with cooked prawns and lots and lots of fresh herbs. An all-time favourite, but specify how spicy you want it.

- Pad Thai
  Fried rice noodles. This is a true Thai concoction, as opposed to most dishes which have either Chinese or Indian origins or influences. The sweet, sour and spicy noodles are sprinkled with peanuts, more chillies and more lime. A favourite lunchtime dish.

- Pad Bai Krapao
  A stir-fry dish of either chicken, beef or seafood with lots and lots of garlic and chillies. This dish is made more intense by an addition of spicy holy basil leaves. It is eaten with plenty of rice (and water!).

- Grilled Chicken and Sticky Rice
  Originally from the north-eastern region where sticky rice is consumed instead of normal rice. A whole chicken (or pieces) is marinated in a mixture of herbs and spices and barbecued. This popular dish is usually bought by the roadside, and is hardly cooked at home—and may pose the sophisticated restaurant some problem. It can be eaten any time, for breakfast, lunch, dinner or as a snack. Particularly good with Thai whisky/soda or beer.

- Som Tum
  A spicy salad of fresh, grated green papaya. Also a north-eastern dish, it usually forms a trio with grilled chicken and sticky rice to make a perfect, balanced meal at any time of the day.

- Gaeng Som
  A clear, sour fish curry, usually served at dinnertime. An authentic Gaeng Som should have three distinct flavours in one, leading with sour, followed by salty with only a hint of sweetness. To master a perfect Gaeng Som is not easy, and a budding cook is always judged by his or her ability to cook this dish well.

- Nam Prik Kapi
  Chilli dip with vegetables. This dish can be as simple or as complicated as the budget or taste buds allow. The pungent dip is made from shrimp paste, chillies, garlic and lime juice. Fresh, steamed or deep-fried vegetable pieces usually accompany this dip.

- Gaeng Keow Wan
  Spicy green curry. This is the national favourite dish, and is usually eaten with rice noodles.

- Kao Kluk Kapi
  An old-time favourite amongst Thais but, due to its strong taste, not too popular with foreigners. Cooked rice is fried with shrimp paste, giving it a distinct pungent flavour. What makes this dish truly unique is the variety of its accompaniments: deep fried, crispy vegetables; thinly fried, rolled omelette; crispy fried small shrimps; sliced shallot; lime wedges; sweet pork cooked in coconut sugar; and, finally, grated green mango.

Eating Out

Eating out in Thailand is a daily event for most people. It may be restricted to one of the snacks offered by street vendors, it may be lunch with colleagues at work, or it may be no more than stopping for *som tum* on the way home or on the way to a restaurant to share the evening meal with friends.

The visitor will be pleased to hear that eating out in Thailand, unless attending a wedding feast (and even then not too much) involves little in the way of protocol and, apart from a reluctance to discuss death or other serious subjects which may grace a Western intellectual's dinner conversation, no real taboos. No food or beverage is forbidden, all can be taken in any order and the eating of one thing does not exclude the eating of another thing. If there are any rules, 'anything, any time, any place,' just about sums them up. A Thai enjoys eating and drinking to the limits of his or your purse, and frequently beyond it.

Buddhist restrictions on taking life do not prevent Thais from enjoying meat and even the monks eat meat. Drinking alcohol is a normal part of social activity for men, not taboo for women, and cigarette smoking remains common among both men and women, although attitudes are changing and smoke-free zones are now to be found in many air-conditioned places in Bangkok. There are occasional half-hearted campaigns to suggest that drinking and driving are not compatible activities, but every driver seems to think these apply to everybody but himself.

Snacks

When not eating, the Thai is discussing his next meal, or at least thinking about it. Often, overcome with these thoughts, he has a snack, which is easy to do because there are food vendors everywhere—not the mechanical ones dispensing stale sandwiches that you are used to back home, but living ones, carrying an entire restaurant bouncing from the two ends of a bamboo shoulder pole.

Restaurants and 'Refined Dining'

Thais entertain at home, but more often in restaurants. They prefer to eat in groups. This satisfies a gregarious nature and permits a variety of different foods to be eaten along with the rice. However, if you have to eat alone, it is quite acceptable to ask for a little of two or three different dishes.

Thai restaurant owners must be among the world's most tolerant. Except for a few pretentious (and expensive) places, you are quite free to take your own alcohol with you at no extra charge and need have no fear of commanding glasses to pour it into and ice to cool it.

Norms are changing; one fancy Patpong restaurant, trying to discourage customers from bringing in their own bottles of cheap Mekhong whisky, has a sign on the wall saying 'Cockage Charge 500 Baht'. The sign has drawn interested inquiries from male tourists.

It is even possible to take your own food into a Thai restaurant, and some hawkers make their living simply going from eating place to eating place selling dried squid, deep-fried birds (crispy all the way through to the beak!) and other delicacies that might not immediately attract the non-Thai. And if one eating shop does not have all that you want, then the chances are the shop next door will have it and somebody will fetch it for you. These norms of Thai restaurant management mean that a variety of good Thai food can be found in most parts of the kingdom. One minus point, for the visitor, is that restaurants which are really Thai (in terms of food and clientele, not ownership, which is most likely to be Chinese) close very early. Thais eat early, usually taking their evening meal at about six o'clock. The result is that most of the cheaper Thai restaurants, even in Bangkok, close at about 8:00 pm. If you go too early, it is crowded, noisy and hot; go too late and there is no food left. You are, of course, no more required to eat at a cheap Thai restaurant than is the average Thai, and you will have absolutely no problem finding places to eat at any hour.

Really refined dishes are unlikely to achieve the sophistication or refinement of the restaurant near soi Convent that claims to serve royal dishes prepared in a traditional way. An equally upmarket but perhaps better value alternative is Cabbages and Condoms, the only restaurant I advertise by giving its name because the customer gets a good deal, and all profits are said to go towards sex education and AIDS-prevention programmes.

Cabbages and Condoms

This famous restaurant is the brainchild of Mechai Viravaidya, who for several decades has led the campaign to make condoms fun, the best way of getting any message across. At first concerned with a runaway population increase as a contribution to poverty, Mechai sought to change the image of condom use. That he succeeded is evident in the fact that the common word for 'condom' in Thai is now 'Mechai'. Just one of his efforts is this excellent restaurant, which would rate among the best for food, location and décor, even without the thought that in paying the perfectly reasonable bill, you are contributing to the prevention of the spread of AIDS and other STDs. Located a very short walk from Sukhumvit on soi 12 [tel: (02) 229-4610], it has some excellent examples of Thai cuisine, yet is also popular with foreigners. One thing I particularly like is that unlike many upmarket restaurants, the atmosphere is informal, prices are reasonable, and Thai whisky is served by the bottle. At the entrance is a gift shop where you can buy some of the most original souvenirs of Thailand you will ever find, and all for a good cause. Booking is sometimes necessary for larger groups. While open for lunch, the one drawback is that it closes around 10:00 pm—but you can finish your meal if ordered before then.

At first, the average Thai menu, especially if it is transliterated or translated into very special English, may sound a bit strange; cow pat, eggs in horse's urine, mouse's droppings and elephant's penis soup may not appeal immediately to every visitor. But after a few experiments involving raw vegetables, burning chillies and various strange parts of unknown animals, many visitors begin to enjoy eating in Thailand almost as much as the locals. Thai cuisine is now renowned worldwide and plenty of Bangkok restaurants now cater for non-Thais to the point of spicing-down Thai dishes to suit an international palate. But if you are in a place with a menu, especially one with some English translation, you have already moved up a notch or two in refined dining.

Eating Habits

Eating habits are informal. Most people eat with a fork and spoon, the spoon held in the right hand and carrying the food, and the fork being used to push food onto the spoon. The one exception to this appears to be spaghetti (noodles by another name), which for some inscrutable reason is eaten with a knife and fork.

In the countryside, the fork is often dispensed with. When eating sticky rice with side dishes, fingers of the right hand are all that is necessary, a manageable lump of rice being broken off, squeezed into a flattened ball in the hand and dipped into a side dish. Chopsticks are rare except in Chinese homes. The Thais use them only for eating noodles and *popiah* (spring rolls). It is also rare to find salt on the table; instead Thais use the salty *nam pla* (fish sauce).

Sitting at a table, or sitting on the floor in a circle around the food, you are free to eat your food with fewer protocol restrictions than exist back home. It is, however, considered odd to eat when standing or walking; unless, of course, you are at a cocktail party.

As in most cultures, it is not polite to talk with the mouth full or to lick fingers; and it is not done to appear to be too greedy, although it is normal to show that you appreciate the food by eating enough of it. The fact that it is all there in front of you means you can pick and choose as you wish and you don't have to worry that another course is coming or not coming (unless eating real Chinese). You also don't have to worry that a delicacy you would rather avoid will be placed on your plate or in your bowl (unless eating with Vietnamese-Thai).

When you have finished the rice on your plate, it is probable that somebody will offer you more; if they don't, you can simply serve yourself. Compliments about the quality of the food are in order, and you should have no problem sounding sincere. Your first ten words in Thai are likely to include *aroy* (tasty), and your second ten words will include *aroy mark* (very tasty). Thais do not expect Westerners to be able to eat spicy hot food (some Thai food is very hot!) and you need feel no embarrassment about refusing something that is too hot for you; in fact, it is sensible to do so.

Paying

You do not, of course, offer to pay for a meal if somebody has invited you to eat at his house. In Thailand, the same convention applies to eating out: the inviter pays. This rule is clear enough between Thais, and should be readily understood by the visitor; if you like somebody enough to invite them to eat, then you foot the bill. There are, however, many situations where no clear invitation has been made. In this case the rule is: the superior pays.

If the eating/drinking circle is composed of near equals (or if you would like to think it is), it is still not Thai custom to 'go Dutch'. The value placed on generosity means that somebody will offer to pay, preferably you. The moment to make this offer is when everybody is ready to leave. Learn fast the Thai for 'bill please', so that, having ensured all have had enough, you can simply ask the waitress and she will bring the bill to you. (The word 'bill'—or *bin* in Thai—will be readily understood in most Bangkok restaurants.) A man who repeatedly fails to pay, or acts in a way that would confuse and even insult his Thai companions by offering to reimburse the payer for his share alone, would be thought of as mean; Thais would refer to him as *khi nio*, which can be translated as 'sticky shit,' the implication perhaps being that it is very difficult to get anything out of him! Such a reputation would not only damage your social life but would seriously affect your social status—and your business opportunities.

Paying for the group is such an established norm that if you board a bus with friends and, as often happens, you get physically separated by the ebb and flow of the crowd, your friends, upon seeing you pay the bus boy, will ignore him when he gets to them. If you find yourself frequently in the position of the superior, at least when the time comes to pay, console yourself with the thought that Thais are treating you with respect by allowing you to treat them with food. If this sounds a bit too much like buying respect and status, then you are already beginning to understand the Thai system.

Refined Dining

Refined dining looks a lot more like the picture on the front of your Thai cookbook than the usual daily spread of the average Thai. Unless it is a special occasion, people do not have the time or inclination to carve their vegetables into flowers before they eat them. The differences between everyday dining and refined dining are not in the order of eating. In both cases, everything is served at once, or almost at once. The main differences are that refined dining includes dishes that often take a long time to prepare (not always, even the common *som tum* has its place in a refined restaurant), and in the presentation.

Somewhat paradoxically these archetypical Thai restaurants usually serve Western wines (Chateau Nongkhai has yet to catch on, but it does exist, give it time). They are expensive and don't really cater for the regular customer. They are, however, places where you can be sure of finding real Thai food, and where you can usually specify with a reasonable degree of accuracy if you want it normally spicy, less spicy or—and this is a bit of a waste—not spicy at all. Menus in such places can be extensive, but they will always include the popular dishes listed in this chapter (refer to 'Ten Popular and Traditional Dishes' on pages 190–191). And if you eventually become more adventurous in your choice of Thai restaurants, you will certainly need a place you can take visitors from home, who will want to experience Thai cuisine, but who will not regret the experience.

HAVING FUN

CHAPTER 7

'Have fun and you will live forever.'
—Sign in English at U Mong forest
meditation temple in Chiang Mai

THIS BOOK, BY ITS NATURE, tends to focus more on problem areas than on aspects of the country which draw visitors to 'Amazing Thailand' (the slogan of the visit Thailand year). Its primary aim is to help non-Thai visitors come to terms with cultural and material differences and to help them settle in as quickly as possible and with as little heartache or hassle as possible. This is not a guidebook advising you on places to visit, stay and eat, although occasionally such advice is included as a way of understanding 'problems' or making the best of them.

With this chapter, I take a more positive approach to enjoying things Thai and Thailand. My assumption is that many of the material and basic cultural problems that you might encounter are now understood and hopefully resolved, or on their way to resolution. I am also aware that Thailand, for Thais and non-Thais is supposed to be *sanuk*—another one of the ten basic words that you will probably pick up within your first few days—which means fun.

You will still be having problems with the Thai language (perhaps until the day you leave!) and you will still be trying to come to terms with Thai business culture, where it differs from your own, but you can learn Thai, even the Central Thai of Bangkok, on a trip to other parts of the kingdom. You need breaks from the office and your work partners, although sometimes it is a good idea to *tio*—another basic word and concept; it means 'trip', usually in the enjoyable sense—with them. Chapters on language, business and work will follow, but let's take some time off now to begin to have fun.

FESTIVALS

While I have not counted, it is possible that Thailand has more festivals than any other country. The dates of festivals may vary, as some are determined by the (adjustable) lunar calendar and some by the Gregorian (Western) calendar. Only those on the Gregorian calendar are given a specific date in the calendar of major festivals and ceremonies in the following pages.

The Tourism Authority of Thailand (TAT, 1600 Phetburi Road; tel: (02) 250-5500, with 22 offices in Thailand and 16 overseas) lists most of the festivals with dates for the coming year in 'Major Events and Festivals'. Thai calendars will carry—on the Gregorian calendar for the year—indication of the dates of most religious ceremonies, some festivals, and full-moon and new-moon days (although some get them wrong). Articles on upcoming festivals are carried in in-flight magazines, particularly the domestic *Sawassdi* (you will probably learn this word even before leaving the plane on arrival, it means hello and good bye and has the same Sanskrit origin as *Swastika*!) carriers.

I have not distinguished too much between festivals (essentially secular) and ceremonies (religious), since there is usually an element of one in the other, and it is convenient to list all at one go. (Almost all, that is, there are too many local ceremonies and festivals to list them all.)

All festivals are—and must be—fun, and many are public holidays, with the banks and government offices closed. This does not necessarily mean you have to give your servant time off (except at Thai New Year), but be aware that for many Thais, there is no such thing as an annual holiday and these events are a Thai alternative. They like to enjoy them as much as they can, so eating and drinking are a part—a large part—of any festival. The fact that some of these festivities are fabricated rather than traditionally spontaneous does not worry the Thais. If there is no festival, the Thais invent one.

MAJOR FESTIVALS
January

- New Year (I January, Gregorian calendar)
  Public holiday. Not traditionally Thai and no religious activity. But lots of parties (just like in the West).

- Phra That Phanom
  During one week, pilgrims come from all over Thailand, and from neighbouriang Laos, make merit at the most sacred *that* (tart), stupa, in the north-east, in Nakhon Phanom.

February

- Chiang Mai Flower Festival
  Date decided by local authorities depending on weather and flower blooms. Chiang Mai has many cool season flowers and this ceremony was created just a few years ago by the authorities as a tourist attraction before the hot season, at a time when most flowers are in bloom. It is now a favourite among Thais and is marked by competition to produce the best flower-covered floats in a long parade that includes the almost inevitable Beauty Queen, chosen for the occasion, and the almost compulsory classic and folk dancing, with plenty of long-drum and *khern* pipes playing, in the streets. Much drinking involved.

- Makha Puja
  The full moon of the third lunar month (the first is in December). Mixes festival and ceremony. Celebrates the first major teaching of the Buddha, when 1,250 monks came spontaneously to visit him. Evening sermons in most wats (temples) are followed by a triple candle-holding circumbulation (*vientien*—always clockwise) around the *bot* holding the main Buddha images. Public holiday.

- Phra Nakhon Khiri Festival
  This is another fairly recently fabricated festival but one of historical and architectural interest, rather than another excuse for a booze-up. Wats are lit up with candles or

electric lights and there is a sound and light show on Khao Wang, a hill overlooking Nakhon Kiri town and the site of a former royal palace. There is much Thai classical dance and drama throughout one week. Tourist bus trips make the run, usually for one day but sometimes with an overnight stay and concentrate on the sound and light performance.

February–March

- Chinese (and Vietnamese) New Year
  Lion dancing and firework displays in most urban centres, where most Chinese live. Lasts three days, during which many restaurants are closed for at least part of the time. At this time, the visitor will realise just how many of his Thai co-workers are of Chinese origin or have Chinese relatives to visit and eat with.

March

- Gem and Jewellery Fair
  A Department of Export creation. Trade shows are held in large Bangkok hotels. If you are in the trade, or just want some sort of guarantee of buying a genuine article, this is useful.

- Phanom Rung (Last week of the month)
  Takes place mostly in a well-restored Khmer temple complex in Burinam Province. With its procession up Phanom hill and impressive sound and light shows, it is akin to the Phra Nakhon festival.

April

- Chakri Day (6 April)
  Commemorates the founding of the Chakri dynasty in 1782. Public holiday.

- Songkran/Thai New Year (13–15 April)
  This is a mixture of the religious and the secular and considered a time for excessive fun by the Thais, although the foreigner might get fed up with the constant throwing

of water. The religious part consists in bathing Buddha images in the main temples (many Thais consider it good luck to do this in nine temples, although some pay children to do it on their behalf) or when they are taken out for a *tio*, receiving blessings from the monks, and releasing fish or birds or other animals into nature (carrying away any bad luck of the last year). At the height of the hot season, Songkran certainly helps you cool off. However, the gentle water-blessings of the past have now given rise to water battles, often by competing pick-up trucks. Things go on for much too long in Chiang Mai, where the population is not only swollen by Chiang Mai people returning from work elsewhere but by many visitors from Bangkok, who drink to excess and find it fun to throw icy water full blast in your face—without taking out the chunks of ice first. Many foreigners confuse the Thai words Songkran (with an 'n') and Songkram (with an 'm'), since final consonants are barely pronounced. An alternative is to say the easier *pi may* (new year). For once, their confusion is understandable. Even the Thais in Chiang Mai are retreating indoors with colds near the end of festivities. Sometimes, the Thais admit, you can have too much of a good thing.

May

- International Labour Day (1 May)
  Public holiday.

- Coronation Day (5 May)
  The king presides at a ceremony at Wat Phra Kaew. Public holiday.

- Visakha Puja
  15th day of the waxing month in the 6th lunar calendar. This single day commemorates the Buddha's birthday, the day of his enlightenment, and the day of his death, all of which took place on the same day of the year. It is worth going to a *wat*, even if you understand none of the sermons, for the chanting (in Pali language) and to see

the Thais in quiet reflective mood. There are hauntingly quiet *vientien* triple circumbulations of the main Buddha image, with each person holding a candle (with paper or card guard to prevent the wax falling on the hands) held in a *wai*.

May-June

- Phi Ta Khon
Held originally in Dan Sai District of Loei Province and beginning to spread to other places. Like many festivals, including Songkran, this has religious origins and celebrates the day many *phii* (spirits) grouped to greet the Buddha. Origins are now largely forgotten, although the legend does reflect the peaceful meeting between animism and Buddhism. In Europe, Christianity was established after five million people were burnt at the stake, in Thailand, non-believers and believers have never shown any antagonism towards each other. This festival is an excuse for a very wild party in which Thais dress as they imagine *phii* would appear, using their imagination and liberal coatings of paint, masks and wearing carved wood and bone phalli (representations of the penis). Visitors in cars may be stopped in the street and asked for money or contributions to buy alcohol. You are, of course, always invited but most foreigners decide that discretion is the better part of valour.

- Boun Bang Fai (Rocket Festival)
Rockets, packed with gunpowder and some so big they can only be transported by pick-up, are taken to open fields in many areas and send off whizzing into the sky, one after the other. The purpose is to attract a good rainfall in the north-east and hence a good rice crop (normally this festival only takes place in the north-eastern, Lao-influenced parts of Thailand). Even if it is absolutely pouring with rain at the time, it still takes place—after all, a lot of work has gone into building the rockets and it is a good show. If you have transport, find a comfortable spot in the field, where temporary cafes will serve you food, beer

and alcohol on tables, with chairs to sit on, and enjoy the free show. It is amazing how every show seems to attract a downpour towards evening—but this is the beginning of the rainy season.

- Royal Ploughing Ceremony
  At a time set by the Court Brahmins (captured centuries ago from Cambodia and of high status), the king begins the official 'first ploughing'. This always takes place on Sanam Luang (Royal Field—open to all), near the Royal Palace and Thammasat University (and Khao San Road!). Thousands of Thais watch and swarm onto the field afterwards to collect the blessed grains of rice, either for their own use or for sale. The field is never used for growing rice, but this provides an occasion to see the king (who is always in public) and one of the oldest and revered ceremonies in Thailand—which remains predominantly agricultural.

July.

- Asaanha Puja
  Commemorates the very first sermon by the Buddha.

- Candle Festival
  In the north-east, the beginning of Phansa (Buddhist Lent) is marked by a parade of carved wax candles, most of them very large and ornate. Especially huge in Ubon Ratchatani. The candles are thereafter placed in the various *wats* during the three-month Lent period.

- Khao Phansa
  The beginning of the three-month Buddhist Lent which coincides with the height of the rainy season. Young men are ordained at this time, particularly if engaged to be married, and should remain monks for the full three months. Civil servants have a right to take leave during this period. Monks should remain in their temples, legend has it to stop them trampling on the rice seedlings! They are not allowed to take part in productive work outside of repairs to the monastery and

At the end of the Royal Ploughing Ceremony, crowds rush onto the field to collect some of the royal grains, which they mix with their seed stick to ensure a good harvest.

teaching (sometimes all subjects in simple village schools). Ordinary people are supposed to spend the time in reflection and listening to the monks. In fact, visits to *wats* increase during this period, at least in part because many Thais have relatives and friends who have ordained and because *boun* made at this time (essentially by giving to the *wat* or its monks) is magnified. Alcohol consumption is said to drop, and there are few large organised parties. Marriages do not take place during Phansa and prisoners on death row are not executed—meaning that the weeks following the end of Phansa are characterised by marriage and execution.

August
- Queen's Birthday/Children's day (12 August)
  A public holiday. The Grand Palace is ablaze with lights. Children's day coincides because the queen is considered the mother of the nation.

September
- Boat Races
  In Bangkok, these spectacular boat races are held on the

Chao Phrya River near the Rama IX Bridge. The swan-neck boats may be inspected in various *wats* near the river and some of the oldest are now in the National Museum. In the north-east of the country, international boat races take place between Thailand and Laos. This is the time when the rivers are full but not dangerous.

- Narathi Wat (Last week of September)
  At the very opposite end of the country, in one of the southernmost towns, there is a week of festivities in which both ethnic Thais and ethnic Thai-Malays participate in a fair which includes boar races, bird-singing contests, handicrafts, and southern dance and music. The king and queen usually attend.

September–October
- Vegetarian Festival
  During nine days in Phuket and surrounding areas, Chinese-Thais may eat occasional vegetarian meals or go the whole nine days vegetarian. Much merit-making in the Chinese temples. At the end of the vegetarian period, many fortune tellers and spirit mediums will demonstrate their skills by piercing the skin and walking on burning coals.

October–November
- Kathin
  A time for making merit after *ock phansa* (the end of Buddhist Lent). Many Thais group together to hire buses or other vehicles to go to a *wat* far from their homes, where they make merit by distributing robes and other needs to monks. This is followed by a string of marriages and marriage feasts.

October
- Chulalongkorn Day (23 October)
  Public holiday in commemoration of King Chulalongkorn, the great reformer, who is now the subject of a cult centred around his statue on Ratchadamnoen Nok.

November

- Loi Khatong
  One of Thailand's most beautiful and peaceful festivals. This is of Indian origin. On the full-moon night, *Khatong* (lotus flower-shaped boats made of banana stems or polystyrene) carry burning incense, candles and a few small coins, together with the wishes of the *loy* (launcher) down to the sea, or as far as they can get before being upended by some small boy who pockets the coins. As some small boys are paid to swim out and *loy* a *khatong* in a river current, their friends are busily emptying the contents intended for the river goddess. Nobody minds. Best in Chiang Mai or Sukhothai.

- Surin Elephant Roundup (Third week of the month)
  Elephants take part in tugs of war, football matches and pretend warfare. This north-eastern town is packed, so reserve accommodation early. Much drinking and while children will enjoy the shows, it may be best to have them back in the hotel at an earlier hour than normal. Be aware also that while elephants are revered and well behaved in general, there have been accidents, often involving children. And one does not argue with an elephant.

- River Khwai Bridge
  The death railway has been cleaned up and tourist rides are now available where a few years ago there was only jungle and all transport was by river. The festival started after the success of the Alec Guiness movie, *Bridge on the River Kwai*. The bridge tourists gaze at is a comparatively new one, the old one being destroyed by allied bombing during WWII. Good sound and light shows and historical exhibitions. The scene may be visited at any time of the year, not just at exhibition time.

December

- King's Birthday (5 December)
  Public holiday. Celebrated throughout the kingdom, with each province putting up large pictures of the king and

holding special events in aid of various causes. There is no better democratic exhibition of the people's love for their monarch.

- Constitution Day (10 December)
  Public holiday that commemorates the establishment of the constitutional monarchy in 1932.

LIFE-CYCLE CEREMONIES

As noted above, ceremonies often carry an element of festival, and festivals often start out as religious ceremonies. There is, however, a clear distinction between those ceremonies related to the life-cycle and festivals open to the public at large. Life-cycle ceremonies tend to take place in the home, although they may progress from the home to the *wat* (from private to public spheres) or from the home to a restaurant (which remains private in the sense of a private party, but is in the public domain).

I make no excuses for including life-cycle rites here. They should all have an element of fun, even funerals, although at the proper time and with appropriate constraints. While essentially private and therefore with an almost obligatory participation of relatives and real friends, the visitor may expect to be invited to such ceremonies of any of the members of his staff, or simply people known well or people who would like to know the visitor. It is at these 'private' ceremonies that the visitor sees the family, and many relatives and friends, and the core of community existence.

Private ceremonies are usually distinguished by invitation— usually an elaborate invitation card in the case of a marriage—but you may equally be invited just the day before or on the morning itself. This is quite normal and the visitor should not feel he has been included as an afterthought. There is no obligation to attend birth celebrations, marriage ceremonies, funerals or others, but the invitation by card, with your name on the envelope, does imply that you will give back the envelope (not another one) with some money inside. How much you give will vary. If you don't know the person and cannot find out who he is, you are justified in forgetting the invite. If the invitation comes from your boss or a close co-worker, such as your assistant or secretary, you are almost obliged to attend, but certainly obliged to give fairly generously (which means more than the Thai will give).

As you continue in Thailand, there may simply be too many invitations, especially during the marriage month, and you cannot accept them all. Some people, however, do manage to fit three or more events into an evening. But don't refuse them all, even if some are more of a chore than an entertainment. They are part of the package that fits you into Thailand and the Thais, and you presumably do not want to remain forever an outsider. Refuse all invitations and you will be cutting yourself off from the important occasions for Thais and losing out on what can be, or should be, fun. And life and work without any fun is just not Thai. People will wonder why you came to Thailand. You might wonder that yourself.

THE THAI-NESS OF THAI CEREMONY

Ceremony, like power, is amoral. It is yet another way of manipulating known and unknown forces. Secret societies, boy scouts, gangsters, spirit mediums, policemen, little old ladies and newborn babies; in Thailand, every organisation and every individual takes part in ceremony. Birth and rebirth cause suffering. The many ceremonies of Thailand are part of man's attempt to overcome that suffering and break the circle.

Private and Public

If you come home to find your colour TV set missing and burning incense and flowers in its place, it is because the *khamoy* (thief) took the time to placate the spirits of the house and ensure his safe getaway before fleeing the scene. He might never have got into the house at all had you gone to the trouble of keeping the *phra phoum* spirits happy, or maybe the real blame lies with the person who built the house, who perhaps skimped on the house-warming ceremony.

Apart from the private *khamoy* escape ceremony, which is dying out as *khamoys* lose their panache, most other ceremonies take place in public either on the street or in the *wat*, or both, and show no sign at all of dying out for at least one very good reason: they are good fun.

No public ceremony is taboo for the (uninvited) non-Thai and your presence will be welcomed, as long as you follow the basic rules of good manners. Not all of these are as easy and obvious as 'shoes off at temple door'.

Comfortable Fun

Strolling through the grounds of an upcountry *wat*, you are welcomed by a group of villagers having lunch and, at the inevitable invitation, you sit down and join them. Bottles of rice whisky are passed back and forth. Cigarettes, hand-rolled in leaves, are lit and relit. People are chatting and joking and everything is very *sabay* (comfortable) and *sanuk* (good fun). What's going on? A wedding, a big win on the lottery, somebody's birthday? No, none of these. Look around you, see people dressed in black and white? Chances are it's a funeral.

Unless you are Irish, you might be a little surprised to see people enjoying themselves at a funeral, or more properly, after a funeral. In Thailand, whenever people get together to eat and drink, it is fun. This in no way demonstrates lack of respect for the dead. Plenty of tears have been shed in private and in public before you came on the scene. Real mourners (close family) have done a lot of work and gone through a lot of ceremony before you came along. On the day of the funeral itself, they will serve breakfast to whoever comes along, friends or relatives, work mates or neighbours. You would certainly be welcome to come, just deposit your envelope, with something inside it, discreetly on the tray at the entrance. This is not the moment to bring out the Johnnie Walker.

Once the body has been cremated at the *wat*, and you have been served cold refreshments, the dead is on his way to a new life. If the deceased was a good person, the next life will be better than the last: reason to rejoice, not to be sorrowful. And if the deceased wasn't all he might have been, it is only good manners to ignore that at his funeral and, for the sake of his family, behave as if you are sure he would be reborn as a prince and not a puppy.

ONE CONTINUOUS CEREMONY

Life in Thailand often seems like one continuous ceremony. There is no end to it. I have place to consider only the major life-cycle ceremonies: birth, puberty, ordination, marriage and death. I pick five out of a multitude not because there are any real do's and taboos (apart from those already mentioned) for the visitor to follow if he should be present at any of these occasions, but because they show us a lot about the Thais. Particularly, they demonstrate the compatibility of Buddhist and animistic (belief in spirits) aspects of life in Thailand.

Some characteristics of Thai ceremony are so common that the visitor cannot help but wonder about them. The most obvious of these are a sacred white thread, the number three, auspicious timing and money.

White Thread

If your wrists are tied up, don't call for the police until you are sure your host is not making a gesture of welcome. Tying pieces of white thread, called *sai sin*, onto the wrists (but not tying the wrists together!) is a way of wishing somebody safety and good health.

The thread is not always white (some monks use red or another colour) but white thread is found in many ceremonies and usually takes the form of a circle. All participants at a pre-ordination ceremony sit in a circle holding a single long thread between the thumb and first finger of both hands, which are raised in a *wai*. At funerals, the thread is carried in a circle three times around the crematorium. At weddings, the thread links the twin circles of the heads of the couple being married.

The white thread works as a kind of spiritual telegraph, carrying merit along a line or around a circle. When circles of this thread are tied on your wrists, they serve to help you retain all your good power, while protecting you from the potential dangers of the spirit world. The circle is particularly

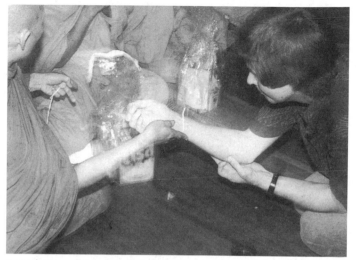

A monk ties *sai sin* onto a *farang's* wrist.

powerful because the protective qualities continue on their trajectory infinitely.

To refuse *sai sin*, if it is offered, is like refusing the person's hospitality. However, although the thread is sacred, or semi-sacred, in Buddhist ceremony, it is only as sacred as good manners when tied around the wrist. One Christian missionary told us he felt as if he were being strangled when *sai sin* were tied on him, but most non-Thais find that the biggest problem with *sai sin* is that they don't know what to do with it once they have got it.

Some visitors find their wrists covered in *sai sin* and, afraid to offend by taking it off, wait forever for it to drop off. One *farang* I know had his wrists tied up just before leaving the north-east, where the custom is particularly rampant, to return home to England. A great lover of the Thais and fearer of spirits, he waited for two threadbare years back in the UK before the circles finally disintegrated and fell off naturally. People looked at him rather strangely in the pub.

It is somewhat rude to take *sai sin* off right in front of the person who has just so charmingly tied it on. But it is quite all right to do so when you have left them and (to play it safe with the spirits) after arriving back home. Ideally, it should be kept on for three days or longer.

Three

Number three, you will notice, occurs time after time and, of course, after time. Buddha, Dharma (the teachings of the Lord Buddha), Sangha (the monastic order). All good things come in lots of three.

Timing

Along with threads and the number three, many ceremonies also have the idea of timing. Everybody, including the king and government leaders, consult astrologers when conducting important ceremonies or implementing important decisions. Important firsts, like putting up a spirit house, laying the first brick or board of a home and sowing the first seed, together with dangerous, 'chancy' things like setting off on an important mission to slay a dragon or getting married, all require trips to the professional astrologer or the local amateur fortune-teller, who will set a propitious time for the event (usually very early in the morning).

If your Thai friend invites you to come to his wedding between 6:19–6:27 am, he means it. This is one occasion

Important 'firsts' (openings, sowing of seeds, new arrivals, etc.) require ceremony. Here, His Holiness the Supreme Patriarch anoints the nose of the Thai Airways Company's third Boeing 737 before it goes into service.

when things happen on time. If you don't want to go to the actual ceremony, it's quite all right to go along to the wedding feast in the evening. In fact, most guests are invited only to the feast, which is a celebration of a marriage already taken place. It is in the evening when you drop your envelope, with your name clearly on it, in the heart-shaped box.

Three Weddings, but No Funeral

During the busiest time for marriages, I was invited to yet another wedding. It was a good friend, so I thought I should go. It was to be held at the first of three hotels, all large and next to each other. I checked with the host, yes it was the first—the hotels all had the same name and owner and were distinguished as 1, 2 and 3. It was definitely the first.

I arrived shortly after time and was surprised when the line-up, just forming, welcomed me and said I was early but never mind good to see you and have a drink. My friend was nowhere in evidence and I recognised no faces. I popped my envelope in the box and sat chatting with other early guests. The food was as bad as always at these occasions, a tasteless potato-based soup, and the bottle of Scotch on the table was a cheap Thai copy. I thought this strange as my friend was very rich. It was only when the party was in full swing that the bride and groom visited each table to share a toast and I realised I knew neither of them.

Enquiries revealed that there was another wedding next door. Nobody minded and I was shown the way to the next-door wedding, which by that time was in full swing. I looked for my friend, couldn't find him and resorted to the mobile telephone. After some confusion trying to meet up in the huge hall, since all wedding parties are built around a dance floor, I discovered I was again at the wrong wedding. Some laughter, no problem, my friend came to get me, two hours late, and already drunk, I arrived at the correct wedding, only to explain that I had put my envelope with 1,000 baht into the box of an unknown couple. He and his new wife found that funny. "I thought you said Number One Restaurant," I explained. "What I said was the first restaurant," he corrected. "But we came from different directions." Anyway, it was fun.

Money

Money, the fourth common characteristic, speaks for itself. It is often in open evidence in Thai ceremonies. Sometimes it is used symbolically, but more often it is simply an ostentatious display of the host's status and power. Ceremonies vary in grandeur according to the wealth of the people involved, but even the very poor have something of a ceremony at important stages in the life-cycle. Money circulates at these events according to well-established norms of reciprocity.

Money usually changes hands inside envelopes. These may be put on a tray or in a box or passed to one side unopened, but someone somewhere will note exactly who gave what in order for the family to reciprocate when roles are reversed and hosts become guests.

The non-Thai visitor is, of course, outside this circle. Never mind, you will still be fed. Without thinking of anything as vulgar as paying for your dinner, you might like to pursue a course of 'instant reciprocity' at ceremonies and related feasts, which can be very expensive for the host. This is quite acceptable. Don't count the money out, but the price of a good meal with drinks is all right (more if a good friend or colleague is directly involved). With or without an envelope, hand the money directly to your host, explaining if you like (although not at a wedding) that you wish to *tham boon* (make merit). He then grants you a favour by accepting your money, rather than you granting him a favour by giving it.

This is very much like the feeling of everybody involved in the giving of food to monks on the morning alms round. Far from begging or receiving charity, the monks provide laymen with an opportunity to make merit; it is the laymen who feel gratitude and offer thanks through the *wai*.

One of the most obvious examples of ostentatious use of money is the taking of a 'money-tree' for presentation to the *wat*. A money-tree is a miniature tree, formed from sprigs of branches, with banknotes stuck on as leaves. It is carried by the family (or leading members of an organisation) through the streets with much dancing and drum playing to make everybody aware of what is going on. If you are held up on the road by spooky dancing 'bandits', faces painted white and whisky bottles passing, you should give a banknote or two to the money-tree.

A public display of pecuniary piety, the money-tree procession builds religious merit for those involved and also increases secular status. Having money, displaying money and giving away money are important marks of status.

Some visitors find this obvious and ubiquitous use of money

Carrying money-trees and new robes to the wat.

conflicts with the romantic idea they would like to have of how Thais live in peace and cooperation. For some reason, the sweet-scented flower garland loses something of its charm when a hundred baht banknote is ostentatiously clipped to it. But without money, there would be no ceremony, no food, no drink and no fun.

Ceremonies, and the reciprocity they involve, maintain Thai communities. Money, instead of destroying social relationships, can help to maintain them. Money is neutral. But the more of it the better.

BIRTH
The precise time of a baby's entry into the world is a key factor in Thai fortune-telling. Karma of past lives causes an individual to be reborn in a certain situation, in a specific place and at a precise time. For this reason, birth time is noted as accurately as possible and will be used 30 days after birth for the first of many fortune-tellings.

Making a Soul
Soon after birth, the baby is the centre of the *tham khwan sam wan* ceremony. The name means literally 'making a

soul (after) three days'. This is the first of many *tham khwan* ceremonies an individual will undergo at important stages in life or whenever he is sick or depressed. On future occasions, he will go to a Buddhist monk to request a *tham* (make, (re)make/sustain) *khwan* (spirit matter, soul) but monks play no role in this first ceremony, which is entirely animistic.

The rationale behind this ceremony is that a baby is sent into his mother's womb by a spirit. It is debatable how many Thais actually believe in this these days when family planning and anti-sexually transmitted disease campaigns include such beautiful Thai-isms as monks blessing piles of condoms, campaigners handing out visiting cards which bear the Buddhist scripture, 'Many births cause suffering' and have a brightly coloured contraceptive attached, and the slogan, 'Space your next pregnancy with a pig' (a reference to the free piglet given in some areas of the country to families who practise family planning) and which is sometimes written on a pig!

A young girl who pleads with an angry father that the baby in her womb was sent by a spirit is, these days, likely to be thrashed until she reveals the name of the 'spirit'. Sceptical as they are of 'immaculate conception', many village Thais still prefer not to risk incurring the wrath of the spirit-mother by forgetting to hold the *tham khwan* ceremony (although few urban Thais now feel it necessary).

The three-day-old child is placed on a wicker winnowing tray and rocked gently from side to side, a symbolic separating of 'grain' from 'chaff' and good from bad, while the spirit mother is told 'three days (old) a spirit child, four days a child of man, whoever's child this is, come take him'. An old woman (never the mother) then 'buys' the child by offering a coin to the spirit. If the spirit tries to get its child back in the future, it will go to the wrong 'mother'. (Sometimes spirits can be very easily tricked, especially when money is involved!) In the past, but rarely today, the child would have a candle burning above its bed throughout the following month. Even if there is no formal third day party, you can drop in anyway. You may give money to the mother or you may give a present—functional things if the family is poor.

Taboos

Pregnant Thai women are traditionally surrounded by many taboos, which, among other things, prevent them fishing, eating chillies, telling lies or visiting the sick and attending funerals. Contravention of these taboos puts the baby's health at risk. Although few women would attend a funeral when pregnant, most, in Bangkok at least, are today quite happy to dismiss the stricture against eating chillies as 'silly superstition'. Very few Bangkok mothers now confine themselves next to a hot, smoky stove after childbirth (this was traditionally required for between 7–21 days), although this is still practised widely in the north-east.

First Haircut

If the child survives a month, the parents give a feast for relatives and friends and the baby has its first haircut. This ceremony is called *tham khwan duan*, literally 'making the soul (after) one month'. As with the first, this *tham khwan* protects the newborn from evil spirits, who like to make themselves at home in the hair. More public than the 'three-day' ceremony, it announces to the world that the baby has been born, has survived the most dangerous period of its life, and is ready to be introduced to the Buddhist community.

Three

The magic number three is very evident in both of these ceremonies, the first taking place three days after birth and the second 30 (in Thai 'three tens') days after birth. This number is also evident in the fact that nine monks are invited to chant from the scriptures at the 30-day ceremony. Nine is clearly three times three; in Thai, the pronunciation '*kaw*' means both the number nine and 'to advance' and is therefore especially significant for marking birthdays.

Naming

A Thai is given his name by the parents, who often ask a monk or an elder to select an appropriate one or the first letter or syllable of the name. This name is of two or more syllables and is used for all official/legal purposes. These names are Sanskrit in origin and always have a good meaning (long life, sun, light of happiness, etc.). In addition to this 'real' name, almost all Thais possess a nickname, inevitably of one syllable and meaning something like frog, pig, rat, fatty or many variations on tiny. The use of a nickname is tied up with the idea of avoiding the attention of spirits. Using a person's real name during the first 30 days of life could cause the spirits to focus their attention on the baby, with unfortunate results. Today, most Thais continue to use their nicknames throughout life and many do not know, or ever think to ask, for the real name of their friends.

Compliment-insults

In addition to the use of nicknames, none of which is complimentary in literal translation, babies might be deliberately referred to in disparaging terms. The origin of this practice is the belief that spirits are attracted to the beautiful. Whether modern Thais believe this or not, it is still possible to hear one mother 'complimenting' another on her *na kliat* (ugly) baby, and just or more frequent to hear someone say 'how cute'.

The process of compliment-insult suffers in translation and the visitor's natural instinct to compliment parents on their beautiful baby is likely to be understood by anybody who speaks enough English to understand the words spoken. Indeed, it is now common for Thais, particularly the younger generation, to ignore the spirits and compliment in much the same way as *farang* do—although not all *farang* would feel particularly complimented on being told how white and fat their baby is. While being aware of the Thai custom (just in case somebody compliments you on your wretched frog of a child), it is advisable to avoid entering into the spirit of things even if you can say it in Thai. "Oh my, what an ugly little monster you have", said in English or Thai, is not likely to endear you to the middle-class Thai who spent ten years at Harvard!

It is considered good fortune if a female baby looks like her father and a male baby looks like his mother. Very frequently one hears Thais say, "She looks like her father"; even when said straight to the mother, it is a compliment combined with something of a blessing. Similarly, telling a father that his son looks like the mother does not cast any doubts on paternity. The visitor, having established the sex of the child, can safely follow this common custom.

BIRTHDAYS

Thais consider every 12th year of life particularly significant and will usually mark it by giving a special party at the house and inviting nine monks to chant. Most important is the 60th birthday, which often marks a withdrawal from the active world.

The visitor should be aware that Thais often invite people to their home on birthdays. They may not mention the reason for celebration when making the invitation, but this may be discovered by asking another guest. No special gifts are required and none are inappropriate. Flowers and fruits are always acceptable on any visit to a Thai home and (Thai) women will often help to prepare food. The woman visitor is not expected to join them, but need not fear insulting her host by bringing along some homemade or shop-purchased cakes.

Please remember that flowers, fruits and Thai cakes are cheap in Bangkok; your gift should therefore be specially

On significant birthdays, nine monks are invited to chant in the home. Note the practice of chanting with faces hidden behind fans and white thread carrying 'good vibrations' from the monks to the lay participants. Note also the sideways sitting position of respect.

packaged with a reasonably expensive presentation. A plastic bag of Thai *khanom*, however delicious, is out, a *farang* cake from a hotel or bakery of repute is definitely in. *Farang* chocolates, in nice boxes, are expensive in Thailand and will be appreciated: they are worth stocking up on during trips overseas. A purse, even a branded one, may be purchased cheaply in Thailand. It is appropriate if there is something in it—nobody wants an empty purse or wallet.

PUBERTY

The visitor may be surprised to see some Thai children with their heads closely cropped except for a long topknot. This is done in preparation for the *khon chuk* or 'topknot cutting' ceremony. At this event, the topknot is ceremonially cut off by a Brahmin priest and the child is blessed by Buddhist monks. Relatives and friends are then invited to a *khon chuk* feast.

This ceremony marks the onset of puberty and takes place either in the child's 11th or 13th year, but never in the 12th. The reason for this is usually explained by the belief that odd numbers are lucky whereas even numbers are generally unlucky. However, the 12th year of one's life is not regarded as unlucky. It is the completion of the first 12-year cycle and a time for celebration. The taboo on performing this ceremony during the 12th year may have something to do with the fact that the 12-year calendar was introduced from China, while the *khon chuk* ceremony (like most Thai ceremonies) is of Hindu-Indian origin. (Some 'Brahmin priests' trace their ancestry back for centuries but they are Thais, not Indians. They remain significant in the royal household, but much of their role in popular ceremony is now performed by Buddhist monks.)

The *khon chuk* ceremony is less common today than in the past and many parents do not bother with it unless their child has been sick frequently, in which case a spirit medium might advise that the ritual be performed. It remains sufficiently popular for large numbers of children to present themselves at a royal-sponsored ceremony for the poor held each March, in which topknots are ritually cut by a Brahmin from the royal household.

ORDINATION

Ordination into the Buddhist order of monks is often seen as a ceremony marking entry into the adult world of responsibilities. Most Thai men *Buat Phra* (enter the monkhood) at some point in life, usually just before they get married. Many remain in the monkhood for only a short period, sometimes just a few days, but more often throughout one Phansa, the three-month Buddhist Lent which coincides with the rainy season. For this reason, most ordinations take place in July just before Khao Phansa (beginning of Lent).

Eligibility

To *Buat Phra*, a man must be at least 20 years old and physically fit and free from contagious disease, must not have killed his parents or a monk, must have obtained his parents' permission and must be free of family and other economic responsibilities and debts. To these traditional requirements a new one has been added: a man must have completed at least four years of schooling.

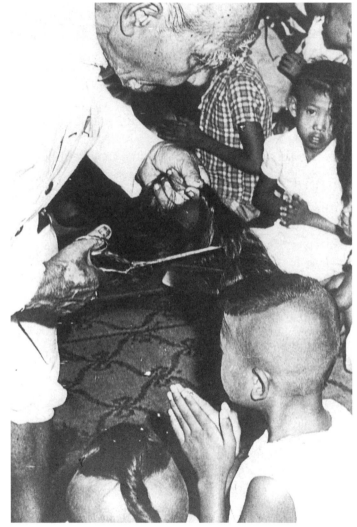

Large numbers of children present themselves at a royal-sponsored ceremony held each March, in whick topknots are ritually cut by a Brahmin from the royal household.

Motive

The purpose of becoming a monk remains what it has always been: to acquire a deeper knowledge of Buddhist teachings through study, self-deprivation and meditation, to progress along the path to enlightenment (the overcoming of all suffering) and to bring merit to one's parents.

Women

Women cannot become monks and therefore try their best to persuade their sons or husbands to ordain. Thai women do not regard this prohibition as in any way 'sexist', although many may tend to compensate for this natural disability by accumulating as much religious merit as possible; the vast majority of people seen offering food to the monks on the morning alms round are women. If a woman creates enough merit in this life, she will be born as a man in the next.

Nuns

Some women become nuns by shaving their heads, wearing white robes and obtaining permission to live in nun's quarters on grounds within the temple. They, too, are fed by the laity but they do not make the alms round. They are supported directly through food, daily requirements and money presented by the lay population to the *wat*. Their daily routine is as near to that of a monk as it can be, much of their time being spent in study, meditation and counselling of lay people.

The vast majority of people seen offering food to the monks on the morning alms round are women.

Although expected to lead good and celibate lives, nuns are not bound to their vows in the same way as monks and they do not officiate at any ritual activity, although they will help out when the demand is simply too great at certain times, e.g. at Songkran, nuns sit nearby the monks and tie on sacred, blessed threads to the wrists of the multitude of devotees. During ceremonies, they sit with the lay people, not with the monks. Some young girls become nuns for a set number of days in order to keep a vow made during a period of sickness or to mentally and socially absolve themselves from the result of past bad actions and present problems and misfortunes. Such temporary nuns do not shave their heads and some are more serious than others.

Nuns must conform to the taboo against females touching a monk or his robes or handing him something directly. This taboo is not extended to nuns—the male or female visitor who wishes to hand something to a nun may do so directly.

Vows

Before a man becomes a monk, he is required to learn by heart the long request for ordination, which he must say in Pali, the language of the scriptures. He should also contemplate the meaning of the 227 rules of conduct a monk is required to keep. The most important of these are the vow of celibacy and the strictures against taking life, eating any food after midday, indulging in magic and taking intoxicants. If any monk feels he can no longer keep his vows, he may request the abbot to release him from them, at which point he returns to lay life.

Sukhwan Nak Ceremony

The ordination ceremony is the most Buddhist of Thai religious rites. It is preceded by a lay ceremony, the *sukhwan nak*, which functions to protect the candidate for ordination from the powers of evil spirits. The candidate is particularly vulnerable to accidents during the period between having the head shaved, which sets him apart from other men, and obtaining the safety of the monastic order. During this period he is known as a *nak*, literally a 'dragon', a name which refers to a Buddhist myth of a dragon who wanted to be a monk. The use of this term emphasises the transitional nature of the candidate who is neither layman nor monk. Perhaps the term functions in the same way as nicknames, to confuse the spirits, who would think twice before attacking a dragon.

The *sukhwan nak* ceremony takes place either in the candidate's home or in the *sala* of the *wat*. If long and elaborate, as it always is for a *phu yai's* son, it takes place on the evening before ordination. Alternatively, it may precede the ordination service and may sometimes be omitted completely, the prospective monk simply having his head shaved by a monk, a relative, or even a barber.

The *nak's* head and eyebrows are shaved as a symbol of repudiation of vanity and sexuality. He is then dressed in white and is the centre of an elaborate ceremony in which no monks participate although they may be present. The *sukhwan nak* is conducted by a professional master-of-ceremonies who, together with his assistant, sings for up to three or four hours, recounting the pain and suffering of the mother in giving birth and emphasising the importance of fulfilling filial obligations.

This ceremony concludes with all relatives and friends sitting in a circle holding the protective white thread and then passing three sets of three lighted candles in a clockwise direction, an action known as *vientien*. (A different form of *vientien* occurs when, instead of passing the candles, these are carried three times around the outside of the *bot*, the central sanctuary of the temple, on the occasions of the Buddha's birthday in May and Khao Phansa in July.) It is customary for guests to give money, either attached to flower garlands and hung around the neck of the *nak* or deposited on a tray provided.

Ordination Ceremony

Any visitor, including women, may attend an ordination ceremony. If invited s/he may contribute to the needs of the monk during his time in the *wat*.

At the *sukhwan nak* ceremony, friends and neighbours give banknotes. These are often attached to flower garlands and hung around the neck of the *nak*.

The following morning, the *nak* is carried on shoulders under tall umbrellas in a colourful procession to the *bot*. After parading three times around the *bot*, the *nak* throws coins into the air, an action which symbolises rejection of material pleasures (a rejection eagerly awaited by little boys who scramble for the money), and is carried over the threshold into the *bot*.

The *nak*, still dressed in white, goes down on his knees in prostration before his father who hands him the saffron robes he will wear as a monk and leads him to the abbot who waits with at least four other monks (usually many more) seated on a raised platform in front of the main Buddha image. After three prostrations to the abbot, the *nak* asks for permission to be ordained. The abbot holds the hand of the *nak*, recites a scripture on the impermanent nature of the human body and places a yellow sash on his body to symbolise acceptance for ordination. The *nak* is then taken out of view and dressed in saffron robes by the two monks who will be responsible for supervising his instruction. He then requests the ten basic vows of a novice monk, repeating each as it is said.

In the past, it was usual to spend several years as a novice before full ordination. Today, the prerequisite of four years' education serves the same purpose and the two ceremonies usually follow one immediately after the other.

The father of the candidate presents the alms bowl and other gifts to the abbot, who places the sling of the bowl over the candidate's head to rest on his shoulder. The candidate then stands facing the Buddha and answers questions designed to make sure the basic conditions for entry to the monkhood are upheld. The two 'teacher monks' then request other monks present to accept a new member and give a sermon on the behaviour expected of a monk.

The ceremony concludes with all monks chanting and the new monk pouring water from a silver container into a bowl as a sign that he transfers all merit acquired through being a monk to his parents, who subsequently perform the same rite to transfer some of the merit to their ancestors (who, of course, have been reborn somewhere and benefit from this action). Thus the central ceremony in the life of a Thai man reinforces his identity as Buddhist, cuts him off from his family and marks adult maturity, and at the same time strengthens the link between generations and emphasises the importance of family and community.

The abbot places the sling of the alms bowl over the candidate's head.

MARRIAGE
Choosing Partners
It is perhaps characteristic of the independent nature of the Thais that an individual generally selects his or her marriage partner without too much outside interference. (Although things are moving in this direction throughout Asia, few Asian families allow their children as much freedom as the Thai.) Parents can, however, influence the choice of partner. This seems to be particularly the case among wealthy or influential families, but it is also true that most marriages in the villages tend to take place between members of two families of similar economic and social status. There are no ethnic or religious restrictions and intermarriage is common, particularly between Thai girls and *farang* men.

Types of Marriage
Wedding ceremonies vary between the very elaborate and the non-existent. A couple may be fully recognised as husband and wife simply by living together for a time and having children. Thus, people can become 'gradually married' without any fuss or ceremony (and, just as easily, become gradually divorced!). However, most parents prefer their children to have some kind of ceremony and within the upper echelons of society, an elaborate and expensive wedding ceremony is essential.

Thais are legally required to register marriages at the district office, although there is no penalty for failing to do so and many do not. Only one legal marriage is allowed at a time. A well-off man may, however, have several *mia noy* (minor wives). *Mia noy* of today have no legal rights, but their children are recognised as legitimate under Thai law. Divorce is easy for either party to a marriage and requires only that both sign a statement of mutual consent at the district office. If only one party seeks divorce, it is necessary to demonstrate desertion or non-provision of maintenance for one year. The divorce rate, official and unofficial, is high by any standards and divorce is usually followed by remarriage.

Wedding Ceremony

Wedding ceremonies are usually held, if at all, only to mark the first marriage. The two families agree beforehand on the expenses of the ceremony and the 'bride price' to be paid. The wedding day begins with the couple feeding the monks in the early morning and receiving their blessings. A procession of gifts from the house of the groom to that of the bride was usual in the past but is less frequently seen today. The wedding consists of the couple kneeling side by side, the groom to the right of the bride. At an auspicious time, chosen by an astrologer or a monk, their heads are linked with joined loops of *sai monkon* (specially prepared white thread) by a senior elder who then pours sacred water over the hands of the couple. The water drips from their hands into bowls of ornately arranged flowers. Guests then bless the couple by pouring water in the same fashion.

Monks may be present, but the Thai wedding ceremony is essentially non-religious and no vows are made to love and cherish (and certainly not to obey!) until 'death do us part'.

Heads linked with joined loops of *sai monkon*, a couple's marriage is blessed by a respected elder who pours water over the hands of the bride and groom.

It may be significant that the white thread that usually unites everybody in a single circle is, in the wedding ceremony, formed into two linked but independent circles. Individual identity is retained but destinies are linked.

Variations on the basic ceremony are many. Certainly, most weddings are much shorter and less elaborate than in the past. In many rural areas, the 'sympathetic magic' of having an old couple, evidence of a successful marriage, 'prepare the bridal bed' continues to be practised. This semi-farce requires the jolly couple to lie on the bed before the newlyweds and chatter away saying lots of auspicious things like 'This bed seems very lucky to me, I think whoever sleeps on it will have lots of children and be rich …'

The old couple then get off the bed and place on it many symbols of fertility and prosperity including a tomcat, bags of rice, sesame seeds and coins, a stone pestle, and a bowl of rainwater. The newlyweds should share their bed with these objects (but not the tomcat!) for three days, which probably explains why most middle-class couples today prefer to leave after the wedding party for a honeymoon in Phuket!

The Inevitable

If you do manage to find excuses to stay on in this wonderland of a country, and learn some Thai, you will become very used to the question, "Married already or not yet?" It is always asked in this way. There is no possibility of escaping the event, it's simply a question of when. If you are unmarried, you are obliged to answer "not yet". This is really the only answer possible in Thai, even if you are a confirmed homosexual. With time, the repeated 'not yet' begins to sound somewhat deviant, particularly if you are 39 years old (and have been for the past ten years).

Finally, you bow to the will of the majority and tie the circles with a Thai. You will still be asked, "Married already or not yet?" but now, a responsible human being at last, you can answer proudly "Married already". The pride will last just until the next question, "Have children or not yet?" And when you do have three little children climbing over you as you wait in the maternity hospital for the fourth to be delivered, the chap next to you will ask, "What your name?", "How old are you?" and "Married already or not yet?"

DEATH

Of all life-cycle rites, Thais consider the *ngarn sop* (cremation ceremony) to be the most important. Funeral rites mark not only the end of a life, but the start of a journey towards rebirth. Death is seen as a transition, a natural and necessary part of life.

Rebirth

If an individual is seriously ill, friends and relatives will help him to direct the mind to the Buddha and Buddha's teachings. This provides the dying with psychological comfort by preparing his mind for a good rebirth.

Belief in reincarnation is essential to the Thai view of life and religion, which maintains that an individual's material existence is determined by a spiritual balance of all of his or her good and bad actions (karma) and that the course of existence, in this life and the next, can be changed by making *tham boon* (religious merit). Because of the importance of these 'rites of passage' from one life to another, they are usually as elaborate as a dead person's relatives and friends can afford.

Preparing the Corpse

After death, the corpse is bathed by members of the family, perfumed, dressed in new clothes and laid out on a mat. Relatives and friends line up to bless the departed soul by pouring water over the right hand of the dead body. A one baht coin is placed in the mouth (to enable the dead to buy his way into purgatory), the hands are placed together in a *wai* and tied with white thread. Between the palms are placed a banknote, two flowers and two candles. The ankles are also tied with thread, the mouth and eyes are sealed with wax and the corpse is placed in a coffin with the head pointing towards the west, the direction of the setting sun and of death.

At the head of the coffin a lamp is kept burning to help the soul find its way to the west. Near it are placed personal objects such as the deceased's sleeping mat, blanket, plates, food and clothing and a knife, for use in purgatory. Visitors help family members to prepare the funeral feast and make merit by giving a small banknote to the family. These notes are often fixed on bamboo sticks and planted like flags into the sides of the coffin.

During the three days following death, monks receive their morning meal from the family of the deceased and chant in the house. In small villages with only one or two monks, messengers are sent out to neighbouring villages to invite monks to attend the funeral. The presence of monks is essential.

The Funeral

The coffin is carried out of the house feet-first. In rural households built on stilts, the jar of drinking water outside the house is turned upside down and the house ladder is reversed in a symbolic negation of the world of the living to discourage the ghost from returning home.

Family members, carrying a picture of the deceased, a tray of tinder to start the funeral pyre and a jar in which the remains will be collected, lead the funeral procession to the

Family members carry a picture of the deceased and monks lead the funeral procession to the crematorium. Behind the coffin walk the men of the village, who are in turn, followed by the women.

crematorium. Behind them, monks, walking in pairs (for funerals only), hold the sacred white thread which is fastened to the foot of the coffin. Behind the coffin walk the men of the village and behind the men, the women. Rice is scattered to placate the many spirits attracted to funeral activities.

On arriving at the *wat*, the coffin is carried three times around the crematorium (which was in the past and still is in remote rural areas, an open funeral pyre). The usual practice of clockwise circumambulation is reversed on this occasion, continuing the symbolic negation made at the start of the funeral procession. Coconut water is then poured onto the face of the corpse by a pair of monks who are followed by a long queue of relatives and villagers who bless the dead by pouring scented water onto the body.

The string is detached from the foot of the coffin and fastened at its head. Monks chant the *suadnitcha*, which tells of the inevitability of suffering and death as the white cloth (symbolising death) is lifted from the coffin by the most senior monk present, the coffin is placed into the crematorium or onto the pyre, and the body is consumed in flames.

It is customary to hold a funeral feast in the *wat* grounds. Everybody is welcome. Guests avoid bright colours, and relatives wear black and white, the colours of mourning, but this feast is not a sad occasion.

That evening, and for the following two evenings, monks will come to the house of the dead person to chant the *suad paritta monkhon* to bless the departed soul and protect the living. Chantings are followed by parties, open to all visitors, when people eat, drink and play games with the direct intention of making family members happy. There is no more reason to be sad; the departed is advancing along the great cycle of death and rebirth towards the ultimate state of existence, the state of perfect peace.

HOBBIES AND SPORTS

Your image of the average Thai is perhaps changing by now. Impressions of the Thais, at least those held overseas, are at best out of date. The image of the laid-back Thai, sitting and watching his rice grow, and tackling problems with a *may pen rai* (never mind) attitude is possibly changing to one where the Thai is very active, often holding down two jobs at a time, studying English and other things in his or her spare time, getting up early to prepare food and feed the monks and constantly engaged in giving and attending ceremonies and festivals. It now seems somewhat amazing that they find the time for a full social and material life, and somehow manage to strike a balance between the two. A few decades ago, any talk of Thai life would have included *may pen rai* from the first page, even within the title. This book has just got around to mentioning that it exists, or perhaps existed, but it is no longer a national philosophy.

Full as traditional and modern-economic life is, many Thais find the time for ever more activities. And these are activities in which the visitor can join in fully, to the extent he wishes to do so and is able to do so. These hobbies, perhaps new to the visitor, will, if he makes a selection, strike that balance that I come to expect in things Thai. At the extremes, we have Thai martial arts and Thai meditation, in between we have *tai chi* (a Chinese import), Thai massage (the traditional kind), classical cooking and food preparation, and the slow dreamy but muscle-stretching Thai dancing. The visitor is not likely to do all of those, and others besides, but there is certainly no shortage of things to do, for both men and women, in Thailand.

Thai Boxing

What could be more Thai than *muay Thai*, or Thai boxing. Fish fighting perhaps, cock fighting, bull fighting? Lots of fighting going on there, but the one that has captured the attention of the sports world, and of a lot of young *farang*, is Thai boxing. This requires a commitment from Thais and the same commitment is expected of foreigners, who must in addition learn enough of the Thai language to get by.

For many western foreigners, conformity poses a problem. The training system, rather like the primary school system, and very similar to Thai meditation practices, is based on conformity, not innovation or the whims of would-be prima donnas. A very basic diet and humble accommodation are part of the whole thing. Not all training establishments will accept foreigners. Those who do usually insist on a residential course. This is cheap at US$ 50–250 per week, including food and accommodation and equipment. The upper-end will have air-con bedrooms; for the rest, roughing it seems par for the course. A fairly full list of training establishments and information on the sport is included at the website: http://www.muaythai.com. Thai boxing is becoming increasingly international, but remains firmly based in Thai traditions and methods. Training is open to both men and women.

Thai Meditation

Foreigners have become respected monks within Thailand. Many Thais even acclaim them as preserving Buddhist teachings and values as so many young Thais rush into modernisation. Such monks are the exceptions. Most foreigners will be more interested in learning meditation techniques to help them cope with, understand and even enjoy the stresses of life, often with a material objective of improving their disposition and thereby their work performance. Others will find meditation fun— a different kind of fun to filling a glass with whisky and soda or sucking on a joint—the fun of seeing a different world, and a nicer one.

There is nothing to prevent a foreigner ordaining as a monk or living as a nun, not even his religious affiliations. One can, as far as Buddhism is concerned, be Christian, Jewish, Muslim, Hindu or whatever. Those other religions might not accept dual-religion with the same tolerance as Buddhism, which is something to think about before getting too involved in the religion/philosophy of Buddhism.

On the other hand, there is no need to ordain in any sense at all. Visitors are welcome to live in many temples and participate fully in life, without taking any vows or changing their clothing. Indeed, many Thais go on weekend retreats to forest *wats* with much the same objectives as foreigners. It may be said that they are addicted to meditation, but this is only to say they are addicted to the search for understanding and eventual peace (which for Christians, but not for Buddhists, passeth understanding). Most temples use a variety of methods, one of the most Thai being perhaps walking meditation, in which every movement of the body is mindful and understood. Several temples have foreign or Thai monks who give special classes in instruction in meditation in English. For more information, read *A guide to Buddhist Monasteries and Meditation Centres in Thailand* from the World Fellowship of Buddhists in Bangkok, website: http://www.dharmanet.org.

Thai meditation employs two basic systems. The first, *samatha*, which is essentially stillness of mind and advanced states of concentration (which of these comes first is part of the thing). This is similar to other meditation techniques employed in different religions and different parts of the world. A more specifically Thai system of Theravada meditation is known in Thai as *vipatsanaa*, which observes and studies the way the mind and body act together through thought and action.

Visas for Foreign Monks

Foreign men intending to study Buddhism through ordination as a monk should get non-immigrant visas, which will probably be renewed as long as the robes are worn. Unfortunately, since there is no official order of nuns, women will need to make the tourist run—unless they are on some other visa such as an over-50 retirement visa.

Massage and Cookery

Not just for the expat's wife, but something that is almost guaranteed to be appreciated by any husband is a course in Thai massage or cookery. Many courses and books exist on these subjects and both may be followed to the extent desired. Learn to cook for your family or friends, or learn a whole new vocation that you can use back home. It all depends how much you want to put into it. The need to know the Thai language is more limited here than in most hobbies. The centre for traditional Thai massage is acknowledged as

Wat Po in Bangkok, although some other schools offer a softer approach that is based on pressure points and finger tips rather than setting one part of the body against another.

There are many schools on cooking, perhaps the most serious is the UFM Food Centre, 29-39, soi 33/1, Sukhumvit; [tel: (02) 259-0620-33]. Language of instruction is in Thai—this is after all a school to produce Thai chefs—but an English-language class can be arranged for at least four English students. Other courses may be advertised in the English-media press and *Yellow Pages*.

Teaching English
This may be approached either as a hobby—the rewards being small but your exposure to Thais being great—or as a profession. For the latter, unless you have the best qualifications and several years experience, you are not likely to earn much more than the basic cost of living, and perhaps to lose in the process any sense of fun. Thais are very keen to learn English and there is no problem in finding private students. Other more interesting jobs (for young foreigners) may be found outside Bangkok, at local schools, where you will receive very little but make many friends. One website that advertises teaching jobs in Bangkok is http://www.ajarn.com. Otherwise, look regularly in the *Bangkok Post/Nation*.

Diving
Diving courses can be found in any place where there is a beach and foreigners. This is, of course, because of the usually ideal diving conditions and the abundance of tropical marine life. Much of the attraction, for marine life as for the foreign observer, stems from the reefs lying offshore. As these get eroded, not least by the activities of divers themselves, the attraction will falter. Some diving schools realise this and teach responsibility as part of a built-in package. Unfortunately, many do not and instruction is widely varied. Try to go with a teacher experienced in the area, who will know the easy dives and the dangers. Similarly, lessons can be taken in windsurfing and sea canoeing. Always make

sure you always go with an experienced person who knows the tides and can not only guide you into an amazingly private little world inside an ocean's rock formations, but also guide you out.

Nightlife

Nightlife is not usually considered as a hobby or sport, although it takes on both roles for a number of expatriate men. But it is, or should be, fun—when there is no drunken brawl or argument going on, which the visitor will find less in Thailand than in some other countries.

Thailand is famous (or infamous) for nightlife and prostitution, and the two usually go together. Bangkok's main areas of bars, restaurants, girly shows and massage parlours are Patpong I and II off Silom, and soi Cowboy and soi Nana on Sukhumvit, areas well-frequented by foreigners. Patpong also has an excellent bookshop (which provides an excuse for frequenting the area!), some good places to eat and a lively open-air shopping area. It also has rows of swallows sitting on the wires overhead to mark every parked vehicle with evidence of a visit to the sin centre of Bangkok.

Generally, foreign women accompanied by foreign men are quite welcome to see what is going on in the bars. One sight not to be forgotten is the huge massage parlours on New Phetburi Road. You may find several guidebooks on the bar scene in Bangkok, Chiang Mai, Phuket and Pattaya. And every Friday in the *Bangkok Post*, Bernard Trink's 'Nite Owl Page' will let you know what is happening in the main nightlife areas of Bangkok. In an attempt by the authorities to keep the whole of Bangkok from becoming one big go-go bar, naughty nightlife is being zoned. Areas mentioned above are all within the new zones. (But new ones have popped up outside Bangkok and cater for the mobile and upwardly-mobile.)

Although it might seem that Thailand's nightlife is all bars and bargirls, this is not so. Hotels have nightclubs and discos, and some bars offer live music. There are some places frequented by gay men and others by gay women, and others almost entirely teenage, and others where all this is mixed up. Reportedly, there is also a place where only straights go, although I have yet to find it.

Museums

Public national and provincial museums are normally open daily except Mondays, Tuesdays and national holidays. Private museums and art galleries, of which there are many, often close on Mondays.

The National Museum is on Na Phra That Road, next to Thammasat University, between Sanam Luang and the Phra Pinklao bridge over the river. New arrivals are advised to see this impressive museum first (and to return periodically). Free guided tours are available in English, French, German, Japanese and Spanish (times vary, so inquire inside). Buy the guidebook to find your way around. If you are interested in being a volunteer guide, ask the management—you would certainly learn a lot.

The museum houses the largest collection of Buddhist art and pre-Buddhist era artifacts in South-east Asia. Originally a palace, the museum opened in 1928 and maintained its spacious and breezy ambience, making this a pleasant place to be. It is closely affiliated with provincial museums throughout the country, many of which try to approach its excellence. You can find information on all the other museums and a range of books and booklets on all things Thai here.

Fitness Centres

The climate and streets of most Thai towns are not conducive to walking or jogging, and many expats prefer to exercise in an air-conditioned environment. If you prefer the lonesome approach to staying fit, and your apartment block does not provide an exercise room, you may profit from the fact that various fitness equipment is made in Thailand, or brought in cheaply from China, and sold at reasonable prices in supermarkets or through advertisements. Most people however, feel the need for some sort of a support group to keep them at it and take out a membership at a large hotel or independent fitness centre, where facilities often include swimming pools, tennis and squash courts, saunas, jogging tracks, and a full range of equipment with trainers to show you how to use them.

There will certainly be a fitness centre near your home or your place of work, and most people follow the recommendations of work colleagues rather than look in the *Yellow Pages* (sensible since there is a large social element to fitness centres and being in a group will perhaps keep you at it longer than the 50 per cent who drop out in the first month). Two of the cheapest places to get your exercise are the YMCA (27 Sathorn Tai) and the YWCA (13 Sathorn Tai). If you rise with the lark and feel a less violent need for keeping the body moving as it should, any park or open space will have *tai chi* sessions (5:00 am–7:00 am), which are really not just for the old and past it.

Cinemas

When not tied to a Thai drama on Channel 7 of their box, Thais love going to the movies. Many cinemas are excellent, with spacious, comfortable and well-arranged seats. But before you get too comfortable, remember to stand up for the national anthem, which is played before the film. Foreign films are usually dubbed in Thai, but cinemas often have an original soundtrack showing. Some cinemas have a sound room where the original soundtrack is played while the rest of the cinema gets the Thai version. Get information on cinemas, what's on, and times of original soundtrack shows, from the English language media. Call to reserve the best seats.

English language newspapers will also provide details of 'minority interest' films screened at the Alliance Francaise, AUA, British Council, D K Film House and Thai German Cultural Association (Goethe Institute).

Arts, Crafts and Enlightenment

The foreigner looking to continue an interest or hobby should have no problems in Thailand. If looking to develop new activities, he or she has a choice limited only by time available.

The Skytrain in Bangkok passing through modern offices and shopping centres. The transportation system in the city is convenient and efficient and adds to the appeal of Bangkok as one of the most popular travel destinations in Asia.

There are many beautiful temples in Thailand which are well worth a visit for their cultural and religious significance, as well as for their unique architecture.

A floating market in Ratchaburi province. Fruits, vegetables and other produce are sold from the boats and the vendors paddle up and down the waterways selling and bartering their merchandise.

Exclusive beach resorts in various parts of Thailand cater to well-heeled travellers and boasts breathtaking views, luxurious surroundings and impeccable service.

Religion plays a significant role in the everyday life of the Thais, particularly in the rural provinces, and monks are held in high esteem.

Many of the activities listed here are available at the YMCA or YWCA. In addition, several institutions offer classes in art, pottery, cooking, Thai music and dance. University and school teachers are also available to teach on an individual or small group basis.

For a more Asian kick, try *feng shui*, *tai chi*, Thai boxing, *tokraw* or yoga. Meditation classes and practices are readily available in English at leading Buddhist temples in Bangkok and Chiang Mai. Many of the teachers are foreign monks or ex-monks with many years of experience in Thailand. Try Wat Bovornivet or Wat Mahatat (inquire from any foreign monk), or contact the World Fellowship of Buddhists on Sukhumvit between sois 1 and 3 [tel: (02) 251-1188].

Reading

Thailand has long had a tradition of reading and prints all Thai-language books within the country. It is normal to see Thais reading (mostly light novels) while waiting for transport or even when hanging on a careering bus. Bookshops and stalls are to be found in most shopping centres. Naturally, the majority of books in any shop are likely to be in Thai, but specialist Japanese bookshops exist in several malls and any bookshop is likely to have an English-language section.

Like any bookshops in the world, books can only be kept on the shelves for so long. But most shops in malls are branches of larger companies and may be able to locate on computer—and have brought over from another branch, if you have time to wait—copies of what you are looking for. Worth asking, and better to write down the author and title than rely on purely verbal communication. The biggest bookshop, in terms of stock, distribution and branches is definitely Asia Books [soi 15 Sukhumvit; tel: (02) 252-7277 is the largest one], with DK a close second in terms of branches (Bangkok, Chiang Mai, Ko Samui, Phuket). Once again, let your fingers do the walking and look to the *Yellow Pages*. While prices of books in the Thai language are usually cheap, English-language books, being imported or of only minority interest tend to be as high as those in Europe.

In recent years, there have been some serious new publishing houses, concentrating on academic Thai subjects in English (White Lotus, Silkworm). Piracy remains a problem, although perhaps a smaller one than in the past (although no case has ever been taken to a Thai court). There has also been an increase in legal reprints of old texts, often with engravings (Oxford in Asia led the way). The academic section remains generally small however (sometimes you might find some out-of-print book in an English-language secondhand bookshop attached to a guest house, worth a browse). Most English-language books fall into three categories: fiction (some good, most international best-sellers, and many written by resident expats who barely step outside Bangkok's bars), books on Thai subjects (including coffee-table photo books, guides and language courses) and books on management (mostly bought by Thais, who seem convinced they will advance in their career by following foreign management methods; rather the opposite point of view to that in this book!).

LEARNING THAI

CHAPTER 8

'Your language shows your country origins.
Your manners show your family origins.'
—Popular saying

THE THAI LANGUAGE

Thai-speaking foreigners are no longer the novelty they were in Thailand, but speaking to Thais in Thai is still necessary in most places not specifically catering for foreigners. In all cases, your efforts to speak Thai will be appreciated and open the way to interaction that is unlikely to be there if very stilted English is all you have between you.

Foreigners, if they are honest and can remember, will tell you that for a Westerner (or for that matter a Japanese, Indonesian or African) who speaks no tonal language, Thai is difficult. Be that as it may, the existence of foreign Thai-speakers stands as evidence that learning Thai is not the quasi-impossibility it was imagined to be just a generation or two ago. Today, many schools, kits and books are available to help you on what remains a difficult and time-consuming task, but one that should bring more joy and fun than grief and frustration.

While you will be busy on arrival and inclined to put off learning any Thai until later, this is not always the best idea. Often, as an expat gets into his work, he finds he has less rather than more time to spend learning Thai, and bosses are always more sympathetic to providing time and funds for language learning at the beginning of a stay. And it is at the beginning of your stay that you are going to be meeting a great number of Thais, not all of whom will speak good English.

Some companies provide a short crash course before their staff arrive in Thailand, or give them a few weeks or months to begin learning Thai immediately after they are in the country.

Thai language schools and private teachers vary between the very good and the very bad. If you pick a bad one, never mind how nice and pretty the teacher is, make an excuse and take another. (Try not to pay for a course in advance, and if taking a 'free' trial lesson, and are satisfied, make sure that you will be taught by that teacher and not another, unless you agree.) Plenty of schools and individuals advertise in the English press. Complete beginners, who can find a few hours a morning or evening might do well to enrol in the consistently good AUA at 179 Ratchadamri Road [tel: (02) 252-8170].

The AUA takes in a new batch of students every five weeks for intensive (three hours per day) or regular evening classes. There is also a full-time course to take beginners through to spoken and written fluency (the *por hok*, sixth grade level, which equips you, if you are so inclined, to work in the government school system, but a complete beginner will need to count on 12-18 months to get there). The choice of learning methods can accommodate a variety of foreigner's needs. You learn in small classes (maximum eight people) of mixed nationalities. And because the school is actually meant for young Thais who wish to learn English, there are plenty of pleasant people on whom you can practise your Thai while sitting in the cafeteria.

A good language laboratory is open at set hours to all students, and offers the best drilling in pronunciation, particularly tones and vowel lengths. The AUA prints course books for learning Thai that go along with the graduated structure of the language lab tapes, and although at first glance most may look dry and unappealing, they offer the repetition that is so necessary to learn any language. So even if you don't attend their courses, consider buying the books (and tapes) from the AUA office. (*Other schools are listed at the back in the* Resource Guide *on page 339.*)

Learning Thai is not usually considered a good enough reason to be in the country to obtain a visa, and even teachers at the AUA and similar schools are usually on regular visa runs to the Cambodian border and back. Those enrolled in full-time Thai studies will have an easier time getting their non-immigrant visas extended.

Characteristics of Writing Thai in English

As if Thai was not difficult enough, there is no official or generally acceptable way of transcribing Thai words into English. There is something called the Royal Thai General System (RTGS), but this does not distinguish vowel lengths and has been heavily criticised for misleading as much as it leads in constructing a real Roman script pronunciation system. For example, every Thai wants to make merit, this merit is called *boon* or *boun* (rhymes with soon) but the RTGS writes it in Roman letters as *bun*, which a Westerner is likely to pronounce as the type of cake that rhymes with fun and sun. Making merit and making cakes are not the same things. It sometimes seems as if foreigners are being deliberately misled. This is not the case, but when a perfectly reasonable Romanised approximation exists (e.g. *meuang* instead of *muang*), failure to use the closer approximation does, at best, lead to further confusion.

Each guidebook or dictionary has its own pronunciation guide. Many, like the AUA, produce nice clear tone marks over vowels and double vowels when long, leaving single vowels to be pronounced short. This is fine for reading, but you cannot reproduce those tonal marks on a regular word processing programme, so to practise writing Thai in English, or I should say Roman script, it is back to pen and paper (not necessarily a bad idea). Other schools and books that use transliteration—and it is very hard to get started unless some form of transliteration is used—invent their own system of tone marks or add a letter after each syllable in parenthesis to show what the tone of the preceding syllable is (or should have been).

Outside of language instructors and instruction materials, which do at least try to produce the sound as a speaker of another language might pronounce it, I enter a fairly wild world where almost anything goes. Often a Thai letter (there are 46 consonants and 24 written vowels) is matched up with what seems to be the nearest English equivalent (in a 26-consonant, 5-vowel alphabet). As an example of what should be easily understood, let's take the familiar *sawatdi* (which, in case you didn't know by now, means hello). This contains three consonants and three vowels in the usual English written transliteration and the same number in Thai. There familiarity ends. Thai has several letters that represent the English 's' sound. Thai uses the 'rising s' when beginning this word in Thai; however, in this particular word (a very simple one), this particular 's' is pronounced with a low, not rising, tone. In fact, the tone is on the vowel, but in this word the vowel 'a', following the 's' in speech, is not written, we just go straight from 's' to 'w'.

This reflects the fact that in Thai, no two consonants are ever written side by side without a spoken vowel, written or unwritten, being inserted between them (and in the rare event that they actually are, they are pronounced as something different to both of them!). Confused yet? Well, let's continue to analyse that simple little word the hostess says to you as you get on the Thai plane in London, Frankfurt or America. It continues with a familiar 'w', which is toneless, or rather takes the tone of its syllable. 'W' in this case is connected to a second rising 's' by a second short 'a'. This short 'a', pronounced the same as the first, is written above and between the 'w' and second (rising) 's', producing another low tone syllable. Then we have the final syllable, 'di', or sometimes a little more accurately, 'dii'. This is written with 'd' wearing a hat of the vowel 'i', which in this case is long, making this last syllable mid-tone.

Let's not go through the entire dictionary. The point is to show you that you have to be very careful when looking at Thai words written in the familiar Roman script. The most usual way of saying 'no' in Thai is *may chay*, both falling tones; this is written in straight transliteration as ay-m-marker above the 'm' to make the tone fall-ay (but a different 'ay' to the first one in the phrase)–ch, with falling marker above it.

This could be written *aym'aych*. Doesn't look a lot like *may chay* does it?

Not difficult enough for you? Thais love to make their language, written in Thai, look like English. Even the airline name 'Thai' is written 'ay-t-y', but the first 'ay' is made to look like an English 't' and the last 'y' is made to look something like an English 'y'. In between is one of the Thai 't', looking like an innocent little vowel, especially if the left loop is exaggerated.

Please don't ask if it is correct to write *sawatdi*, *sawatdii*, *sawasdii* or, as the in-flight magazine has it, *Sawassdii*. The only answer is that all and none are correct. Write it and any other Thai word however you like it. This goes for name cards too. It is a good idea to check out how the Thai side of your name card sounds to a Thai reading it. It may approximate your name, it may not, but even if it does, it may have some barely-hidden meaning. Surprise is not only for non-tonal speakers. It was years before a Chinese ambassadress named Hoy Keng realised that her name had been written in Thai as Hoy (rising) Kheng (rising). *Hoy*, literally shellfish, is a very colloquial word for the most private part of a woman's anatomy in Thai, and *kheng* means hard, or in slang, ready for sex. Worth checking things out with someone you can trust!

> The Thai King's name is transliterated as Bhumibol. A 'correct' Romanisation of the Thai way of pronouncing this best-known name of all, would be nearer to Phumiphon—keeping in mind that 'ph' in Thai transliteration is always breathy, like the English 'p' (not like the French), and never like 'f' (as 'ph' always is in Vietnamese), and that 'u' is like 'oo' in look, not like 'u' in put.

Of course, the real answer is for the Thais to get around to making a realistic, accurate and official transcription of words. This was in fact considered in the 1870s and rejected as unnecessary. Meanwhile, Vietnamese has had an European-type alphabet for centuries, China has introduced one in the last century, and Malaysia has given up on trying to write Malay in Arabic alphabet and went straight to English.

Another answer might be for those wishing to learn Thai to learn international phonetics first. This is actually a lot easier than it looks, as such phonetics are based entirely on the Roman alphabet. However, it is practically impossible to find any course or course books or teachers who know the system, which requires a computer programme of its own.

So, you are stuck with transliterations that might or might not approximate the Thai pronunciation, but never render it as it should be. Thus, if you are remotely serious about learning Thai, take a bit of time to learn the letters. Learn them in words, not in isolation. You can have fun trying to read the signs on Coke bottles and above shop doorways—many of which are English words written in Thai script. You also have a double chance when tackling a dictionary, even one written in translation, since the Thai script is often there alongside the transliteration, and with a bit of practice (not that much), you will soon be able to decipher without too much pain. Then you are ready to learn Thai.

Thai is a relatively clear and relatively simple five-tone language. Of course, everything is relative. If you have learnt Chinese (Mandarin), you will have no trouble with the tones, since they are essentially the same, the mid-tone taking the place of the neutral and there being no formal tone changes as in Mandarin. (The problem for the Chinese speaker is more likely to be vowel length.) The five Thai tones are represented graphically, if imaginatively and approximately, in the chart below.

Peculiarities of the Thai Language

```
HIGH          FA
               L
               L              G
MID            I              N
                 N          I
                  G        S
                          I
LOW                    R
```

For those who have no idea what a tonal language is: each syllable, or syllables within a word, has a fixed tonal rendition. If you are looking for Noy (falling), you are enquiring after a different person from Noy (low), and if the visitor seeks to clarify by putting a rising inflection on the word—'you know, Noy (rising)'—he is likely to be told, 'sorry, no Noy (rising) here'. If you do find Noy (falling) and, in your very limited Thai, tell her (or him) they are *suway*, you will either be saying the person is beautiful or bad luck, depending on the tone you use. There are indeed a lot of people who are both beautiful and bad luck, and many of them are called some form of Noy. Noy, if exposed to the foreigner's funny way of talking might well give you the benefit of the doubt. But there is a tip even here, when you know you are likely to be saying things wrongly. This is it: there are often two ways of saying the same thing in Thai, as in most languages; Thai often joins the two together (but don't count on it). Thus they might, in saying 'beautiful' say both the Central Thai modern *suway* and the (originally north-eastern) more ancient *ngam*, making *suway-ngam*. Say that, even with tones all over the place, and you will be understood. (Of course, you have to learn to say the initial *ng-*!)

In addition to being a five-tone language (at least Central Thai is, other Thai dialects have different tonal patterns and one or two more tones to cope with—so think yourself comparatively lucky), Thai also possesses aspirated and unaspirated consonants and long and short vowels. All of these are almost impossible to transcribe satisfactorily using the English alphabet, as we have seen above. The best transcription can make nonsense of Thai, as in *klay* meaning near and *klay* meaning far, or as one of the early question-answer drills in the AUA course demonstrates:

Q: Mai mai mai mai
  Does new silk burn? (or Does new wood burn?)

A: Mai, mai mai mai mai
  No, new silk doesn't burn.

Now, as if that's not enough to put you off, imagine the above example written without any gaps between the words or punctuation:

Maimaimaimaimai

If written in Thai, that's how it would look, with Thai letters of course. Thai rarely uses punctuation, although it's creeping into novels. Instead, they simply have a short break when they feel something has changed about the written piece. One would think that Thai should take up half the printed space of English, since syllables are short and there are so few gaps. Wrong again, a page written in English will take more than a page when translated into Thai. This is mostly because although the sounds are often short, the way of writing them is not. Vowels can be written before, after, above or below consonants, or all around it, although they are pronounced after it and syllables read from left to right.

However—and thank heavens there is always a however—while Thais rarely leave gaps between written words, this is not the way they speak (unless you are a Channel 7 news reader!). Indeed, spoken Thai requires gaps (French: please pay attention). Thais speak pretty much the same way as other people, leaving gaps between words (indeed, since each syllable in a multi-syllable word has a tone and small gaps between syllables). Once you are tuned in, not just to the words, but also to the gaps, you will begin to pick out words and phrases—you are learning Thai.

Things getting a little happier? They get better. While written Thai has so few gaps and punctuation, spoken Thai is absolutely full of them. This helps to break up what people are saying into nice clear sentences, and adds meaning to the sentences at the same time. Central Thai in particular, being based so rigidly on the status system we have looked at earlier in this book, ends almost every sentence with *khrap* (man speaking) or *kha* (woman or transvestite speaking). These two little words mean nothing and everything. For most Thais, they are respectful speech habits; and they will become your Thai speech habits far more quickly than you could ever imagine. They are also the normal way of saying 'yes' or simply agreeing with the speaker to keep him going through a pause. You can't go wrong with *khrap* or *kha*.

Khrap on the Telephone

A foreigner was overheard speaking Thai into the telephone. A Thai seated nearby listened attentively. He could only hear the foreigner's half of the conversation.

"Hello (rising)"

"Khrap (high)"

"Khrap"

"Khrap"

"Hello"

"Khrap"

"Khrap"

"Khrap. Sawat-dii khrap."

As the foreigner hung up, the Thai nearby said, "My goodness, you do speak good Thai."

These useful little words tend to get dropped between friends and family and the further you are *ban nok* (upcountry), and the north-east doesn't use them at all when speaking dialect (so don't expect to hear the girls and boys of Patpong use them between themselves, although all will use them with you). Never mind. There are plenty of other particles (little words of speech) that help break things up nicely for you. One of the most useful—and overlooked in language courses—of words for the foreigner is the little *leu* (almost rhymes with fur), always spoken with a rising tone and while the vowel is long anyway, you can make this one even longer. It translates as 'did you say?', the word you are asking about going before not after: '*maa* (rising) *leu* (rising)' 'Did you say dog'? An advanced use of this little word can be very useful when listening for tones and meanings: '*maa* (rising) *leu* (rising) *maa* (high, meaning horse)'. If you don't quite catch the reply, just ask again using the simple formula: *maa leu*. Fortunately, the Thais are a lot more patient with this sort of thing than most Europeans.

USEFUL WORDS, PHRASES AND EXPRESSIONS

Learning new Thai words in established phrases is the easiest way for a speaker of an intonation, rather than a tonal, language to come to terms with Thai and begin to use the language. Thus, don't just learn and try to say 'toilet', but the sentence, 'Where is the toilet?' This will (believe it) help the Thai listener understand what you want and help you quickly build up vocabulary. 'Where is the toilet?' can easily be transformed into 'Where is the Post Office?' It makes sense in any language –imagine walking up to a stranger in England and saying the one word 'toilet'.

Having said that, I shall now not quite practice what I preach and give you a short but possibly helpful wordlist. The newcomer to Thailand should not rely on such lists. It is better to buy yourself a dictionary that has a reasonable system of reproducing Thai using the English alphabet and also has words written in the Thai alphabet, so that a Thai, not a book, can tell you how they should be pronounced. Many expats find Gordon Allison's *Jumbo English–Thai Dictionary* comprehensive enough for most eventualities, yet not of a size that prevents it being carried around easily.

Since most words have only one syllable and each syllable has a tone, sentence pattern stress does not exist in the same way as in European languages. Words with more than one syllable are usually foreign and are stressed on the last syllable. Thus, if somebody doesn't understand when you ask for a PEP-si, ask for a pep-SII and you might get it. If you manage to put a falling tone on -SII, you almost certainly will get it (most Western-origin words end in a falling tone).

The list is very limited but it is not meant to teach you Thai. Rather, it is to demonstrate that quite a lot can be communicated with just a few words. And in case you are already thinking that Thai is the most difficult language in the world, it will give you an idea of just how simple it is in terms of grammar. Thus, the time you spend learning the tones and vowel lengths is in part at least compensated by the very easy grammatical structures of the language.

As I have stated, the list is of limited use. It will be somewhat more useful if you can find an English-speaking Thai to tell you how the words should be pronounced. This pronunciation guide may be of some help if you have an idea of languages other than your own.

Vowels

- **i**   *i* as in *in*
- **ii**   *ee* in *feet*
- **ai**   *i* as in *pipe*
- **aa**   *ar* as in *father*
- **a**   short version of *aa*, as in *cat*
- **e**   as in *hen*
- **ay**   as *a* in *hate*
- **oe**   as *ur* in *turn*
- **u**   as in *flute*
- **uu**   as in *food*
- **eu**   as *ur* in *fur*
- **ao**   as *ow* in *now*
- **o**   as *on* in *bone*
- **oh**   as *o* in *toe*
- **eua**   dipthong of *eu* blending into *a*
- **ia**   dipthong of *i* into *a*
- **ua**   dipthong *u* and *a*, as in *tour*
- **uay**   *u* into *uay*, e.g. *suay*
- **iu**   as *ew* in *yew*

Unless words end in a vowel, or a nasal (*m*, *n*, *ng*) the end-consonants will be pronounced as *p*, *t* or *k*, however they are written in transliteration. You will often see the frequent male particle *khrap*, written as *khrab*: it is , however, always pronounced *khrap*.

Consonants

k   very similar to an English *g*. There is no separate *g* in Thai, so there is a tendency for foreigners to substitute *g* wherever they see *k*. This is not quite right but a lot nearer than pronouncing like the English *k*. So *kin* (eat) is pronounced more like 'gin' (but not the drink!). I call this an unaspirated and unvoiced letter.

p   close to the French *p* and half-way between an English *b* and *p*, e.g. *pay*, which means go.

t   close to the English *d*, but not quite there (Thai has a clear *d*). Unaspirated, unvoiced.

r   has made a comeback in Thai and is now sometimes over-pronounced, particularly in the media. There remains a large tendency to pronounce it as *l*.

kh   as the English *k*.

ng   can occur at the beginning of words, where it causes most trouble to foreigners. English has the sound, but in the middle of the word e.g. singer (English southern dialect only), NOT ginger.

LEARNING MORE ABOUT THAII AND

As a foreigner, you are quite free to take a course at what is the Thai equivalent of Oxford or Cambridge universities: Chulalongkorn University (always written in that word order, whether in Thai or English). Chulalongkorn—or Chula as it is affectionately known—is the only Thai university where the name precedes the word University. So (in Thai and often translated in that order) we say and write the University of Thammasat, University of Chiang Mai, etc., but always Chulalongkorn University, never the University of Chulalongkorn.

This course might be a straight academic course on a variety of subjects or it could be a course specifically for non-Thais wishing to learn more about the kingdom. Courses vary between a two-week intensive course on just about all things Thai, offered once a year in July (accommodation at the university is available), and a two-year Masters in Thai Studies (for which you should already have a first degree in any subject from any university). The two-year course is conducted primarily in English, but includes the chance to learn to read and write Thai and instruction is available from some of the leading experts on Thai culture, philosophy, politics and economy.

Contact the university directly or visit the Thai Studies Section in the Faculty of Arts. Chulalongkorn University is conveniently located if you or your spouse are living and working in the Silom-Sukhumvit area, and anybody can eat in the students' cafeterias there. The university also has several libraries, which might at first need a little orientation but can be very useful for writers and researchers; obtain permission first, usually this is no problem if you have the support of a department head.

If your interests are more directly academic and specific, don't forget the following sources of information:

- **The Siam Society**
  131 soi Asoke, Sukhumvit, closed Mondays
  Tel: (02) 661-6470
  Sponsored by the royal family, you can apply for membership and contribute to its prestigious *Journal of the Siam Society*, or you can ask to use the reference library (monographs are also on sale). The grounds also accommodate Ban Kamthieng, of interest primarily to ethnologists.

- **The Neilson Hays Library**
  195 Surawong, closed Mondays
  Tel: (02) 233-1731
  The oldest English-language library in Thailand. Beautiful colonial building right next to the British Club.

- **The National Library**
  Samsen
  Tel: (02) 281-5212
  Huge collections dating back centuries. You have to be a member, but membership is free.

THAI BUSINESS

CHAPTER 9

'If you have silver, I count you as my little brother.
If you have gold, you are my big brother.'
—Old Thai saying

THOSE COMING TO THAILAND TO WORK, or those interested in the business culture of Thailand, are strongly advised to obtain the companion volume to this one: the 2004 revised version of *Thais Mean Business: the Expat's Guide to Doing Business in Thailand* (*refer to* Further Reading *on page 343*). I cannot reproduce here all of what is said there, but can point out that anybody working in Thailand (even, theoretically, if doing voluntary work and certainly if they are staff of an NGO) should have a work permit, along of course with the appropriate visa. This chapter, in keeping with the aim of this book, will concentrate on explaining those aspects of Thai business culture that most help the expatriate achieve a comfortable fit in a reasonable time schedule.

There are institutions overseas and in Thailand that provide some exposure to the Thai business world before playing for real. The investment in such orientation, given that the average expat manager is here for a 3–5-year term, seems like a pretty good deal. Not everybody shares that view. Some HQs are even afraid that knowing too much about Thai ways might compromise the loyalty of the individual to his company or country. Views change and vogues disappear to reappear. I am not sure that current thought is moving towards helping the expatriate into Thai ways of doing business—that would seem to be in everybody's interest—but it is up to the individual companies to decide if it will increase their profits and the well-being and motivation of their personnel. With lots of foreigners now speaking Thai to some degree and lots more Thais now proficient in English, many cost-conscious foreign companies and agencies see little need for much more than a briefing on the work to be done.

In the 1970s and 1980s, Peace Corps volunteers received several months intensive training and cultural orientation before arrival, and more once they arrived in Thailand, before going off, probably to teach English in a Thai school. Very good. As we advance into the 21st century, many new expat managers, perhaps responsible for a budget of millions of dollars, are—in my view, all too often—expected to pick things up as they go along.

BUSINESS AND CULTURE

Thailand, like several other East and South-east Asian countries, has developed very rapidly in recent years, attracting substantial foreign enterprise and investment. Just about all foreign companies setting up in Bangkok feel the need to appoint at least one expatriate manager. Unfortunately, they often fail to equip the manager with the linguistic and cultural knowledge which would help him do his job in a strange country. Many Japanese and Korean companies now provide cultural orientation and Thai language training to all staff coming to Thailand. They are the exceptions. And they are doing well.

International companies and organisations, used to rotating expatriate management staff between countries, rarely furnish much in the way of orientation. Most embassies consider it enough to have one or two of their nationals conversant with Thai, Thailand and the Thais, the rest of their expat staff is provided with a cultural bubble within which their social and material needs are met more or less as they are back home.

Almost all embassies have national clubs and organisations which are overwhelmingly expat and usually open to anybody living in the country. They might conduct classes in English, French, Japanese or German culture and language for Thais. They are, with some exceptions, unlikely to provide any class in Thai culture and language for their expat nationals.

Fine, if the expat is here to attend expat social functions and play with fellow expats. Not quite so fine if he is intent on educating Thais in the ways of his country. Not fine also even if his business is wholly orientated towards the expat community. Not at all fine if the expat is here to manage Thais at work, to reach annual objectives and to make money.

Thais mean business. Not all of them are willing or able to cope with a range of expat cultures, attitudes and languages in order to do business with foreigners. If foreigners want the business, they will have to be prepared for the fact that norms of business management are not always the same in Thailand as in the West.

THE EXPAT MANAGER

Forget any ideas about 'one-minute management' and be prepared to spend time with your staff, mostly on an individual basis when directly related to work tasks, and on a group basis for social occasions. There is a place for the weekly staff meeting which will serve for you to provide information received from headquarters and summarise local events of the week, with praise when due but not criticism. Such meetings should not be seen as a short cut to delegating work for the week ahead or appraising in any but the broadest sense the week gone past. A few questions might be raised, but don't expect much in the way of 'brainstorming'.

In addition to managing your staff, you will, to a varying degree depending on the nature of business, need to be in touch with Thai business contacts, government officials and influential people. You will need to build alliances and know your enemies and how to neutralise them. You will need an information system which amounts to a genteel spy network. In all of this, you will certainly need some capable and well-placed assistance.

The Compradore

All of the successful earlier foreign business enterprises in Thailand survived because they worked through a Thai compradore, a person of influence who owed his loyalty to Thailand but who received money from foreigners. A compradore held an important and respected position.

The term 'compradore' is still in use in English and in Thai. In English, it now has pejorative connotations related to the spread of European imperialism. In Thai, it has lost its original meaning and usually now refers to a financial broker (without any pejorative undercurrents). Although use of the term had best be avoided lest HQ calls back its nutcase representative, the foreign entrepreneur or manager will certainly need a modern compradore of some sort if he is to survive and prosper. Call him what you will—partner, deputy, assistant, consultant, or even secretary—but know that an efficient compradore is necessary to operations.

The role, power and recompense of the compradore will vary according to the reasons he is employed. However, even those foreigners who have established successful small enterprises in the kingdom entirely through their own efforts need a Thai partner. A foreigner might have lived in the country most of his life, speak totally fluent Thai, and be accepted by Thais as Thai. He could even have a national reputation and access to the highest of social circles. (Bruce Gaston, the musician, comes immediately to mind.) He thinks Thai, and because of this, he plays it safe. Let others, preferably Thais, praise him if they will; he will humbly and publicly attribute everything he has achieved to his Thai mentor.

For most expat managers in Thailand, there is no question of fame and real fortune. They are interested in the shortest route to efficient and profitable management. Your compradore will tell you the way. Day-to-day bureaucratic problems, which can stifle your company and you, will disappear. When you come to the table to sign contracts, it will be for symbolic discussion, probably some last minute light-hearted ritual of bargaining and commemorative photographs; all the work has been done behind the scenes but not behind your back by your compradore and the person in the other camp with whom he or she went to school. Problems of project implementation, import and export regulations, building permits and so on; your compradore is there to smooth things over.

Your modern version compradore will owe loyalty to you as well as the company. Most likely, he or she has been running the Thailand part of the empire for years already and you have only to fit in and make yourself liked. If such arrangements already exist, count your blessings. Disrupt them at your peril.

If you find yourself replacing a failed manager, there may be nobody performing the compradore's role. Look carefully around your staff. They were probably recruited because of high education and proficiency in English, qualities which are becoming increasingly available but are still very much valued. Just a few years ago, a really well-educated Thai was rare enough that he or she was likely to know personally many of the like-educated (and well-placed) and to be related to at least some. Pay particular attention to the middle-aged. Decide as quickly as you can if you simply need someone who knows his way around customs procedures or if you are flying much higher. A compradore with court connections is not a must if you are managing a restaurant on Patpong: an ex-policeman could be helpful.

If there is no one available to fill the role, you will have to recruit. Be careful: employ a Thai only because of good social contacts and he could turn out to be inefficient, dishonest and hard to get rid of. The surest way to get the reasonable assistance of a good compradore is to poach one from another foreign company, which is not easy and will definitely involve offering much more money and non-taxable incentives.

Reorganising

However good your compradore, he will not manage your staff and is not likely to be doing much in the way of routine office work. Hopefully, routine administrative work will be carried out efficiently with a minimum of checking. If it is not, very discreetly switch functions around a bit with your staff until you are satisfied. Take your time, but not too long. It is expected that a new boss might have some changes to make.

The good manager will make it look, at least on the surface, as if everybody involved in the changes is getting increased responsibility that will place them in line for promotion. Let your staff come to understand, without telling them, that within the limitations set by company budgets, rules and regulations (and up to you to decide how far these can be bent—in the company's interest, of course), you will follow traditional Thai patronage practice and reward those who follow and obey. Showing maximum concern for those who work well and support you does not, of course, mean you ignore production. It will be fully understood that those who do not follow and obey will be exterminated (speaking figuratively, of course).

Having satisfied yourself that your organisational structure is sound, you can sit back and appear to relax. You have time now to get to know your staff a bit. Not too much; be friendly but not friends, and make the workplace more pleasant and yourself more popular. Time to enjoy it all and at the same time really get down to work. Of course, as you might have guessed by now, getting down to work doesn't mean quite the same thing for the Western manager and his Thai staff.

WORK

The Thai word *ngan* means both 'work' and 'party'. It does not follow from this that Thais cannot distinguish between work and party and it certainly should not be assumed that Thais would just as soon go to work as they would go to a party. Rather, it implies that whenever it is possible to turn work into a party, Thais will do so.

The industrial mind, more used to thinking of work and party as opposites, may find this single Thai concept somewhat inscrutable at first. The origin of the term fully explains the mystery.

In the agricultural setting, where most Thais grew up, people come together in groups linked by kinship, residence and friendship to do difficult jobs or the work requiring a larger workforce than one family can provide. Thus, *tham ngan* (to work) means literally 'to make (up a) party'.

'Our backs to the sky, our faces to the ground...forever' is a farmers' saying.

Cooperation

In the modern urban setting, an invitation to *ngan* in a friend's house does not mean that everybody should come armed with a spade and ready to dig in the gardens; but it still implies an element of collective work. Such work, like most work in Thailand, is done by the women. The men might help out to the extent of rigging a tarpaulin outside so that they can sit in the shade and drink Mekong whisky while waiting for the women to prepare the food. Work done together is much more fun than the usual daily cooking chores.

Most people would much rather prepare a party than transplant rice seedlings. Work in the fields is never likely to be much fun, but working together at least makes it bearable. Certain economic benefits are to be gained from cooperative patterns of work organisation, but it is noticeable that the total number of people coming together is usually much greater than the minimum number required to reap these benefits. Nobody wants to be left out. This is not because of any altruistic feeling of helping one's neighbour, since all labour contributed by one family to another is precisely and directly reciprocated in kind. To be left out of the work would mean being left out of the party.

Cooperative 'labour exchange' involves the host's family feeding all of the work-party before and after work; roles are reversed as hosts change from day to day. Thus, at certain times of the year at least, 'work' and 'party' are, if not exactly the same, very much interrelated.

During the working day, backs are bent but there is always the chance to assess the strength and patience of a possible future bride or son-in-law. And when backs stretch up and sit down in a patch of shade for a while, there are friends to chat and eat with.

This Thai woman, like most Thais, live and work in an agricultural setting, where people come together to *tham ngan* (work), or literally 'make up a party'.

Motivation

Often people working side by side on transplant or harvest enter into friendly 'competition' to be first to finish a line. Like bus-drivers racing side by side in Bangkok, such contests add a fun element to what would otherwise be a hard and dreary job, and provide short-term incentives to work hard when one man alone might feel an overwhelming desire to sit under a tree and have a smoke.

These traditional patterns of motivation are often lacking in an urban work situation. The Thais will try as best they can to recreate them. Successful offices and factories are usually those where people enjoy their work and have plenty of opportunities to come together for social activity. The expat manager working in Thailand, used perhaps to treating his long-industrialised workers to one office bus-trip to Brighton each year and a barrel of beer for Christmas, might be advised to allow a somewhat greater percentage of running costs to be spent on fun and games.

In Thailand, few workers are happy with purely economic incentives if a job is no fun. Fortunately, plenty of occasions exist for organising parties, and the expat manager's role is usually limited to sitting back and enjoying it, perhaps giving a short speech praising the work of everybody and indicating future expansion of the company and, of course, picking up a large part of the bill when the party is over.

When work stops being fun, it rapidly slows down and sometimes stops completely. The Thais have, after many years, developed a name for producing quality products in a reasonable time, but they do not yet have an international reputation for discipline and staying power. New activities may be enthusiastically taken up only to be dropped when rewards are not immediately forthcoming or when work becomes too boring. In the agricultural setting, social pressures from family and neighbours might be enough to keep the individual at the job until the next party comes along. Such pressures cannot exist to the same extent in offices and factories.

> For any opening enterprise, or one reopening, relocating or building a new wing or branch office, nine monks will be invited to bless the new adventure/location; the monks will be fed, then the workers.

Fun at Work

The Khatin outing in November/December is the nearest the Thais get to the day trip to Brighton. At this time, in almost every workplace employing Thais, an organising committee will be formed almost spontaneously. People on this committee will tend to be the natural social leaders of any office or workplace. The department manager might not be on it; the receptionist might.

The Kathin outing committee will arrange hire of a bus, collect money from all employees, buy the new robes and other things to be presented to the monks (this is the purpose of Kathin), and make absolutely sure there is plenty to eat and drink for the merit makers. Then everybody goes off on a fun trip. They could simply go to the *wat* next door, but the chances are they will drive across the country and make the donation at a wat few of them have ever seen before. These trips and similar activities serve to make a place of work a place of fun.

Family

Most large-scale urban work situations involve bringing people who have no common links of kinship or neighbourhood into daily interaction. Even so, a surprising number of established institutions in Bangkok are staffed largely on a family basis. If the newcomer goes to learn Thai at the AUA, he will find that just about all the Thai teachers seem to be related. In that situation, something of a family enterprise has been recreated and has been working extremely well for a long, long time. Teachers help each other out and are obviously enjoying what would otherwise be a very dull job indeed (repeating the same lessons over and over every five weeks for years on end). Both teachers and students benefit from the pleasant relationships existing between staff members.

Apart from the universal small family business and some noteworthy exceptions, relationships engendered in the family village setting have no obvious application to most urban patterns of work organisation. However, they remain important to an individual's chances of finding work. A villager from the north-east could arrive in Bangkok one day and, if his uncle is a taxi driver, be driving a taxi the next (even if he has to ask his passengers the way!).

Family relations can help 'productivity', as in the case of the AUA, and they can help individuals (but not necessarily taxi passengers); they can also create some problems.

Nepotism

Nepotism (favouring family members over strangers) can influence job opportunities and selection of contract tenders. The non-Thai executive will not be under social pressure to help his relatives (unless he marries a Thai) but he should be aware that the Thai he asks for advice may be socially obliged to place personal relationships before questions of productivity.

Nepotism is not necessarily negative. It could be seen as an attempt to recreate something out of the rural ideal, where economic and social relationships are not separated as they are in an urban environment. Modernisation and urbanisation have tended, in a very short time, to reverse the ancient and natural social order of the Thais. To a Thai, a life spent more in the company of complete strangers than together with trusted family members is an unnatural and insecure life.

A sales manager who passes over better qualified and more experienced applicants in order to give the vacant assistant sales manager's job to his nephew, may get a very good assistant he can trust. However, if he knows full well that his nephew is lazy, unintelligent and would do the job badly, he is still likely to feel some obligation to support his application, although with somewhat less enthusiasm.

In our view, nepotism is a very natural thing in any country with a strong agricultural tradition. While managers must obviously be aware of its possible negative effects, too strong an attempt to stamp it out might seriously disturb the workplace and retard the development of a 'working community'.

Job Accumulation

While nepotism may be natural and, under certain conditions, might lend stability and continuity to a labour force, it is difficult to see any advantages to that other prevalent urban work habit, job accumulation. The sleepy-eyed government clerk may be selling real-estate at night. The fact that your executive secretary stays late in the office after you have gone home may have nothing to do with her official workload but a lot to do with the private typing and telephoning she does on the side to help her husband's business. The public relations officer who disappears for two hours every Thursday might be giving English lessons to the Thai boss of the office next door. The girl who gets in early to clean the office floor might be an usherette in a cinema in the evening.

The reason so many people are working so long, if not so hard, is a very simple one: money, or lack of it. Thailand is at a point in its development where cars, condominiums and other goodies churned out at a furious pace during the big boom remains tantalisingly in reach for many, but only if some protracted stretching takes place.

Even the rich go in for job collecting. The motive for doing so is, however, likely to be status rather than, or as well as, money. In 1973, shortly before he was overthrown from power, the Field Marshal was referred to as Field Marshal Prapass, Deputy Prime Minister, Interior Minister, Acting Director-General of the Police Department, Deputy Supreme Commander of the Armed Forces, Commander-in-Chief of the Royal Thai Army, Chairman of the Board of Directors of the Bangkok Bank, and Chairman of the Hill Tribes Development Committee in the Communist Suppression Operation Command. Imagine trying to take that lot seriously.

CRITICISM

In Thailand, face-to-face criticism is seen as a form of violence. It hurts people and threatens superficial harmony. Disturbance of the peace is, for the Thai, a totally negative concept. Open criticism is therefore rarely, if ever, entered into with any positive intention of improving a conflict situation. The act of criticism is at best a sign of bad manners, at worst a deliberate attempt to offend.

Constructive Criticism

In the West, it is thought (or pretended) to be possible and even admirable for two people to disagree in public, be critical of each others' ideas in a meeting, agree to disagree or to reach a constructive compromise, remain friends and go off for a drink together after work. Maybe some *farang* do manage this extraordinary feat, which smacks of sado-masochism to the Thai way of seeing. Do not expect Thais to behave in the same way. The difference is an essential part of the great divide between conflict-resolution and conflict avoidance. In the West, difference of an opinion may be intentionally aired in public. This is considered a healthy state of affairs. If critical opposition is lacking, one person may deliberately take the role of the 'devil's advocate', setting out the 'other side of the coin' in the interests of 'fair play'. A synthesis of opposing views or a choice between two or more alternatives would ideally be made when all facts and viewpoints have been clearly stated.

In Thailand, differences of opinion exist but critical expression of these differences is carefully avoided. Resolution, if any, of conflicting points of view is less a matter of dialectical debate than of behind-the-scenes manipulation.

Criticism is not only disliked, it is also regarded as destructive to the social system. The superior is supposed to decide, the inferior is supposed to obey. To criticise a superior is to question the idea that the superior is always right. To criticise an inferior would suggest either the inferior is responsible for making decisions or that the orders given to him by the superior were inadequate or that the superior had made a mistake in entrusting the job to somebody who was incompetent to do it. Criticising an inferior in public would also impress on all present the superior's bad manners as much as the inferior's inefficiency.

If a superior is criticised, he would most likely respond by removing the source of criticism. Even if the inferior's comments make sense and could have saved a lot of money and a lot of lives, they are unlikely to be considered. In the unlikely event that such criticism is acted upon, the inferior is likely to gain nothing and is more likely to be sacked, demoted or transferred than praised and promoted.

The inferior criticised by a superior cannot remove the source of discomfort but he can remove himself. As fast as possible, flee the scene. If he does not, he has to accept public shame. Such public acceptance is inevitably accompanied by private resentment. A Thai can brood for months. During this time, orders received from the superior-critic may be slowly executed, deliberately delayed or delegated to people not equipped to do the job, perhaps with a comment like, 'the boss told me to give you this to do'.

The taboo against open criticism to an individual's face does not extend to covert criticism behind the back and a prolonged gossip campaign could reduce a superior's popularity and harm productivity. Such passive resistance is very difficult to counter. Certainly, it cannot be removed by further doses of criticism.

Indirect Criticism

What then is the poor *farang* boss to do in Thailand? Must he put up with lateness and poor quality work and make no complaints that could possibly be construed as criticism of individuals?

Maybe. Although you, in turn, risk criticism from your peers and bosses for failing to do your job as manager, putting up with it might be more profitable than trying to put it down. At least, recognise that you are in a very different work situation. The boss respected by the workers as 'hard but fair' back in Germany is not likely to accomplish great things in Thailand unless he wears a muzzle. The successful *farang* boss in Thailand is often the one who is very popular

TRIGG

with the workers and interferes with them as little as possible. Certainly, he does not roll up his sleeves and show them how to do their job. Instead, he might take a lesson from the white elephant and criticise by praising while punishing through kindness.

White Elephants

White elephants, when born or found, are given to the king as a mark of respect. Symbols of national peace and prosperity, they are well looked after according to a set and expensive procedure.

In the past, a king would honour his nobles by giving them white elephants to look after. The expense involved in maintenance would pose no problems for those who held favour in the court since a gift of land would also be made. It has been suggested, however, that white elephants were a double-edged sword. They could increase a noble's status or they could drain the purse of the lesser noble, perhaps trying to climb a bit too fast above his station.

A noble who had gained the court's displeasure need not be criticised. He would simply be sent a white elephant (without a gift of land). The 'honour' could not be refused. The elephant would do no work and could not be sold or given away. The offending noble would take care to avoid receiving any similar honours in the future by adjusting his behaviour or ambitions.

White elephants are not recommended as gifts to subtly put the maid back in her place or reduce the secretary's trips to the canteen, but the principle of indirect criticism is appropriate.

Open or public criticism by Thais, of the kind one politician will make of another to the media, is tantamount to an act of war—hopefully of the cold rather than the hot type. It takes place all the time between individuals belonging to rival groups. It does not take place publicly between members of single group. Neither does it take place within a group, unless the group is splitting up or an individual has decided to attach himself to a patron in a contending faction.

Ticking Off Gently

Being indirect does not mean being sarcastic. Thais have a great sense of humour but they don't like sarcasm. "Did your bus get cut in half by a train again this morning?" is not an example of indirect criticism and it is likely to make a worker later the next morning and not earlier.

In the West, an employee late for work is ticked off immediately on arrival. The crime is fresh, the punishment is given and hopefully all can then get down to work. In Thailand, the employee could wait until after lunch or even the next day, then receive some praise for good work. This praise would be followed up by a few questions of a personal nature which might bring the reply 'mind your own business' back in Islington but which, in Thailand, would be regarded as a superior showing interest in the welfare of his subordinates. Is everything all right at

How to Criticise

Indirect criticism is a subtle art and the same format cannot be followed time after time. But following basic ground rules should act as some kind of guide.

- Avoid public confrontation at all costs.
- See the person yourself.
- Pick the best time for the talk, preferably when things are going well, never when you are angry.
- Balance any criticism with praise using a ratio of ten parts praise to one part criticism.
- Be indirect and diplomatic, offering criticisms with praise as suggestions if possible and obtaining verbal agreement.
- Be nice all the time and buy lots of cream cakes for everybody.

The most important of these rules is the last one. Being nice instead of asserting your authority nearly always pays.

home? Has the baby recovered? Are you still living at the same place? That's a long way, isn't it? And if you really need to drive the message home, nothing stronger or more sarcastic than—how long does it take you to get to work?

That should be enough. If it is not and the offender keeps right on offending, decide whether the deviant behaviour is really upsetting the work schedules. If it is not and you are simply enforcing the rules in order to maintain overall discipline, you might be better off back in Germany. If there is some real reason to make somebody turn up at 7:30 am instead of 7:50 am, make a point of 'seeing' the person involved alone. Be indirect, even at this stage. If you are told a list of personal problems which seem to have no bearing on the offending behaviour pattern and which you suspect are complete fabrications, listen sympathetically since this is a mark of a correct superior-inferior relationship (the superior does not tell his problems in return).

At some point in this quiet chat, you do have to mention clearly the subject involved. A *farang*, trying to be reasonable, might think the best way is to explain the importance of keeping the rules—you have to be there at 7:30 am, otherwise Nit and Noy cannot get it and Lek and Toy might miss the mailman. A better way might be to fall back on the 'leader principle' and bring the whole weight to the Thai system to your aid. Everybody has a superior; make full use of yours.

Passing the Buck

Make it clear that your superiors hold you responsible for your workers' behaviour. If your secretary doesn't turn up on time, you, not her, are going to get into trouble. Nit and Noy and Lek and Toy are not as important to her as her boyfriend who keeps her up late at night, but everything and everybody is less important than the system.

For this technique of passing-the-buck-to-the-superior-once-removed to work properly, the superior making the complaint must be liked by the person being indirectly criticised. So following through with some praise for things done right is a good move. If you can't find anything to praise, cream cakes will make most people like you.

Being liked, or at least not being disliked, is a very important part of management technique. If your staff member hates you, he or she will not be moved by recourse to the system, and if your anonymous bosses in another land cause you trouble because of his or her actions, so much the better. Be aware that without an expatriate manager

If you want to express dissatisfaction with a maid's services, the same process of 'setting out the system' can be used. The *farang* wife tells the maid that the master is unhappy with the wife, who should be running the house. If you are single you are unlikely to have any problems, but you should, of course, get married as soon as possible before your entire life is taken over by your maid. Marrying the maid is not the answer; many *farang* have tried and all find they gain a wife but lose a maid.

hearing a single word of it, he can suddenly find himself replaced by HQ. Visitors come from HQ, a few of your staff might even have relations of sorts with people in HQ that extend back long before you came on the scene. If you are nasty to your Thai staff, or they think you are being nasty, they will find a way to get you or get rid of you.

COMPLAINTS

When you buy a new clock and it falls apart after two days. When the plumber repairs the leak by tying one of your handkerchiefs around the water pipe. When the car comes back from repair with an extra 1,000 km on the clock. Complaints are in order.

In circumstances like these, it is not easy to be polite, friendly and private. But if people like you, they will do things for you or knock something off your bill or do it right the next time. There are, of course, limits to being nice. Thailand may teach you yours.

QUESTIONS

The Thai reluctance to criticise is extended to asking questions, if doing so could in any way imply a criticism. Since any question asked in a lecture hall or seminar room would suggest that either the lecture speech was less than perfect or that the questioner was incapable of understanding, very few questions ever get asked. University lecturers can ask after every lecture 'Any questions?' and never get one. Some may get a few questions a couple of days or a couple of months after the lecture is over. Such questions are always asked in private and always wrapped up in a way that demonstrates quite clearly that the wretched student is too dim to understand the clear and brilliant lecture given.

Although *farang* lecturers and teachers love to bemoan the 'lack of intellectual stimulation' and complain among themselves of the rote-learning system which discourages critical evaluation and punishes originality, they all enjoy working in Thailand; most of them enjoy it precisely because the students are so uncritical and well-mannered.

If these teachers are good at their job, they allow time and make opportunities for students to consult them in private and incorporate any points raised in such talks in the next lecture without making any direct reference to the questioner. Working within the system in this way takes no more time than the lecturer spends back home trying to be smarter than everybody else in the lecture hall. It is certainly a lot easier on the nerves and, when the answer to a question is not known, a lot safer.

Other foreigners who come to work in Thailand generally get much better pay than lecturers and teachers, but enjoy a much lower status (although probably a higher one than they had back home). If you like to pretend that you could not give a fig for questions of status and just want to do the best job possible, you are thinking very differently to the way Thais think. Such different thought patterns are almost bound to conflict eventually.

Teachers at tertiary level in Thailand are referred to as *ajarn*, an honorific title that can also be used for monks. The term *ajarn* simple oozes with respect and status, although a bit less so than it did a few years ago. The businessman's title of *nai hang* does imply respect, but it has nothing like the same status. The businessman has mere money to compensate him for the fact that meetings, conferences and seminars involving Thais are almost always dull affairs.

Anything interesting and important seems to get said over tea before or after the ritual coming together of 'the seminar'.

Any damp fireworks during meetings are inevitably thrown by a couple of *farang* while Thai participation is often limited to an occasional yawn.

CONFORMING TO THE TABOO

For a *farang* working in Thailand, understanding Thai sensitivities and the criticism taboo is one thing, conforming to it, (or, as some say, 'pandering' to it) is quite another. Some would argue that the *farang* should not change his behaviour since he was recruited precisely because of his ability to analyse critically and to act on his analysis in a way that a Thai would find difficult to do.

Some *farang* would go as far as to suggest that Western professional standards contain a ethic which requires open criticism. The line would go that the needs of patients in a hospital and students in an university must come before personal sensitivities of the staff. What is a *farang* doctor to do if he sees a senior Thai doctor prescribing a lethal dose of arsenic? What is a *farang* lecturer to do if he discovers a university professor delegating the marking of examination papers to his maid?

Perhaps the first thing you should do if you find yourself in either of these unlikely situations is to decide exactly what your motive is in making an intervention. Is it to belittle the doctor or professor and publicly prove yourself superior (an acceptable game in the *farang* world but not in the Thai) or is it to help the patients and students in question? If you have the first motive, any boost to your ego is temporary and the longer term effects on your career in Thailand could be disastrous. Whether you intend to help yourself or to help the students or patients in question, open criticism may not be the best way of doing things.

Quiet Intervention

Even in these extreme circumstances, the Thai in your position is likely to look for a way to remedy the situation while avoiding confrontation.

The doctor is most unlikely to leave the victims to their fate with, "Well, must be their karma, guess they had it coming." He would try to intervene quietly. Perhaps he would simply change the prescription from arsenic to aspirin after the senior doctor had left the room and ask him later how long it had been since he had a holiday. Or, in an examination case, a Thai lecturer might offer the professor, who of course has a thousand demands on his genius, the lecturer's own services in helping the professor mark the papers: "I hesitate to offer, but I am sure I would learn a great deal if you would allow me to work through those scripts." Situation corrected and career enhanced. A million times safer and more effective than sending a pile of your own unmarked scripts to the professor's maid.

If each subtle intervention is impossible, other tactics are required. As the senior doctor measures out the arsenic while insisting that the patient drinks it all immediately, the junior doctor, before the lunge to save the patient's life, might try the self-ignorance ploy which would allow his senior to change his mind without losing face: "Excuse me, sir. What is that patient taking? Did you say ascorbic acid, sir? What sort of effect does ascorbic acid have in cases like this, sir?" With any luck the senior might reply, "Ascorbic acid? No, I didn't say that. That would have no effect at all. I said aspirin, but I seem to have got hold of the wrong bottle. Nurse, where is the aspirin?" Such subtlety saves lives, makes friends out of enemies and helps your career by making you look like a fool. "Arsenic? Wouldn't rat poison be better?" is not the thing to say.

Graft

Few Thais favour bribery and corruption but few would refuse a present offered for a small service rendered. Western businessmen are reluctant to admit participation in such activities, but most are aware that if they want to be sure goods get to the port in one piece, are cleared in time and are loaded onto the right ship,

The Thais say, 'Look after an elephant and eat its poo-poo.' This definitely loses a little in translation but, basically means that if you care well for something valuable, certain valuable droppings will (legitimately) come your way.

they must have somebody, somewhere, looking after their interests with an incentive greater than that inspired by the basic wage.

Bribery

Gunnar Myrdal suggests in his famous *Asian Drama* that among multinational companies in Asia, the Japanese are the most willing to pay bribes to secure trading and manufacturing advantages over their competitors and to ensure smooth day-to-day running of their organisations. They are closely followed by the Germans, French and Americans. Large-scale bribery usually involves 'go-betweens'. In this role, the compradores serve much the same functions as marriage go-betweens did in the early stages of marriage negotiations in the past, to prevent embarrassment to either party.

Opening the Mouth

I have already emphasised that a good go-between can be invaluable to the foreign businessman who would otherwise waste much time and money locating the key man in a government department or in a rival agency. The efficient compradore will let you know in confidence when somebody requires 'money to open the mouth' (to speak in favour of, and actively pursue, your interests).

In the absence of a professional middleman, who looks after the company's interests generally and might be given a highly-paid 'consultant' position, specific-purpose middlemen arise from time to time. A clerk in a government office might turn up on behalf of his superior and inform the foreigner that a specific sum of money is required before a service can be performed. There is, of course, no way of knowing if the junior is telling the truth and this is why the major portion of the bribe is only paid upon successful completion of the service. A middleman is a speculator. If he fails to achieve the results, he gets nothing.

Money doesn't always go to the top man of an organisation. A junior member drawing up bids for a contract can provide one bidder with valuable information on the competition and present one bid in a more favourable way than others. When the bids get to the committee stage, one member 'opening his mouth' might be enough. No point in bribing all committee members if you can bribe one man who has the chairman's ear. Having the chairman's ear is most likely to mean that the largest cut will find its way to the chairman. A junior who acted on his own initiative and pocketed the cash would lose job and career if discovered.

Expat companies and organisations not only take part in bribery, they are victims of it. The foreign manager should be aware that a sub-contract does not always go to the most efficient company. Attempting to limit the consequences of this possibility, some companies prefer to split the work into two or more contracts, intending to maintain certain competition for a period before making a firm decision in favour of one party. This can be a dangerous course of action. The companies involved might spend more time trying to knock out the competition than in actively doing the job.

Alternatively, they might cooperate and agree to up the price while sharing the benefits. This is particularly likely when the two competing companies just happen to have the same directors, a coincidence which seems to happen a lot in Thailand.

Invisibility

Bribery is as invisible as the spirit world. Certainly it exists, but it does not appear at the end-of-year accounts. It is therefore very difficult to guess whether the incidence of bribery is higher in Thailand than elsewhere. Even if everybody knows exactly where the money for Boonpop's holiday in Phuket came from, nobody talks about it,

The act of taking bribes is referred to in Thai as 'eating'. Everybody has to eat.

FAST FACTS AT YOUR FINGERTIPS

CHAPTER 10

'Time is money.'
—An English saying that is, perhaps
surprisingly, also an old Thai saying.

Official Name
Thailand

Capital
Bangkok

Administration
76 provinces, each subdivided into *amphoe* (district), *tambon* (sub-district) and *muban* (village)

Surface Area
517,000 sq km (199,614.8 sq miles)

Time
Greenwich Mean Time plus 7 hours (GMT + 0700)

Telephone Country Code
66

Earliest Known Facts
Inhabited some 10,000 years ago. Possibly the world's first agriculturists (4,000 years ago) and metal workers

Climate
Monsoonal. Wet: June–October, dry: November–May. Hottest: March–June, with temperatures in the top thirties. Cooler in

north and in highlands, particularly December–February. Humidity high at 66–82 per cent average

Population
62 million, one-third in urban areas. 75 per cent ethnic Thai divided into four dialect groups. Chinese and Malays form the largest minority groups, with significant hill tribe presence in the mountains

Religion
Some 95 per cent are Theravada (aka Hinayana) Buddhists, the remainder are Mahayana Buddhists (mostly Chinese) and Muslims (mostly Malays), with a 0.5 per cent Christian representation (Chinese and Thai and hill tribe)

National Language
Thai (Central). Significant variables in regional dialects. Chinese (dialects) widely understood in shops. English taught as a second language, not widely spoken

Currency
Thai baht

Credit Cards
Acceptable in the more upmarket outlets, supermarkets, restaurants and hotels. Three per cent normally added to price. May be used to withdraw money at most banks

Debit Cards
Can be used at ATM machines anywhere in Thailand to withdraw money from the home account with no (or sometimes a tiny) charge. Not every ATM machine takes all cards

Cheques
Not widely used

Bank Accounts
Foreigners may open accounts but only non-interest savings accounts if not a resident

Water
Drink only bottled or boiled

Gross Domestic Product (GDP)
US$ 524.8 billion (2004 est)

Industries
Tourism, textiles and garments, agricultural processing, beverages, tobacco, cement, light manufacturing such as jewellery, electric appliances and components, computers and parts, integrated circuits, furniture, plastics, tungsten and tin

Exports
Textiles and footwear, fishery products, rice, rubber, jewellery, automobiles, computers and electrical appliances

Imports
Capital goods, intermediate goods and raw materials, consumer goods, fuels

THE GOVERNMENT SYSTEM

- Thailand has been an independent country since AD 1238 and is the only country in the region to have avoided Western colonisation.
- Since 1932, the country has been a constitutional monarchy, initially inspired by the British model.
- The 500-member house of representatives is elected, along with the prime minister, through four-yearly national polls.
- A senate votes on any constitutional changes.
- Thailand has a multi-party system. Currently no parties are illegal. The four major parties in terms of representation are the Democrats, New Aspiration, National Development, and Thai Nation.
- After many years of struggle, pro-democracy groups achieved, on 27 September 1997, Thailand's 16th Constitution was voted in—for the first time by a civilian government. It contains articles to allow the

monitoring of elected officials and the protection of human rights.

- The 'People's Constitution' as the 1997 reforms have become known, makes voting compulsory, provides free public education for 12 years (nine of them compulsory), establishes several 'watchdogs', including the constitution court, the anti-corruption commission and the human rights commission.

- The military, in the form of generals, self or popularly elected, has commanded the premiership of Thailand for most of the years since the 1932 transition, often seizing power in military coups. With modernisation, the growth and internationalisation of the economy, membership of ASEAN and widely supported constitutional reform, coups should now be a thing of the past. Some people see them as a historical accident bridging the absolute monarchy before 1932 and the constitutional monarchy introduced at that time.

- All judges sitting on Thailand's supreme court are appointed by the king.

- The king takes no active role in government but, in a society that continues to be based strongly on status, he and the royal family remain the most respected members of society. As such, his opinion and example is most important to all Thais. King Bhumibol ascended the throne in 1946 and remains influential and very much in public contact with Thais in each of the four main parts of the country. There is no serious anti-monarchist movement and the king's political role has been largely one of example. Perhaps the best example of his style and respect is the military coup attempt of 1981. As the 'Young Turks' sought to take over, the king and the royal family, together with Prime Minister Prem, simply left the capital and installed themselves temporarily in Khorat. The coup collapsed.

- The Crown Prince Maha Vajiralongkorn was officially designated heir on reaching 20 in 1972. Thus, the Chakri dynasty is assured a peaceful continuation in the future.

FAMOUS THAIS
His Majesty King Bhumibol Adulyadej

His Majesty Bhumibol Adulyadej, whose name is occasionally spelled Phumiphon Adunlayadet ('Strength of the Land, Incomparable Power'), is also known as Rama IX, 9th King of the Chakri Dynasty. He was born 5 December 1927, in Cambridge, Massachusetts, US, and became king of Thailand in 1946. A grandson of King Chulalongkorn, he married Princess Sirikit Kitiyakara on 28 April 1950, and was formally crowned on 5 May 1950. The absolute monarchy having been abolished in 1932, King Bhumibol wielded little real political power. His most important function was to serve as a living symbol and a focus of unity for the Thai nation. The king has always led an active ceremonial life, frequently appearing in public and moderating between extreme parties in Thai politics. Bhumibol designated his only son, Vajiralongkorn, as crown prince in 1972; he also has three daughters.

Her Majesty Queen Sirikit

Her Majesty Queen Sirikit was born on 12 August 1932 in Thailand. Her father was a Thai ambassador to England and France, and Mom Rajawongse Sirikit Kitiyakara, as she was then known, accompanied him on his various European postings. It was in Paris where she met the future Thai king, King Bhumibol. They returned to Thailand to get married, just a week before the king's coronation.

Queen Sirikit works tirelessly alongside her husband in improving the welfare of Thai citizens, especially that of the rural women. Under her initiative and patronage, traditional craft and textile projects have been set up to promote and improve the livelihood of rural Thai women.

Their Majesties the King and Queen have four children:

Princess Ubol Ratana

Born 5 April 1951 in Lausanne, Switzerland, Princess Ubol Ratana graduated from Massachusetts Institute of Technology in the US with a Bachelor of Science in Bio-Chemistry in 1973. She married Mr Peter Jensen and now resides in

Thailand with her children, Khun Ploypailin Jensen, Khun Bhumi (Poom) Jensen and Khun Sirikitiya Jensen. Sadly, Khun Poom Jensen died in the tsunami disaster that hit Phuket in December 2004.

Crown Prince Maha Vajiralongkorn

Born 28 July 1952 in Bangkok, Crown Prince Maha Vajiralongkorn graduated from Australia's Royal Military College and serves in the Royal Thai Army. He was conferred the title of Somdech Phra Boroma Orosadhiraj Chao Fah Maha Vajiralongkorn in 1972, making him heir to the throne. He is married to Princess Somsavali, and together they have a daughter, Princess Siribha Chudhabhorn.

Princess Maha Chakri Sirindhorn

Born 2 April 1955 in Bangkok, Princess Maha Chakri Sirindhorn holds a bachelor degree in Ancient-Oriental languages, and a doctorate in education and development. Princess Sirindhorn is the driving force behind many of Thailand cultural preservation projects. She teaches history at the Royal Military Academy, writes books in her spare time, and heads many charitable foundations.

Princess Chulabhorn

Their Majesties' youngest child, Princess Chulabhorn was born 4 July 1957 in Bangkok. A gifted scientist, she received a PhD in chemistry. She set up the Chulabhorn Research Institute to promote scientific research in Thailand. She is married to Flight Lieutenant Virayuth Didyasarin, a fighter pilot, and has two daughters, Princess Siribhachudhabhorn and Princess Adityadornkitikhun.

Thaksin Shinawatra
Thai Prime Minister 2001–Coup of September 2006

Thaksin Shinawatra (pronouned chin-na-wat) was born in Chiang Mai in 1949 to a rich merchant family. He studied at the Thailand Police Academy, and went on to obtain law degrees in the US, finishing with a PhD in Criminal Justice from Sam Houston State University in Texas in 1978.

Back in Thailand, he started his career as a police officer. After 14 years, he left to set up his own telecommunication business operating mainly media and communication networks throughout Asia. Born to be an entrepreneur, Thaksin was fast to spot the potential new marketing items. Pagers, mobile phones, software and communications satellites were among many of his business enterprises.

In 1994, Thaksin went into politics under the Palang Dharma Party led by Chamlong Srimuang, and became foreign minister. He then headed the party when Chamlong resigned, and served as the deputy prime minister under the Chavalit government in 1997.

In 1998, Thaksin formed the Thai Rak Thai party which won a landslide victory in the election of January 2001. The same year, he became prime minister of the 54th government of Thailand. He was re-elected for another term in March 2005.

Phra Payom Kalayano

Phra Payom Kalayano is an outspoken, activist Buddhist monk. He believes the Buddhist message is best conveyed through storytelling. A master entertainer and eloquent speaker, his sermons are full of humorous anecdotes and tales. Thais love them for their directness, practicality and their entertaining twists. His sermons are recorded and sold as cassette tapes that, at times, top the sale of the most fashionable Thai pop music.

Phra Payom is not only a spiritual leader, but also a grass-roots activist who believes in equality for everyone. At his temple of Wad Suan Kaew in Nonthaburi, the Abbot Payom set up a school giving vocational training to hundreds of the unemployed. What marks Phra Payom out from other Thai social activists is the fact that he is an ardent environmentalist as well. At the same temple, he set up modest recycling plants where discarded waste is sorted out, and either reused or recycled. As the only temple to offer such a service, Phra Payom hopes to raise environmental awareness of the Thai people who, according to him, are fast becoming indiscriminate consumerists.

Phra Payom earns tremendous support and respect of the country through his tireless work on issues such as education, environment and the role of Buddhist monks. Outspoken and fearless, he never hesitates to openly criticise powerful monks who abuse and exploit their respectable position to their advantage.

In the land where the faith in Buddhist monks is sometimes thought by Thais to be in decline, Phra Payom's ideals inspire the rediscovery of the teachings of the Buddha.

Kukrit Pramoj (1911–1995)

Kukrit was a prominent statesman and literature figure of Thailand. This great grandson of King Rama V is often coined 'renaissance man' for his interests and achievements, which range from classical dance and drama, to politics and literature.

Kukrit was educated in Oxford, UK. He started his career writing for the respectable *Siam Rath* newspaper. His writings soon multiplied and he authored many important Thai literary works. Among those written or translated into English are: *Many Lives*, *Red Bamboo* and *Four Reigns*, the last multi volume work considered to be the most significant. Set among the political turmoil of the 1930s in which one king was dethroned and another assassinated, *Four Reigns* tells the story of courtiers who live among the fear and the uncertainty of changing times. Most of all, it is a tale of the unaffected love and fierce loyalty Thais have for the royal family. The scope and style of this book rightly places Kukrit at the forefront of Thai writers.

In the 1940s, Kukrit went into politics and became prime minister, serving Thailand from 1975–1976. As a great statesman, his achievements include taking a significant role in producing the Thai constitution of 1974 and, in 1975, establishing diplomatic ties with China after a long period of antagonism between the two countries.

Kukrit died at the age of 84, in 1995, the year when he was granted the title Thai National Artist of the Year.

Prateep Ungsongtham-hata

The story of Prateep reads like a sad novel with a happy ending. Prateep was born in 1952 and grew up in the slum of Klong Toey harbour, south of Bangkok. At the age of ten, she scraped rust off ships to earn food money for her family. However, what young Prateep wanted to do most of all was to go to school. After a lot of hard work, saving what she could of her hard-earned money, and only in her early teens, Prateep was finally able to attend night classes.

In the 1970s, there were about a million slum dwellers in Bangkok. The largest group lived in dubious legality on Prateep's vast and unhealthy wasteland near the harbour. There was no government welfare available to them, and the authorities turned a blind eye to their existence. With no school to go to, the children roamed the streets and became criminals, often involved in drugs or prostitution.

Young Prateep resolved to get these youths off the streets and into education. At the age of 16, she turned her scanty house on stilts into a makeshift nursery and classrooms. She and her sister took turns teaching the neighbourhood children, charging just 1 baht per day to cover costs. Far from receiving national or international assistance at that stage, Prateep constantly had to fight with the Thai authorities who threatened to close the school and arrest her for what they called unlawful undertaking. Prateep's fight with the officials went on for eight years until the government finally acknowledged her work and officially recognised her school. When news spread of Prateep's struggle, donations poured in from kind-hearted well-wishers. The money was used to set up the Duang Prateep Foundation (meaning 'the lantern of life'), a charity that looks after the welfare of the Klong Toey's squatters up to this day.

Teacher Prateep, or *Kru* Prateep as she is known to the Thais, was awarded the Ramon Magsaysay Prize for Public Service in 1978. She married a Japanese businessman but still lives and works in Klong Toey. It is largely thanks to her efforts, and the support of other Thais, that the people of Klong Toey now have the rights of other Thais and live in reasonable conditions. Think of Prateep before you ever say a Thai will do anything for money.

Sulak Sivaraksa

Sulak Sivaraksa, born 1933, is a prominent Thai intellectual and social critic, well known in Thailand for his at times controversial views. Educated in England and Wales, Sulak returned to Thailand, or Siam as he prefers to call his country, at the age of 26. He founded the *Sankhomsaat Paritat*, an intellectual magazine that covered political and social issues. Later, he helped set up many non-governmental organisations (NGOs) involved with human rights struggles and grassroots development.

Sulak never hesitates to criticise what he thinks is fundamentally wrong—an attitude that has made him some powerful enemies but also many supporters. His stand against the many unlawful military *coups d'etat* led to him being arrested, jailed and his bookshop burnt down. Twice he had to flee to exile, once in the US and once in Europe. He was able to return to Thailand in 1992. Through his numerous publications and involvement with NGOs, Sulak continues to lay the foundation for social change in Thailand.

An intellectual Buddhist and democrat, Sulak believes that meaningful social change can only be effected by individual human beings. He has written widely on the principles and practices of Buddhism, and the values of other religions as vehicles for non-violent change. To him, religion goes hand in hand with social change,.

In 1995, Sulak was granted the Right Livelihood Award, also known as the Alternative Nobel Prize.

Chamlong Srimuang

A Thai press editorial once observed that Thai politicians fit neatly into two categories: they are either *naklengs* or monks. This view, if somewhat simplistic, is not simply the Thai equivalent of hawks and doves. The *nakleng,* or 'tough guy' in English, is epitomised by the strings of army commanders that ruled the country since the birth of Thai democracy in 1932. Monks, it is observed, are politicians who usually have strong moral principles where honesty and social issues are concerned. Whilst *naklengs* are men of action, monk politicians are honest and peaceful, but hardly ever deliver.

Chamlong Srimuang, born 1935, embodies both traits. Trained as a soldier early in his career, he managed to discard the military image when he entered politics in the 1980s. Neither did his earlier position in the army stop him from siding with and standing up for the students' revolt against the military coup of 1992.

At the time when Thais were fed up with military rule and corrupt politicians, Chamlong offered a fresh alternative. Nicknamed 'Mr Clean' by the Thai press, he was honest, modest and transparent; qualities rare in the Thai political arena. Also a man of action, Chamlong delivered. As the governor of Bangkok between 1985–1992, he brought order and cleanliness to Bangkok streets, canals and public markets. He managed to control the perennial problems of floods and traffic jams faced by desperate Bangkokians. His fierce anti-corruption drive earned him respect from Thais and put some credibility back into the Thai political system.

Chamlong is a devout Buddhist. He practises *samatha*—humility and austerity. He lives simply, dresses simply and eats only one vegetarian meal a day. He has been compared to Ghandi. Winning the Magsaysay Award for Government Service, Chamlong retired from politics in the mid-1990s only to return, at the request of the current Prime Minister Thaksin Chinawatra, in 2000 as the PM's aide.

Pridi Panomyong (1900–1983)

In 1932, Pridi Panomyong, a Sorbonne graduate Thai lawyer, led a revolution that was to change the fabric of the Thai political system forever. The then king Prachathipok was stripped of his power, and Thailand went from absolute monarchy rule to constitutional democracy. The king went into exile in Britain and Pridi served the Thai government at various ministries before he finally became prime minister in 1946.

His life and work was devoted to the betterment of underprivileged Thai people. However, the sensitivity of Thais where royalty was concerned meant that Pridi was never popular in the country. And when he was alleged to have been involved in the assassination of the succeeding king, King Rama VIII, he fled to France where he died in 1983.

To commemorate his achievement, UNESCO, in 2000, posthumously named Pridi one of the great personalities of the 20th century. Younger generations of Thais now feel in debt to his contribution to the country.

Ad Carabao

Ad Carabao led a seven members rock band that was formed during the students revolt against military regimes in the 1970s. Carabao means buffalo, and the group likened this animal to the poor agrarian Thais, whose voice they represented. Carabao's lyrics were activist and revolutionist in nature, with titles like 'The Beggar', 'The Commoner', 'Made in Thailand' and 'Democracy', among many others. The political dissent and nationalist messages that underpined Carabao's lyrics mean that their band is inevitably synonymous with social struggle, inequality and grass-root dissent.

Unlike many Thai personalities that are only known within Thailand, Carabao is famous internationally, playing as far afield as England, Germany and France. Although the group disbanded in 1996, some members, notably the iconic lead singer Ad Carabao, went on to rally politically through song writing and singing.

Sunthorn Phu (1786–1855)

This 17th century Poet Laureate is sometimes hailed as the Thai answer to England's Shakespeare. It is true that Sunthorn Phu is a national treasure, but his strength lies in his simple literary style and language. At the time when courtier protocol dictated high art and ornate literary style, Sunthorn Phu broke away from it, and wrote popular poems using simple language to reflect the reality of life, romance, hard times and lost love. His work, therefore, appealed to the more popular taste.

Sunthorn Phu was a poet prodigy, able to recite verses as a matter of routine. He served the court of King Rama II in the early 1880s, the time considered the golden age of art and culture. Amongst his many oeuvre was *Nirats*, a kind of travelogue in verse, proverbs, plays and song recitals. However, he is most known and loved through his epic tale of *Phra Aphai Mani*, an adventure of a magical flutist who uses his music to lure lovers and kill demons.

Sunthorn Phu is virtually unknown outside Thailand due to the lack of translations of Thai literature in general. However, in 1986, the bicentennial of his birth, UNESCO officially recognised his importance and designated Sunthorn Phu a classical imminent poet. His birthday (June 26) is celebrated in Rayong, his birthplace, with cultural performances, poetry recitals and puppet show playing *Phra Aphai Mani*.

Bird Thongchai McIntyre

Nicknamed 'Bird', Thongchai McIntyre, born 1958 to a Thai mother and Scottish father, is an extremely popular and endearing actor and singer. He has starred in many movies and television dramas and is best known for his music. His sweet lyrics are simple and direct, with which most Thais identify. Coupled with his mellow good looks and his approachability, Bird is one of the all-time favourite pop singers Thailand has ever produced. During his career that spans three decades, he has sung hundreds of hit songs, and at the age of 46, his music still tops the chart, and touches the heart of the whole nation. There are hardly any Thais who do not know Bird's songs.

CULTURE QUIZ

To function positively and effectively in a new culture requires much more than simply learning a list of social taboos. To be successful, you must get a 'feel' for situations so that 'correct' behaviour comes almost naturally. This, of course, is something that can come only with time and experience, after plenty of mistakes and much frustration. To get you thinking in terms of social situations rather than rules of 'what not to do', this section is devoted to a Thai culture quiz. Situations 1–9 are likely to be met by any visitor; situations 10–17 are geared towards the expat manager.

Human beings being what they are, there is no absolutely correct response to any particular situation. Judgement of 'right' and 'wrong' is therefore bound to be somewhat arbitrary and subjective. Culture is learnt but it is by no means static enough to quantify, except for fun.

Answers are graded on a scale of 10, from –5 to + 5 (with the occasional –10 for real bloomers). Neutral responses are given zero. The childish use of plus and minus signs is to emphasise that whatever your response, it has positive or negative influences on the development of a situation.

There are several ways of tackling the quiz. The simplest way is to follow the instructions ('choose one', 'select as appropriate', etc.), note the response you think correct and check the score given. Score zero and you are safe; a minus score and you should read this book again before you are completely floored by culture shock, or the Thais are floored by you.

If you don't feel like doing a quiz, don't do it. Nobody's watching. Simply read through the situations and comments. Even if you disagree with what I say, you will be thinking situationally. If you are two or more, or a classroom, compare your views—it's more fun. If you want to do the test 'fairly', cover the score column and 'Comments', where the answers and rationale for the answers are written. Use a pencil to permit somebody else to do the quiz.

Don't take the marks too seriously; I didn't.

SITUATION 1

Having paid the bill in a restaurant, the waitress brings your change on a tray. You pick it up, leaving behind a reasonable tip. She smiles beautifully and *wais* you before picking up the money. Do you: (choose one)

A Ignore her.
B Put another 5 baht on the tray.
C Smile and carry on talking to your friends.
D Stand up and return the *wai*.
E Raise your hands casually in a low *wai* while remaining seated.

Comments

Only **A** and **C** are normal. **E** would be odd and **D** could be interpreted as sarcasm and, therefore, rude. To do **B** would certainly invoke a further beautiful smile and *wai*. It would, of course, bring you back to the beginning but might be worth the money if the waitress is genuinely amused. I have given this response a minus because there is a suggestion of playing with people for your own amusement. If your friends laugh, the waitress could be embarrassed.

Score

Ⓐ   0
Ⓑ   −1
Ⓒ   + 5
Ⓓ   −5
Ⓔ   −3

SITUATION 2

You call on a Thai friend to invite him out to eat. He accepts and you are just about to get into the car when his Thai friends draw up. They explain to him that they are going to Nick's Restaurant and ask him to join them. Your friend says, "Meet you there." As you drive off, wondering how much your friend's largess will cost you and what kind of a boring time you are in for with everybody speaking Thai except for you, your friend says, "Where shall we eat, how about the Sorn Daeng?" Do you reply: (choose one)

Ⓐ Of course not, you just told your friends we would be at Nick's.
Ⓑ OK. Let's go there.
Ⓒ Good idea, we can always drop by Nick's later on.
Ⓓ Yes, I'd like to go there. But won't your friends be waiting for us at Nick's?
Ⓔ If you don't want to meet your friends, why didn't you just say we were going to dinner somewhere else and leave it at that?

Comments

An Ⓔ type reply would be very bad manners, however good a friend he is. It betrays a stark Western reasoning; by all means think it, but don't say it. The accusing tone is quite unjustified since your friend was simply trying to be polite to everybody. For him to tell the others that the two of you were going to dinner without inviting them along would suggest that both of you had no time for them; since eating together is a mark of friendship, this suggestion could be interpreted as a repudiation of their friendship. To invite someone to eat with you is a very basic part of Thai personality. It is also a speech habit and the words are therefore not as literally meaningful as the translation would be in the West.

D sounds reasonable but contains an element of criticism. It also places your friend in a difficult position, making him choose between your wishes and meeting his friends. **A** is out because it directly criticises your friend. **B** is fine, assuming you really don't want to be with his friends. **C** is best, since you reaffirm your friend's invitation to his friends. (You do not, of course, remember to drop by unless you want to.) If you do walk into the Sorn Daeng and find your friend's friends there, you smile and join them for dinner!

Score

A   −3
B   + 4
C   + 5
D   −2
E   −5

SITUATION 3

While visiting the grounds of a *wat*, a group of friendly people sitting in the *sala* invite you to sit down with them and eat hot curry and drink rice wine. You dislike both and have no wish to join the group. Do you: (choose one)

A Lie and say you have just eaten.
B Say you are sorry but you don't have time.
C Refuse, explaining that you cannot take curry and rice wine.
D Eat a little bit, hoping to get away quickly.
E Ignore them and hurry away.

Comments

In Thai, invitations to eat are as frequent and as sincere as inquiries after the state of one's health in English. 'Eaten already' (**A**) is the standard polite response. Not having time for something or for somebody (**B**) is no excuse at all in Thailand; this response implies a mild indirect insult to the inviters. **C** is sensible, but your would-be hosts are likely to find other things that they think you would like. **D** is polite but unnecessary; it is also very difficult to leave quickly and gracefully after eating a little. Ignoring them (**E**) is not likely to bother the group very much, but if you hurry away from every situation like this one, you will not benefit at all from your stay in Thailand.

If you do wish to join the group, it is polite, but not essential, to excuse yourself and wait for the invitation to be repeated; at which point, sit down and tuck in. In more formal situations (if you are attending a family ceremony, for example), the 'eaten already' excuse is not acceptable and to refuse to eat for any reason would be bad manners.

Score

A + 5
B – 1
C   0
D   0
E –2

SITUATION 4

You stop a young Thai man in the street and ask him the way. He points in the direction he is walking and offers to show you. As you are walking and talking, he takes your hand. Do you: (choose one)

A Pull your hand away and walk off by yourself.
B Grin and bear it.
C Explain that you are not used to this kind of thing and gently withdraw your hand.
D Grin and enjoy it.
E Ruffle his hair with your free hand.

Comments

Taking the hand of complete strangers is not standard behaviour in Thailand, but if you are a man, be prepared for it to happen more often than back home. The action does not in itself imply homosexuality.

Man answering:
If you do enjoy it, **D** is right for you. If you do not enjoy it, or if you are worried about what your *farang* friends will say if they see you, there is no need to put up with it (**B**). Taking the **C** path while maintaining a friendly manner will save everybody embarrassment; for once explanations, or attempted explanations, are in order. A safe and inoffensive alternative is to occupy your nearside hand by carrying something in it.

Woman answering:
The stranger is being rude to you. Hesitancy will encourage his advances. Time for action. Even if you do enjoy holding hands with strangers (or friends) of the opposite sex, the street is not the place for it!

Either sex:
Ruffle hair and you are, of course, asking for all the trouble you might get.

Score

	Man	Woman
A	–5	+ 5
B	0	–5
C	+ 4	–
D	+ 5	–5
E	–10	10

SITUATION 5

Choose the most appropriate way of saying 'thank you' in each of the following situations from the following responses:
(i) no reaction
(ii) smile
(iii) smile and nod
(iv) 'thank you'
(v) *wai*

A A taxi driver gives you change after you pay the fare.
B A monk gives you something.

◉ A hotel boy opens the door for you.

◉ You buy something from a street vendor who says 'thank you' to you.

◉ Your maid informs you that she has just killed a poisonous snake about to bite your son.

◉ A stranger points out the location of a shop you are looking for.

◉ A polite immigration officer extends your visa to stay in Thailand without making you come back the next day.

Comments

This exercise should show that the form gratitude expression takes in Thailand depends partly on the service performed (as it does in the West), but much more on the status of the doer. Other factors, not included here, are age and likeability. For the same service, the elderly are thanked somewhat more than the young. If you like a particular taxi driver and he has performed well, a verbal 'thank you' is not out of place.

SITUATION 6

You are sitting with a Thai friend and his seven-year-old child on a crowded bus, when an old man enters. Would you: (choose one)

◉ Do nothing.

◉ Ask the child to give up his seat to allow the old man to sit.

◉ Ask your friend to put his child on his lap to make room for the old man.

◉ Give up your seat for the old man.

◉ Give the old man your seat and pay his fare.

Comments

You give up your seat for the old man (**◉**)because of respect for his age. Since children are valued more than anything else, they are given the comparative safety of a seat on the bus and not expected to stand for their elders. **◉** is therefore out. If your friend spontaneously puts his child on his lap, that's fine. But suggesting he do so (**◉**) implies criticism. Doing nothing (**Ⓐ**) is, in today's world, not too bad. Paying the old man's fare, unless he asks you, is insulting. If he does ask you, don't give up your seat.

Score

Ⓐ   0

Ⓑ   −5

Ⓒ   −2

Ⓓ   + 5

Ⓔ   −2

SITUATION 7

You are wandering along, minding your own business, when a stranger sitting at a stall by the roadside says 'You!' at you. Do you: (choose one)

Ⓐ Assume he is looking for trouble and hurry on by.

Ⓑ Say 'You!' in return.

Ⓒ Carry on walking.

Ⓓ Tell him that it is rude to say 'You!'

Ⓔ Point your foot at him.

Comments

'You!', 'Hey, you!' or 'Mister!' could be the first English words you hear spoken by a Thai—small words that leave a bad impression on thousands of foreign visitors every year. However tolerant you are, 'You!' is almost certain to annoy. However, pointing a foot at the offender (**Ⓔ**) is about as appropriate as giving a *wai*, and likely to get you into lots of well-deserved trouble.

   Ⓐ is playing it safe, but it is wrong to assume the caller is looking for trouble. Unless you can say it in Thai, telling him it is rude to say 'You!' (**Ⓓ**) will not get you far, since Thais who say 'You!' rarely speak more than six words of English (all of them annoying); you will also have got yourself into a rather negative situation instead of neutralising an annoying one. Saying 'You!' in return (**Ⓑ**) is not likely to get you into trouble, but it is likely to reinforce the unfortunate behaviour pattern.

If you want to attract somebody's attention, it is acceptable to say the Thai equivalents of 'You', 'Mister' or 'Lady'. Thais do it. But they inevitably pick a polite word for 'You' and add the respect suffix. And, most importantly, they have some reason for attracting attention (just to see the *farang* turn round is not a good reason). So, although the caller is unlikely to wish to be rude, this is really a time for the neutral response. Give a flimsy smile if you like, but walk on by. Don't let an inappropriate response to such a tiny thing spoil one second of your stay in Thailand. Remember, 99 per cent of Thais would never dream of saying 'Hey, you!' and most of the 1 percent would rather say 'Excuse me, Sir', if only they knew the words to use.

Score
- **A** 0
- **B** −4
- **C** +5
- **D** −1
- **E** −5

SITUATION 8

When assessing your relative status, a Thai is likely to consider which of the following points? (Select as many as you think appropriate.)

- **A** Social connections
- **B** Family
- **C** Education
- **D** Wage/wealth
- **E** Occupation
- **F** Dress and manners
- **G** Age
- **H** Car and house
- **I** Religion
- **J** Race
- **K** Ability to speak Thai
- **L** Friendliness

Comments

Almost everything is a pointer to your status, particularly the first five points on this list. However, religion, race, linguistic ability and friendliness play no part. Flattery about fair skin or exaggerated compliments on your ability to say a few words in Thai should not be confused with status.

	Selected	Not Selected
A	+1	−2
B	+1	−2
C	+1	−2
D	+1	−2
E	+1	−2
F	+1	−2
G	+1	−2
H	+1	−2
I	−5	+1
J	−5	+1
K	−5	+1
L	−5	+1

SITUATION 9

A foreigner who wants to make himself popular with Thais should follow which of the following maxims? (Select as many as you think appropriate.)

A Never do or say anything to cause offence.
B Be honest and say exactly what you think.
C Be yourself and people will respect you for it.
D Be generous.
E Do as the Thais do.
F Smile and take it easy.

Comments

In any particular situation, the amount of damage done by 'saying what you think' (**B**) and 'being yourself' (**C**) would depend on what you think and what you are. As a guiding principle covering all situations, it is much safer to avoid making a bad impression (**A**) than to pursue popularity. The foreigner who really craves popularity can buy it (**D**), although generosity without politeness will not achieve very much.

Doing 'as the Thais do' (**E**) is the most dangerous advice without the rider 'as Thais of equal status do'. You do not sit cross-legged in front of a monk, although he is sitting this way. You do not return the same *wai* you receive, etc. If really in doubt about what to do, do nothing; just smile and take it easy. This is the safest and surest way to popularity.

Score

A	+5
B	−5
C	−5
D	+5
E	−5
F	+5

SITUATION 10

You are working in Thailand. You visit a project site where the work is a year behind schedule. During a tour of the site, you find no good reason for the delays. After the visit, you are invited to give your impressions to the Thai manager and staff of the project. Do you: (choose one)

A Tell them the rate of progress is appalling and if they don't pull up their socks, they will all be sacked.

B Ask them collectively the reason for the delays.

C Single out the project manager and ask him to account for the slow progress.

D Go through the aims and history of the project, pointing out all difficulties, however minor, and praising the team for overcoming these difficulties to the extent that work can now proceed as originally planned.

E Make an unfavourable comparison with progress on a similar project and give a mild pep talk.

Comments

The rule here, as everywhere, is to avoid direct criticism. If your words are to have any positive impact, you must be respected and liked. Respect is granted automatically because of your status, but make yourself unpopular and you are unlikely to get very far. The **❶** approach is ideal for situations like this, where you have as long as you like to talk to a captive audience without interruption. Be careful that praise for very minor achievements does not lapse into the kind of sarcasm which could draw a relaxing laugh in the West but would fuel the tension in Thailand.

The real advantages of the **❶** technique is that it gains you popularity with the entire workforce, makes it clear that whatever happened in the past was nobody's fault and need not affect the future and leaves you in a good position to work closely with the project manager. When alone with him, and if you are sure he likes you, you might consider mentioning that the really big bosses are making things difficult for you by always asking for reports on this project (the 'they don't understand the difficulties' approach). Singling out an individual for public criticism (**❸**) would certainly not improve his performance and is likely to cause further delays in project implementation. Similarly, collective criticism, whether direct (**❹**) or indirect (**❺**), will have the opposite effect to that intended (especially if they do not wear socks).

Asking the reason for delays (**❷**), even in a 'let's tackle this problem together' spirit, is most likely to draw an embarrassing silence that is difficult to follow; the silence may be due to reluctance to speak out in public; it could, however, be interpreted as implying that no good reason exists for the delays. The fact that you found no reason for delays during a brief guided tour for big shots does not mean no reason exists. If people like you and find you sympathetic, they will find ways of letting you know if the foreman is pocketing 20 per cent of the workmen's wages.

Score

- **❹** −5
- **❷** 0
- **❸** −10
- **❶** +5
- **❺** −1

SITUATION 11

You receive a printed invitation to an administration clerk's wedding to take place early Saturday morning. You want to maintain good relations, but this is the third wedding in one month; you do not know her family or the groom and you would much rather stay at home, get up late and play with the kids. Do you: (choose one)

Ⓐ Make the effort to go in order to maintain good relations.

Ⓑ Thank her for the invitation and simply not turn up.

Ⓒ Drop by for a short period and leave.

Ⓓ Give her an envelope with a sizeable amount of money inside and say you are sorry you cannot make it.

Ⓔ Give the envelope to a colleague who is certain to attend.

Comments

Any occasion with printed invitations, particularly weddings, cannot simply be ignored (**Ⓑ**) in the same way that a casual verbal invitation could be. Putting yourself, and your family, out in order to attend (**Ⓐ** and **Ⓒ**) is not necessary. It is, however, necessary to give money and not a miserly amount. This can either be given to your clerk (**Ⓓ**) or to a colleague (**Ⓔ**) who will put it on the special tray provided. Your envelope should, of course, be clearly marked with your name so that your generosity is credited (and excellent relations maintained).

Score

Ⓐ   0
Ⓑ   −5
Ⓒ   0
Ⓓ   + 5
Ⓔ   + 5

SITUATION 12

A young staff member never speaks to you and seems to have avoided you ever since you arrived. When he has work to give you, it is usually passed through another person. His work seems all right. At first you thought he was simply shy. But you see him happily chatting with other staff members and even outsiders. You begin to feel that unwittingly you might have offended the staff member. Do you: (choose one)

Ⓐ Call the person into your office for a coffee and a chat and discreetly ask if everything is all right.

Ⓑ Ask your secretary to find out what the problem is.

Ⓒ Encourage more interaction by giving the person duties that require more contact.

Ⓓ Make a point of speaking socially to the person whenever you pass him/her.

Ⓔ Let things continue as they are.

Comments

It is perfectly normal and proper in a Thai work setting for an inferior to maintain social distance from the boss. Individuals vary, but some degree of *krengjai* feeling should be there if you are getting due respect. This does not mean that your staff should be afraid to talk to you; with some you might get more talk than you want and with others, like this staff member, hardly any communication at all.

Deliberately trying to make the individual 'open up' (**Ⓐ**) is likely to leave your staff member confused and wondering if he/she has done something wrong (or if you are making sexual advances). **Ⓑ** will definitely suggest that you are not satisfied (and that therefore the staff member is at fault). **Ⓒ** or **Ⓓ**, while not too bad, would mean singling out the staff member.

If you have the time and inclination to speak a few words to staff members when you pass each of them, try not to ignore this one because of seeming lack of response. Treat him as you would anybody else. Let things continue. You probably have not offended anyone—the person was always reserved (if a normally chatty person suddenly clams up, however, do begin to wonder if there is some reason that could include you). While Thais are becoming increasingly used to working with *farang* and many adjust their behaviour accordingly, some cannot. Please don't push them to do so.

Score

Ⓐ   –5
Ⓑ   –5
Ⓒ   –1
Ⓓ   –1
Ⓔ   +5

SITUATION 13

One of your office staff asks to see you and informs you that a driver is stealing office supplies regularly. You ask how he knows and he claims to have witnessed, along with other staff members, at least one theft. However, he explains that the driver has a reputation as a tough guy and that everybody is afraid to confront him. He also asks you not to involve him in your investigations. Do you: (choose one)

Ⓐ Sack the driver.
Ⓑ Insist that the informant confront the accused in your presence and if he refuses, ignore the matter.
Ⓒ Call in the police.
Ⓓ See all your staff one by one and ask them if they have seen anything.
Ⓔ See all staff together, including the driver, for a showdown.

Comments

This is serious. You must come to a quick decision which your staff will accept as fair. You cannot sack one man only on the word of another (**Ⓐ**). Thieves are often tough guys and it is sensible to a Thai to avoid any possibility of personal reprisal, so don't blame staff for not wanting to point a finger at the accused. Seeing everybody together (**Ⓔ**) could be taken as a sign of the suspect's innocence, since quite possibly nobody will speak up, yet you cannot simply ignore the matter (**Ⓑ**).

If the driver is accused of murder or rape, then do not hesitate to call in the police but in this case, office supplies have been stolen. The police might well find no witnesses; even if they did, office harmony will have been destroyed. You are the boss and you will have to handle this. Start by knowing that such an accusation is unlikely to be fabricated: the staff member might be trying to ingratiate by informing you of the theft but he would have nothing to gain if it were untrue and he would risk the wrath of an angry driver. On the other hand, the staff member could be mistaken or perhaps unintentionally exaggerating a petty theft.

Before any of your staff can go sick or otherwise flee the scene, make it known to everybody in the office that they are to stay put until they are called, one by one, to see you. Then get the driver in. The last thing you want is for him to hear what is going on, before you are ready for him, and drive off with your Mercedes (or Toyota). Tell him that stock is missing and he has been accused. For once some straight speaking. If by chance he admits it, it would probably save a lot of trouble by letting him resign. If he denies it, have him wait outside your room. Let him hear you give orders for all stock records to be brought up. Make sure he sits there throughout your inquiry. Call all staff in one by one. Even if they have nothing to say, keep them ten minutes. Having heard everybody and had the stock records or whatever other pieces of what might be evidence brought conspicuously into your room, decide if the driver is guilty or not before you call him in.

Even if you found no real evidence against him, don't immediately say so; if he is guilty, he probably thinks you have evidence—all those stock books open on your desk for a start. If he pleads not guilty but resigns on the spot, accept immediately. No notice, pay him off. If you have real evidence, tell him he has been seen by so many witnesses, etc. and that therefore you are dismissing him. No notice. Make sure he returns any keys, identification, etc. and get him out immediately. And know that your staff will credit you for your decision. You will probably have a happier office, since nobody likes tough guys. And know also that, even if the driver left humbly and gave you a *wai* (which you do not return!), you have made an enemy for life.

Score

Ⓐ　10

Ⓑ　−5

Ⓒ　−4

Ⓓ　+5

Ⓔ　−5

SITUATION 14

Your secretary, a reliable source of office gossip, tells you one day that the administration assistant is pushing for his brother to be recommended to you for employment in the vacant driver's job. He is treating the personnel officer, whom you rely on for recommendations, to lunch almost every day and at one lunch introduced his brother. Do you: (choose one)

Ⓐ Tick off the administration assistant and say that you cannot allow nepotism.

Ⓑ Tell the personnel officer to remove the brother from the list of applicants.

Ⓒ Wait until you get the recommendation, look at the other applicants and choose one.

Ⓓ Tell your secretary to mind her own business.

Ⓔ Pay special attention to selection and, with the personnel officer present, pick the one you consider the best candidate.

Comments

Duty to a brother comes before duty to the company: not that there need be any contradiction. It is perfectly normal (in a sense admirable) that the administration assistant wants to help his brother. So **Ⓐ** is really out. **Ⓑ** is almost as bad, since your action will be interpreted as criticism. Quietly choosing a different applicant (**Ⓒ**) is neutral and nobody need lose face. If you are really against nepotism, that's for you. Your secretary, although she really knows what is acceptable and might or might not have questionable motives for her disclosure, at least came to tell you; probably she likes you, maybe she has been reading up on modern office management. Don't ever tell her to mind her own business. She probably does, but she minds your business as well. Go ahead and choose the best candidate, and if it's the administration assistant's brother...never mind and maybe so much the better.

Score

Ⓐ −10
Ⓑ −5
Ⓒ 0
Ⓓ −10
Ⓔ +5

SITUATION 15

You are visiting upcountry, examining the administration of a small, entirely Thai-manned new branch of your Bangkok-based office. You know none of the staff personally. You have a budget of 7,000 baht for the local purchase of a small refrigerator. Do you: (choose one)

Ⓐ Tell the staff member responsible for administration that he should go out and buy a fridge up to 7,000 baht and give you the receipt.

Ⓑ Send two members of staff independently to get quotations on fridges.

Ⓒ Send the administration officer to get specifications and prices so you can, if necessary, check with Bangkok and see if it is cheaper to send one up.

Ⓓ Buy it yourself.

Comments

You are the visiting boss. You do not go out and buy a fridge or anything else (**Ⓓ**). Apart from the question of status, there is the pragmatic aspect of making such purchases after you are gone: this is your chance to see how your team will operate. Giving the administration officer full responsibility (**Ⓐ**) is not a bad choice. You can always check later if the fridge really cost 7,000 baht. However, this response does not make it clear to the administration officer that he, like you, is finally responsible to Bangkok office or headquarters. **Ⓒ** sets out this structure without showing suspicion of anybody, as would be the case in **❸**. It is as well to be careful. Trust your staff to a reasonable extent but be aware that if you quote a ceiling budget, receipts are likely to reflect that ceiling precisely to the baht.

Score
ⓐ   0
ⓑ   −4
ⓒ   + 5
ⓓ   −5

SITUATION 16

Visiting a reasonably important Thai for official or business matters in his office, you are received and invited to sit. A girl enters with a tray, sinks to her knees and places a cup of coffee and a glass of water in front of you. Your host has nothing. You do not drink coffee and are not thirsty. Do you: (choose one)

ⓐ Inform the girl that you would prefer tea.
ⓑ Inform the host that you would prefer tea.
ⓒ Leave both coffee and water untouched.
ⓓ Drink the coffee rather than risk offence.
ⓔ Take a sip of the coffee and leave the rest.
ⓕ Drink the water and leave the coffee.

Comments

Puzzling over such petty etiquette shows at least that you are analysing situations. The offer of a glass of water is ubiquitous courtesy. There is no need to drink it. This courtesy has been extended to include coffee, which raises the status of the occasion. Whether you drink, sip or leave either or both will not offend or please your host. However, the coffee has been provided by the host so telling the girl to bring you tea (that is what it comes to) is not on. It is quite all right to tell the host you do not drink coffee, especially if you are to be a regular visitor, but say you prefer tea only if he asks. If either the girl or host asks you if you want coffee or tea, then you are, of course, free to state a preference or decline both. It is traditional to wait until invited by the host before drinking. If you don't want to drink, you can simply say 'thank you' and leave it at that.

Score

A	–5
B	–1
C	0
D	0
E	0
F	0

SITUATION 17

Returning from a successful field visit in the north of Thailand with some important local Thai business contacts, on your way for a social drink, everything around you stops moving as if spell struck. The driver slows and looks at you for instructions. Faintly, through the glass windows, you hear loudspeakers. It is 6:00 pm. Do you: (choose one)

A Ask the driver what is going on.
B Tell the driver to pull over.
C Say, "Go on, what are you waiting for?"
D Carry on speaking and leave the driving to the driver.
E Tell the driver to stop immediately.

Comments

In rural areas more distant from Bangkok, and in some parts of the capital, the national anthem is played over loudspeakers at 8:00 am and 6:00 pm. No need to pull over. Impress your associates and enjoy a quiet minute by stopping right in the middle of the road. Open the window and listen to the music. It is perhaps going too far to open your door and step out to attention. If you ignore this moment of simple national respect (**D**), you are showing at best your ignorance of local custom. You only have a minute, so asking the driver (**A**), while an understandable reaction, is an unnecessary waste of time—now that you know.

Score

Ⓐ   –1

Ⓑ   0

Ⓒ   –5

Ⓓ   –2

Ⓔ   +5

And now to carry on in the same vein, with questions aimed more at young readers.

TWENTY QUESTIONS

This true/false quiz is intended for children of all ages. If you want to do so, tick in either T for true or F for false after the questions. One mark on your score for each correct answer, one mark off for each wrong answer. For those who find this too simple—which should be all of you—supplementary questions are added in brackets. The quiz can be given verbally to several children at one time and they can be invited to add to the supplementary questions as far as they can go.

	Question	T	F
1	Eating in *wat* grounds is forbidden. (Is any food forbidden to Thais?)		
2	Shoes must be removed at the *bot*. (Where else should shoes be removed?)		
3	Menstruating women are not permitted inside the *wat*. (What are the rules, if any, controlling entry?)		
4	Monks do not eat after noon. (What are the five most important rules for monks?)		
5	One should not sit cross-legged in audience with monks. (How does sitting position relate to status?)		
6	Most Thais work in the rice fields. (What is Thailand's principal export?)		

	Question	T	F
7	All Thais are called *Khun*. (How can *Khun* be translated in English?)		
8	Only special friends should call a Thai by his nickname. (What is the likely origin of Thai nicknames?)		
9	Hats should be removed when entering a Thai home. (Describe the relationship between hats and shoes.)		
10	Most Thais use water and the left hand to clean their backsides after defecation. (How do toilet habits relate to social action?)		
11	Thai Buddhist monks do not eat meat. (Why do they/don't they?)		
12	It is forbidden for a woman to touch a monk or his robes. (How should a woman pass something to a monk?)		
13	Hair is considered unclean by the Thais. (Explain the taboo against touching hair and heads.)		
14	During Buddhist Lent, Thais do not drink alcohol. (When is Buddhist Lent?)		
15	Anybody can become a monk. (What are the requirements?)		
16	All Thai girls who wear cardigans back to front are defending themselves against evil spirits. (Why should such behaviour offer any protection?)		
17	One Thai mother can compliment another on her 'ugly' baby. (How do childbirth ceremonies relate to belief in spirits?)		
18	The inferior always pays for the superior. (What is the etiquette of paying in restaurants?)		
19	Thais believe in fair criticism. (What are the 'ground rules' for indirect criticism?)		

	Question	T	F
20	Thais generally feel that no problem is too big for them to tackle. (Describe Thai norms of conflict avoidance.)		

Answers

True: Questions 2, 4, 5, 6, 9, 10, 12, 17
False: Questions 1, 3, 7, 8, 11, 13, 14, 15, 16, 18, 19, 20

No answers are given for supplementary questions, but they are all in this book somewhere. Having read this book and completed the quiz, you will almost certainly find yourself in situations that I haven't covered. You are you and your situations are as unique as you are.

When you find yourself swimming in a new situation and you begin to get that sinking feeling, write your own quiz. Think of all your possible responses and, using your knowledge of Thai behaviour, evaluate these responses in positive and negative terms. Then follow the most positive alternative.

Some people find this approach to understanding a new culture somewhat over-analytical and even 'cold-blooded' or 'Machiavellian'. Others find it greatly increases their power of awareness of what is going on around them and their place in it all. Perhaps the greatest benefit of this situational approach to culture learning is that it can turn the most depressing situation into a game and even make it fun. Seen from this viewpoint, culture shock is both productive and positive, providing food for thought and action.

Life in Thailand is an endless, fascinating game. I have set out in this book some of the rules of this game. If there is one cardinal principle holding the whole glorious experience together, I would guess it is something like the sentence I cited earlier:

Life is very fun why quickly to go.
Have fun and you will survive forever.

DO'S AND DON'TS

DO'S

- Do avoid things, people and situations you don't like rather than moan about them or try to change them.
- Do keep Buddha images in a high place and treat them with great respect. It is against the law to take or send them out of the country except under very special circumstances and with permission.
- Do beckon waiters and servants with the hand, palm downwards, fingers straight and waving rapidly. Don't clap, snap fingers or hiss.
- Do make payment only after eating and drinking, not before. The inviter pays; if no clear invitation was made, the superior pays. Going Dutch is rare.
- Do practise discretion as it is admired as maturity.
- Do dress your status and dress appropriately at parties. Women do not wear shorts or revealing clothing.
- Do eat after the monks during ceremonies.
- Do eat with a spoon and use a fork to load it.
- Do reply with 'eaten already' when greeted with the casual invitation to eat.
- Do keep your feet to yourself and not on your desk.
- Do flatter whenever possible. Thais love it.
- Do be generous. It is a sign of an important person.
- Do open gifts in private.
- Do address social inferiors first when making introductions.
- Do use a person's first name, not the family name. Adults should be addressed as *Khun* unless a title is used.
- Do use an invitation card if attendance and punctuality are important, as invitations are less specific in Thailand.
- Do have a meal prepared should you specifically invite someone to your house. They expect to eat there.
- Do lower the body a little when passing in front of, or between, people.
- Do treat monks with utmost respect at all times. Touching of a monk or his robes by a woman is strictly taboo.

- Do pass objects with the right hand and touch the left hand to the right forearm if extra respect is required. Women never pass directly to monks.

- Do treat royalty with the greatest respect. Do stand up when images of the king or royal family appear on the cinema screen.

- Do remove your shoes at the door of the main temple building and at all homes.

- Do sit in the place you are directed to. Superiors in front, inferiors at the back.

- Do speak gently and do not raise your voice.

- Do smile and people will like you. A smile can be used to excuse small inconveniences, to thank for small services and to return the *wai* of children and servants.

- Do keep your temper.

- Do *wai* monks, old people and your social superiors.

- Do walk slightly behind monks and old people.

DON'TS

- Don't point your feet at anybody. Don't step over anybody or anybody's food.

- Don't point your fingers at anybody, though it is acceptable for objects and animals.

- Don't touch hair and heads. If you do so by accident, excuse yourself.

- Don't cross your legs whether sitting on floor or chair in the presence of monks.

- Don't wear black unless at a funeral (or at a trendy teenage party).

- Don't throw rice away in front of Thais. Rice is the lifeblood of Thailand.

- Don't throw objects. Throwing any object is bad manners.

- Don't *wai* servants, labourers and children. The lower the head, the more respect is shown. The inferior initiates the *wai*. Whatever the *wai* received, reply with a lesser one.

- Don't be surprised if your laundry is done by a man and he refuses to wash a woman's underclothes.

GLOSSARY

USEFUL WORDS AND PHRASES

chuay-duay	help! (If you are under attack)
chuay	help (when requesting assistance)
chuay noy	please help me (polite)
mor/phaet	doctor
rong paya BAN	hospital
sa-BAY/sa-BAY dii	well (healthy)
sa-BAY dii may?	are you well?
may sa-BAY	(I am) not well
jep	hurt/pain
jep nii	(I) hurt here
prik	chillies
say prik	put chillies
may say prik	don't put chillies!
dii	good
dii may?	is it good?
may dii	bad/not good
suay	pretty
suay may?	is she pretty?
may suay	not pretty/ugly
suay dii	very pretty
he-LOW	hello (on the phone only)
sa-WAT dii	hello (face to face)/I am well
sa-WAT dii may?	how are you?
khao jai	understand
khao jai may?	do you understand?
may khao jai	(I) do not understand

tao rai?	how much?
paeng	expensive
may paeng	not expensive
paeng may?	is it expensive?
arai?	what?
arai-na?	What did you say?
cheu arai?	What's your name?
bpai	go
bpai nai?	Where are you going?
khun	you/Mr/Mrs
khop khun	thank you
aroy	tasty
aroy mark	very tasty
aroy may	is it tasty
may aroy	not tasty (but better not say it)

NUMBERS

soon	zero
neung	one
sorng	two
sarm	three
sii	four
har	five
hok	six
jet	seven
peht	eight
gow	nine
sip	ten
sip et	eleven
sip sorng	twelve
sip sarm	thirteen

sip sii	fourteen
sip har	fifteen
sip hok	sixteen
sip jet	seventeen
sip peht	eighteen
sip gow	ninteen
yii sip	twenty
yii sip et	twenty-one
yii sip sorng	twenty-two
sarm sip	thirty
sarm sip et	thirty-one
sarm sip sorng	thirty-two
sii sip	forty
har sip	fifty
hok sip	sixty
jet sip	seventy
peht sip	eighty
gow sip	ninety
roy	one hundred
sorng roy	two hundred
sarm roy	three hundred
pahn	one thousand
sorng phan	two thousand
meun	ten thousand

RESOURCE GUIDE

The expat elect and the newly arrived visitor are likely to be initially gripped more by the worldly needs of everyday life than by the wonders and wormholes of Thai culture. Thus the reason for this easy reference resource, placed at the back of the book, is for it to be consulted preferably before departure or soonest after arrival.

I made two polls of new arrivals in Bangkok. These polls were ten years apart and had very random samples, although I tried to include most nationalities. I asked new expats to place, in order, their main concerns about moving to Thailand. Results show an amazing consistency over a ten-year period and almost all respondents agree that their priorities lie in health and education. Chief on the worry list is, "What are the medical facilities like?" For those with children, this is followed closely or given equal place with, "Where can my child go to school?"

To help the new expat in Thailand, and the prospective expat planning his move, I set out in the following pages to assist with these and other immediate concerns. All information is up to the minute at the time of going to press. Of course institutions change names, addresses, services on offer and contact details. Your comments to the authors, through the publishers, on this section are particularly welcome.

THAILAND CALLING CODES
To call Thailand you will need to dial:
Exit country code + 66 + city code + telephone number

Use the following chart to help make your phone call.

City Code

Bangkok	2
Buriram	44
Chanthaburi	39

Chiang Mai	53
Chiang Rai	54
Chon Buri	38
Hatyai	74
Kamphaengphet	55
Lampang	54
Nakhon Sawan (Nakhonsawan)	56
Nong (Nongkhai)	42
Pathumthani	2
Pattani	73
Pattaya Beach (Phattaya)	38
Phetchaburi	32
Phitsanulok	55
Phuket	76
Ratchaburi	32
Sara Buri (Saraburi)	36
Songkhla	74
Tak	55
Trang	75
Ubon Ratchathani	45
Udon Thani	42

EMERGENCIES AND HEALTH

As English on emergency numbers might be limited or non-existent, have an English-speaking Thai or a Thai-speaking foreigner make your call if this is at all possible.

General Emergency

Dial 191 and specify if you need the police, ambulance or fire brigade and leave your phone number and address. 199 can also be used for cases of fire.

Ambulance

Mark the number nearest to your home (Bangkok only. For other towns, see Hospitals).

- **Bangkok General Hospital**
  soi Soonvijai, New Petchburi Road
  Tel: (02) 310-3456
- **BNH Hospital**
  Convent Road
  Tel: (02) 632-0582-6
- **Bumrungrad Hospital**
  Sukhumvit soi 3
  Tel: (02) 667-2999
- **Samitivej Hospital**
  Sukhumvit soi 49
  Tel: (02) 39211
- **St Louis Hospital**
  215 Sathorn South Road
  Tel: (02) 675-5000
- **Thai Nakarin Hospital**
  345 Bang Na-Trat Road
  Tel: (02) 361-2712-61
- **Samitivej-Srinakarin Hospital**
  Srinakarin Road
  Tel: (02) 731-7000

Snake Bites

Keep the victim still and the affected area below heart level. Wash the bite with soap and water. Call an ambulance or go to the emergency department of the nearest hospital. If you are able to bring the snake, dead or alive, for identification, so much the better. If you live within the range of The Chulalongkorn Hospital Emergency Department on Rama IV Road, opposite the Dusit Thani Hotel, they have an excellent supply of antidotes on hand. Open 24 hours. Tel: (02) 256-4214.

Medical Evacuations

Many people from surrounding countries evacuate into Thailand because of the scope and quality of medical services provided at reasonable prices, particularly in Bangkok. But should evacuation out of Thailand become essential, it may be arranged through the treating hospital. Be aware that this is always expensive. However, insurance is available to cover the costs involved from a number of sources, including:

- **International SOS Services**
  Tel: (02) 256-7146 (24 hours)
- **Pacific East Assistance**
  Tel: (02) 645-3877 (24 hours)

Hospitals (Bangkok)

The following list is a selection of hospitals that regularly use English and are accustomed to treating foreigners. They have all received the highest grading from the Thai Red Cross, which considers them as good, if not better, than the hospitals in Europe and the US. It is quite normal to seek help directly from the hospital without the need for referral by a general practitioner. Indeed, many hospitals function as a one-stop shop for all the family. Current favourites are Bumrunggrad and BNH; in both establishments the latest equipment is available, doctors are often trained overseas, accommodation and facilities are first class and there is a progressive policy of explaining to the patient the nature of problems and treatment. Be prepared to tell the receptionist the essentials of your problem.

- **Bangkok Adventist Mission Hospital**
  430 Pitsanulok Road, Dusit (near Khao San Road)
  Tel: (02) 282-8181
- **BNH Hospital** (Bangkok Nursing Home)
  Convent Road
  Tel: (02) 63252
- **Bumrungrad Hospital**
  Sukhumvit soi 3
  Tel: (02) 667-1000
- **Samitivej Hospital**
  Sukhumvit soi 49
  Tel: (02) 731-7000

Hospitals (Outside Bangkok)
Chantaburi

These two hospitals provide primary care.

- **Taksin Chantaburi Hospital**
  25/14 Taa Luang Road, Chantaburi 22000
  Tel: (039) 351-467
- **Sirivej Hospital**
  151 Moo 7, Trirat Road, Chantaburi 22000
  Tel: (039) 344-2415

Chiang Mai

The hospitals listed below are considered by the Thai Red Cross Society to be of European/US standard. They provide ambulance and emergency services.

- **McCormick Hospital**
  133 Kaew Navarat Road, Chiang Mai, 5000
  Tel: (053) 241-177
- **Chiang Mai Ram Hospital**
  8 Boonruangrit Road, Chiang Mai, 50200
  Tel: (053) 224-861
- **Lanna Hospital**
  1 Sukkasem Road, Kwang Nakornping, Chiang Mai, 50300
  Tel: (053) 357-234-53

Chiang Rai

Care is reasonable here, but surgery cases are often evacuated to Chiang Mai or Bangkok.

- **Overbrook Hospital** (Protestant Mission)
  17 Singhaklai Road, Chiang Rai 57000
  Tel: (054) 711-366
- **Kasemrad Sriburin Hospital**
  111/5 Moo 13, Tambon Sunsai, Chiang Rai 57000
  Tel: (054) 717-499

Khon Kaen

- **Khon Kaen Ram Hospital**
  193 Srijaan Road, Khon Kaen 40000
  Tel: (043) 333-800. Provides primary care only.

Korat

- **Pho Phaet Hospital**
  45-52 Chainarong Road, Nakorn Ratchasima, 30000
  Tel: (044) 251-070. Rated by the Red Cross as being on
  par with hospitals in Chiang Mai.

Nongkhai

- **Nong Khai Wattana Hospital**
  1159/4 Prachak Road, Nong Khai 43000
  Tel: (042) 465-201. Many patients come from neighbouring
  Laos. This is a very friendly hospital and has ambulance
  and emergency services and a dental unit. More serious
  cases are referred to Udorn, 45 minutes away on a very
  good road.

Pattaya

The following hospitals are rated adequate to good.
- **Bangkok Pattaya Hospital**
  301 Moo 6, Sukhumvit Road (KM 143) Muang Pattaya,
  Chonburi 20150
  Tel: (038) 427-770/427-7515
- **Pattaya Memorial Hospital**
  328/1 Pattaya Klang Road, Pattaya, Chonburi 20260
  Tel: (038) 429-422
- **Pattaya International Hospital**
  255/4, Pattaya Road 2, Pattaya, Chonburi 20260
  Tel: (038) 428-374/427-5756

Phuket

Hospitals here provide good treatment and complex
problems are easily transferred to Bangkok or Singapore by
regular flights.
- **Bangkok Phuket Hospital**
  2/1 Hongyokutis Road, Phuket 83000
  Tel: (076) 254-421
- **Phuket International Hospital**
  44 Chalermprakiat Road 9, Phuket 83000
  Tel: (076) 249-400/249-383

Songkhla/Had Yai
These hospitals have been rated good.
- **Bangkok Had Yai Hospital**
  54/113 Moo 3, Klongrean 1 Road, Had Yai, Songkhla 90110
  Tel: (074) 365-7809
- **Rajyindee Hospital**
  119 Rajyindee Road, Had Yai, Songkhla 90110
  Tel: (074) 220-300

Surin
The list below provides primary care.
- **Surin Hospital**
  68 Lakmuang Road, Surin 32000
  Tel: (045) 518-4246/514-125/511-757
- **Surin Ruan Phaet Hospital**
  378 Moo 9, Surin-Lamchee Road, Surin, 32000
  Tel: (045) 516-108

Udorn (Udon Thani)
- **Aek Udon International Hospital**
  555/5 Phosri Road, Udon Thani 41000
  Tel: (042) 342-555. It offers some of the best medical
  services in the north-east, with a range of specialities.

Dental Clinics, Opticians and Cosmetic Surgery
All of the above listed Bangkok hospitals and many of those outside the capital provide a 'one stop shop'. They contain very good dental clinics and opticians, and have staff available who speak English and sometimes French and German. In addition, there is an English-speaking specialist in children's dentistry available in Bangkok from 5:30–7:30 pm at Rak Fun (Love Teeth) 59/22 soi Muang Thong Thani 3, Chaeng Wattana Road; tel: (02) 573-6747.

Outside Bangkok and Chiang Mai, dental facilities are not always as good and you should always check that anything going into your mouth is either disposable or well sterilised. Compared to European and American equivalents, dental and optical work is of a similar quality at a fraction of the cost. In addition to getting your teeth and eyes sorted out, Thailand is also the place where you can get rid of that wart on your nose or the mole on your cheek. If you want to add a few inches or take them up or off, it can also be arranged in a nice place, at a price you can't afford to miss.

UTILITIES

- **Electricity Authority of Thailand**. They are likely to give you a local number when you call, tel: 31424
- **Bangkok Water Works Emergency Department**, tel: 1125
- **Bangkok Water Works Main Office**, tel: (02) 504-8285

COURSES AND EDUCATION
International Schools

To facilitate your search for an international school, I have provided a list here. This list comes without comment since all provide much information by post, fax or internet. They are grouped below by national curriculum. Some are fairly recent annexes of famous schools abroad and have waiting lists and are expensive (but not if compared to back home). It will take time to go through replies, but a group email to all schools of interest is not a bad first move; all should invite you to visit the school during school hours. A few have scholarships and in some, fees are negotiable to an extent. On the other hand, there are often hidden charges for extra activities and 'voluntary' contributions to development funds might be included in your bill. Pay special attention to the range of examination preparation on offer—no child likes to leave at age 14 to board in the 'home' country—and to the practicalities of getting to school and home again, particularly if evening activities are likely to be involved.

UK

- **Bangkok Patana School**
  2/38 Sukhumvit soi 105, Bangkok 10260
  Tel: (02) 398-0200; fax: (02) 399-3179
  Email: registrar@patana.ac.th
  Website: http://www.patana.ac.th

- **Dulwich International College**, 59 Moo 2, Thepkrasattri Road, Koh Kaew, Amphur Muang, Phuket 83200
  Tel: (076) 238-750
  Email: info@dulwich-phuket.com
  Website: http://www.dulwich.ac.th
- **Garden International School** (Bangkok), 2/1 Yen Akart soi 2, Yen Akart Road, Bangkok 10120
  Tel: (02) 249-1943/240-1307; fax: (02) 249-1943
- **Garden International School** (Rayong), 188/24 Moo 4, Pala Ban Chang Road, Tambon Pala, Amphur Ban Chang, Rayong 21130
  Tel: (038) 880-3603; fax: (038) 630-735
  Email: gisrayon@loxinfo.co.th
  Website: http://www.geocities.com/collegePark/Residence/6000/
- **Harrow International School**, Bangkok Garden, 289 soi New Sathorn Road 24, Yannawa, Bangkok 10120
  Tel: (02) 672-0123-6; fax: (02) 672-0127
  Email: his@loxinfo.co.th
  Website: http://www.harrowschool.ac.th
- **International School of the Regents** (Bangkok and Pattaya campuses), 592 Pracha-Uthit Road, Huai Kwang, Bangkok 10320
  Tel: (02) 690-3777 ext. 202/303; fax: (02) 690-3778
  Email: enquiry@isr.ac.th
  Website: http://www.isr.ac.th
- **Modern International School**, 127, 129, 133 soi Prommitr, Sukhumvit 39, Klongtoey, Bangkok 10110
  Tel: (02) 258-8222/258-8216; fax: (02) 258-8219
  Email: misb@samart.com
- **Pomdee International Home School**, 52/1 Sukhumvit soi 53, Bangkok 10110
  Tel: (02) 258-7964-5; fax: (02) 258-7706
  Email: tlpihs@ksc.th.com
- **Sarasas Ektra School**, 336/7 soi 20, Sathupradit Road, Bangpongpang, Yannawa, Bangkok 10120
  Tel: (02) 213-0117/212-0157; fax: (02) 674-0499

- **St Andrews International School** (Bangkok), 9 soi Panitkun, Sukhumvit soi 71, Bangkok 10110
  Tel: (02) 381-2387-8/390-1780/391-4845
  Fax: (02) 391-5227; email: bangkok@st-andrews.ac
  Website: http://www.st-andrews.ac
- **St Andrews International School** (Rayong), Rayong Green Valley Estate, 23 Moo 7, Ban Chang-Makham Road, Rayong 21330
  Tel: (038) 893-716-9; fax: (038) 893-720
  Email: rayong@st-andrews.ac
  Website: http://www.st-andrews.ac
- **St John's International School**, 1110/3 Lad Prao Road, Bangkok 10900
  Tel: (02) 513-8575-90/513-0579; fax: (02) 513-5273
  Email: sjiadmin@stjohn.ac.th
- **St Michael International School**, 400 Sukhumvit Garden City, Sukhumvit soi 79, Prakanong, Bangkok 10250
  Tel: (02) 332-7890-9; fax: (02) 311-7412
- **Traill International School**, 34-36 soi 18, Ramkamhaeng Road, Huamark, Bangkok 10240
  Tel: (02) 314-5250; fax: (02) 318-7194

UK and Thai

- **Rasami International School**, 48/2 soi Rajvithi 2, Rajprasop Road, Bangkok 10400
  Tel: (02) 644-5291/644-5292; fax: (02) 640-9527
  Email: rasami@rasami.ac.th
  Website: http://www.rasami.ac.th
- **St Stephen's International School**, 107 Vibhavadi Rangsit Road, Lad Yao, Chatuchak, Bangkok 10900
  Tel: (02) 513-0270-1/661-6800; fax: (02) 513-0265/661-6824
  Email: richard@ocean.co.th

US

- **Ekamai International School**, 57 soi Charoenchai (Ekamai 12), Sukhumvit 63, Khlong Toey, Bangkok 10110
  Tel: (02) 391-3593; fax: (02) 381-4622

Email: eissdabk@samart.co.th
Website: http://www.ekamai.com
- **International Community School**, 72 soi Prong Jai, Sribumphen Road, Thungmahamek, Sathorn, Bangkok 10120
  Tel: (02) 679-7175-7; fax: (02) 287-4530
  Email: icsbkk@loxinfo.co.th
- **International School Bangkok**, 39/7 soi Nichada Thani, Samakee Road, Pakkret, Nonthaburi 11120
  Tel: (02) 583-5401/583-5420; fax: (02) 583-5431-2
  Email: jamess@isb.ac.th; website: http://www.isb.ac.th
- **International School Eastern Seaboard**, 282 Moo 5, Tambon Barwin, Banglamung, Si Racha, Chonburi 20150
  Tel: (038) 372-591-4; fax: (038) 345-156
  Email: ise@loxinfo.co.th
- **Ruamrudee International School**, 42 Moo 4 soi 184, Ramkamhaeng Road, Minburi, Bangkok 10510
  Tel: (02) 518-0320-29; fax: (02) 518-0303
  Email: director@rism.ac.th
- **The American School of Bangkok**, 900 Moo 3, Bang Na-Trad Km 15, Amphur Bangplee, Samut Prakarn 10540
  Tel: (02) 312-5660-2; fax: (02) 312-5795
  Email: info@asb.th.edu
  Website: http://www.asb.th.edu

Language of Instruction Other Than in English
French
- **Lycee Francais de Bangkok**
  29 Sathorn Tai, Bangkok 10120
  Tel: (02) 287-1599; fax: (02) 679-2059
  Email: lfbangkok@a-net.net.th

Japanese
- **Thai Japanese Association School**
  258 soi 4, Rama IX Road, Bangkok 10320
  Tel: (02) 314-7334-53/314-7797-8
  Email: kosum@mozart.inet.co.th

Swiss (German and French)

- **Ruamrudee International School Swiss Section**
  42 Moo 4 soi 184, Ramkamhaeng Road, Minburi,
  Bangkok 10510
  Tel: (02) 518-0340/518-0343/518-0344; fax: (02) 518-0341
  Email: thomas@ksc.ll.th.com;
  Website: http://www.rism.ac.th

Chinese (and English)

- **Thai Chinese International School**, Km 12 Bang Na-
  Trat Road, Kwaeng Bang Phli Yai, Khet Bang Phli, Samut
  Prakarn 10280
  Tel: (02) 751-1201-7;
  Email: tcis@schoolmail.com

International (English Language, International Baccalaureat)

- **New International School of Thailand**, 36 Sukhumvit soi
  15, Bangkok 10110
  Tel: (02) 651-2065/253-0109/251-6397-8; fax: (02) 253-3800
  Email: admissions@nist.ac.th
- **Rose Marie Academy**, 39/6 soi Nichada Thani, Samakee
  Road, Pakkret, Nonthaburi 11120
  Tel: (02) 960-3661-3; fax: (02) 960-3664
  Email: rma@loxinfo.co.th
- **Universal International School**, 49 Moo 4, Thanarat Road,
  Tambon Nong Nam Daeng, Amphoe Pak Chong, Nakhon
  Ratchasima 30130
  Tel: (044) 328-334/43; fax: (044) 313-519
  Email: hands@mozart.inet.co.th

Universities in Thailand

While most universities teach in Thai, their libraries are
almost entirely in languages other than Thai. With little or
no knowledge of the Thai language, it is possible to pursue
certain courses at some Thai universities. Postgraduate
studies by thesis may be completed in English (even Thais
write their thesis in English—although this is no longer a
requirement). A three- to four-year tour of duty in Thailand

might take on a completely new meaning for a dependent spouse or older child if a university course is pursued. Costs involved might be much less than those at home.

By the way, many British expats are ignorant of the fact that if they and/or their offspring have been out of the country for some time, they are likely to be charged full fees for entry to a UK university, even if they have returned home (check with your embassy). Information on universities is available from the following websites:

- **Ministry of University Affairs**
  http://www.inter.mua.go.th
- **Asian University of Science and Technology**
  http://www.asianust.ac.th
- **Assumption University**
  http://www.au.ac.th
- **Bangkok University International College**
  http://www.bu.ac.th
- **Chulalongkorn University**
  http://www.chula.ac.th
- **Kasetsart University**
  http://www.ku.ac.th
- **Khon Kaen University**
  http://www.kku.ac.th
- **King Mongkut Institute of Technology**
  http://www.kmitnb.ac.th
- **Mahidol University International College**
  http://www.mahidol.ac.th
- **Prince of Songkhla University**
  http://www.psu.ac.th
- **Ramkhamhaeng University**
  http://www.ru.ac.th
- **Stamford International College**
  http://www.stamford.edu
- **St. John's College**
  http://www.stjohn.ac.th
- **Thammasat University**
  http://www.tu.ac.th
- **Webster University**
  http://www.webster.edu

Libraries

Some excellent libraries, often including serious video and music rentals, photocopy facilities and sometimes Internet access and a snack bar, exist in Bangkok, but are rare outside the capital. Approach your embassy for details of any libraries serving your language—some smaller embassies provide this service, mostly part-time and on a voluntary basis. The most well-known libraries in Bangkok are listed below. Do note that all require some sort of membership, which might involve a fee. Libraries are a good source of leads into special interest organisations, hobbies and what's on in Thailand—and sometimes a good place to escape the heat and meet friends.

- **Alliance Francaise**, 29 Sathorn Tai
  Tel: (02) 213-2122-3
  The combination of a library, language school, theatre, cinema and cafeteria makes this a bustling place, and a good meeting point for the French and Francophiles.
- **AUA** (American University Alumni), 179 Rajdamri
  Tel: (02) 251-1607
  For students of English and Thai, and general English language.
- **British Council**, 254 Phayathai soi 64, Siam Square
  Tel: (02) 252-6136-8/252-6111/252-6830-9
  Full range of subjects and facilities including educational opportunities in the UK, correspondence courses and information on many UK-Thai matters. Day membership is available for short-term visitors.
- **Japanese Cultural Centre**, 10th Floor, Sermmit Tower, 159 soi 21 (soi Asoke) Sukhumvit
  Tel: (02) 260-8560-4
  Japanese, Thai and English represented. Free screening of Japanese movies.
- **The Neilson Hays Library**, 195 Surawong Road
  Tel: (02) 233-1731
  Website: http://www.neilsonhayslibrary.com.
  Open everyday except Monday. Many out of Bangkok members benefit from an extended loan of two months.

- **Siam Society**, 131 Sukhumvit soi 21 (soi Asoke)
  Tel: (02) 259-4999/260-2830-2; fax: (02) 258-3491
  Email: siams@telecom.scb.co.th
  Website: http://www.siam-society.org.
  For those interested in all things Thai. Members only.
  Regular talks, field trips and cultural programmes.

Thai Language Schools

- **AUA Language Centre**, 179 Ratchadamri Road
  Tel: (02) 252-8170
- **Chulalongkorn University**, Tel: (02) 218-4888;
  Email: tkongkar@chula.ac.th.
  Intensive Thai Office, Faculty of Arts
- **Nisa Thai Language School**, YMCA Collins House, 27
  Sathorn Tai
  Tel: (02) 286-9323
- **Siri Pattana Thai Language School**, YWCA 13 Sathon Tai
  Tel: (02) 286-1936
- **Union Language School**, Christ Church Building, 109 Surawong
  Tel: (02) 252-8170

EXPAT CLUBS

There is almost a club for every nationality in Bangkok.
There are also clubs principally for expats engaged in certain
professions (e.g. The Foreign Correspondents' Club). There
are simply too many to list here and details change. Generally
membership is required against some form of payment, use
of basic facilities is thereafter free, and there is some form of
restaurant and library or newspaper access with video/DVD
rental in your language. Some of the bigger hotels also have
clubs or provide what for many is all they need of a club: a
good Sunday lunch and a swimming pool. Your embassy (or
the embassy that handles the affairs of your country) should
give you full details of official clubs. Hotels advertise fitness
and other clubs in the English press.

EMBASSIES

Embassies are not just there to complain about. They can and
should provide advice on clubs, legal representation, prison

visiting, trade agreements, chambers of commerce, births and deaths overseas, marriage and divorce, voting rights, requirements to pay for higher education back home, taxation, and a gamut of routine information, including any voluntary agencies that might benefit from your assistance.

This, of course, is not the primary job of any embassy, which is there to represent the home country in all matters with the host country, which includes assistance to its citizens in trouble. Contrary to popular opinion, diplomatic life is not simply composed of movement from one cocktail party to the next. Many embassies suffer from severe financial restraints and are expected to more or less pay their way in terms of trade deals and promotion of exports, including education. Many charge for small services at rates set from the home country and intended to cover costs.

Many expats complain about their embassies doing nothing for them, but do not even bother to register their residence in the country. Registering is entirely in the expat's own interests and ensures rapid assistance should it be required. It also gets you invited to events such as national days, and keeps you up-to-date on free emailed 'advisories'. The 2004 tsunami disaster caused unnecessary suffering to relatives of foreigners living in the area because many had failed to register with their embassies, making contact doubly difficult. Registration costs nothing and requires only the filling in of a simple form. Get the number of your embassy from the *Yellow Pages*.

PLACES OF WORSHIP
Buddhist

Ninety-five per cent of the population of Thailand is Buddhist. There are Thai Buddhist temples (*wats*) in every town and in almost every village. There are over 400 in Bangkok alone. Thus, for a Buddhist, a variety of places of worship abound. The non-Buddhist, whether male or female, is fully at liberty to visit any *wat*. Plenty of the more established temples in Bangkok and Chiang Mai provide courses on Buddhism in English and welcome all. If you are looking for a type of Buddhism other than Thai, or want information on such things as ordination as a monk, try the **World Fellowship of Buddhists** between sois 1 and 3, Sukhumvit; tel: (02) 251-1188.

Chinese Buddhism is different from the Thai, although many Chinese-Thais will worship equally at both Chinese and Thai temples. There are Chinese temples in most towns, especially in Bangkok's Chinatown.

Christian

All denominations of Christianity are represented in Bangkok and Chiang Mai. Church services are in Thai, including those in Catholic churches, unless otherwise specified. English language newspapers provide details of services in the weekend edition. Services in English, French, German and Swedish can be found within Bangkok.

Muslim

Muslim communities are well integrated into Thai life in Bangkok, Chiang Mai and some smaller towns. In the south, bordering Malaysia, several million Muslims live in communities where Malay is the common language used. Within the Thai constitution, the right of Muslims and all religions to practise in peace (but not to seek to convert) is guaranteed. For locations of mosques, inquire at any embassy of any Islamic country or turn to the *Yellow Pages*.

Jewish

There is a **Jewish Community Centre** located at 121 soi 2, off soi 22, Sukhumvit; tel: (02) 662-0244; fax: (02) 663-0245.

Hindu

Several temples exist. Perhaps the most famous is the Phra Sri Maha Uma Devi Temple on Silom Road near the junction with Pan Road.

Sikh

The Sikh communities are found mostly within Bangkok. Many go to the Sri Gurusingh Sabha Temple off Chakraphet Road near Chinatown.

FURTHER READING

PEOPLE AND CULTURE

Thailand: Its People, Its Society, Its Culture. Wendell Branchard. New Haven: HRAF Press, 1958.
- Now dated but still one of the most comprehensive books on Thailand. If you can find a copy (and libraries have them), it will provide an idea of how things have changed and have not changed over 50 years.

The Hmong: A Guide to Traditional Lifestyles. Robert Cooper. Singapore: Times Editions, 1998.
- A detailed guide to the culture of Thailand's largest and most famous hill minority. Contains the author's much-acclaimed photographs.

Phai Daeng (Red Bamboo). Kukrit Pramoj. Bangkok: Progress Publishing Co, 1961.
- The ex-prime minister of Thailand authors this very readable novel about Thai villagers. The story is identical to the Don Camillo series, but the characters come through as 100 per cent Thai. Also by the same author, the famous four-volume *Si Pandin (Four Reigns)*.

Everyday Life in Thailand: An Interpretation. Neils Mulder. Bangkok: Editions Duang Kamol, 1985.
- One for the specialist. Mulder writes for the Thai scholar. If you already have quite a good knowledge of Thai society, this book could increase it.

Phya Anuman Rajadhon.
- A huge collection of books and pamphlets on many aspects of Thai culture. Concentrates on ceremony. Just ask for his works at any good bookshop or library.

Thai Ways. Denis Segaller. Bangkok: Post, 1993. A must. Read also his following book *More Thai Ways* (Post, 2000).

■ These books reprint articles on Thai culture published in the *Bangkok World* since 1975. They are a mine of information, open them anywhere and you learn something new.

WORK AND BUSINESS

Thais Mean Business. Robert Cooper. Singapore: Marshall Cavendish, 2004.

■ A humorous A–Z for the expat manager and businessman in Thailand.

Mai Pen Rai Means Never Mind. Carol Hollinger. Bangkok: Asia Books, 2001 (4th edition).

■ An autobiographical account of an expat's experiences living and teaching in Thailand. The funniest and best introduction to the Thais available. While the days of *may pen rai* might be numbered, this book, and its humour, refuse to date. It will help you enjoy your culture shock.

Conflict or Communication. William Klausner. Bangkok: Post, 1977.

■ Deals specifically with the meeting between Thai and *farang*. Very readable and informative. A must for expat businessmen and anyone (teachers, trainers) in regular contact with Thais.

GUIDES

Insight Photo Guides: Thailand.

■ Updated every year, one of the most useful and certainly the most beautiful of the many guide books to Thailand.

HEALTHCARE

Healthy Living in Thailand. Thai Red Cross Society. Bangkok: Asia Books, 2001.

■ Written by doctors from the Thai Red Cross, this book offers practical advice on preparing for your move to Thailand and staying healthy in a tropical climate. Provides information on vaccinations, food and nutrition, tropical diseases, and much more. Full list of hospitals in Thailand by town. Offers a rating for most hospitals.

USEFUL WEBSITES

- http://www.bangkokpost.com
  Offers a daily update and summary of Thai local news and business news in English. Also entertainment and feature articles. For those who read Thai, a Thai language summary of *Matichon* (Thai newspaper) and TV3 is available.

- http://www.biz-in-thailand.net
  Very useful to the businessman. Provides useful tips for new arrivals and those thinking of doing business in Thailand.

- http://www.bangkokatoz.com
  General information about Bangkok nicely arranged in A–Z format. Has audio-files to help one pronounce basic Thai words and phrases. Also features editorials, local book reviews, photo galleries of streets and places in Bangkok, and a listing of businesses on Sukhumvit Road. Provides a useful list of further websites.

- http://www.mahidol.ac.th/Thailand
  Look for what you want using keywords.

- http://www.tat.or.th
  Tourism Authority of Thailand website gives up-to-date situation reports on regional areas, press releases and tourism statistics.

ABOUT THE AUTHOR

Robert is a British subject who has lived overseas most of his life. He received a Ph D in Economic Anthropology after living for two years with Hmong villagers in Northern Thailand and Laos. Following publication of *Resource Scarcity and the Hmong Response* (University of Singapore), he was elected Fellow of the Royal Anthropological Institute in 1979.

In 1980, Robert left an academic career in anthropology that included lectureships and fellowships at Singapore, Chulalongkorn and Chiang Mai universities to join the United Nations High Commissioner for Refugees. He has served with the UN in Laos, Geneva, Malawi, the Philippines, Bangkok, Chiang Kham in northern Thailand, Nepal, Bangladesh and Indonesia. In 2000, he joined the British Foreign and Commonwealth Office as Head of the British Trade Office in Laos. He spent a year in Vietnam advising the government on poverty reduction, before returning in 2005 to live and write in the Lao People's Democratic Republic.

In addition to writings on Thai culture, Robert has written two books on the Hmong: *Resource Scarcity and the Hmong Response* (Singapore University Press) and *The Hmong* (Times Editions). He is the author of the companion volume to *CultureShock! Thailand*, entitled *Thais Mean Business* (Marshall Cavendish), in which he encourages the expat manager working in Thailand towards a middle path of hands-off management. He has also written cultural guides to Bahrain, Bhutan, Croatia, and Indonesia and three novels set in Asia and the UK—*Red Fox Goose Green* (Marshall Cavendish, 2004), *Professor Dog* (pending publication) and *Red Flag Blue Member* (Coolskin Publications, 2005).

Robert currently manages Book-Café Vientiane, the largest bookshop in Laos, located in the centre of Vientiane.

INDEX

Titles in the CultureShock! series:

Argentina	France	Russia
Australia	Germany	San Francisco
Austria	Hawaii	Saudi Arabia
Bahrain	Hong Kong	Scotland
Beijing	Hungary	Shanghai
Belgium	India	Singapore
Bolivia	Ireland	South Africa
Borneo	Italy	Spain
Brazil	Jakarta	Sri Lanka
Britain	Japan	Sweden
Bulgaria	Korea	Switzerland
Cambodia	Laos	Syria
Canada	London	Taiwan
Chicago	Malaysia	Thailand
Chile	Mauritius	Tokyo
China	Morocco	Turkey
Costa Rica	Munich	United Arab
Cuba	Myanmar	Emirates
Czech Republic	Netherlands	USA
Denmark	New Zealand	Vancouver
Ecuador	Paris	Venezuela
Egypt	Philippines	
Finland	Portugal	

For more information about any of these titles, please contact any of our Marshall Cavendish offices around the world (listed on page ii) or visit our website at:

www.marshallcavendish.com/genref